# THE HUTTERIAN PEOPLE

## RITUAL AND REBIRTH IN THE EVOLUTION OF COMMUNAL LIFE

## Peter H. Stephenson
University of Victoria

UNIVERSITY PRESS OF AMERICA

Lanham • New York • London

Copyright © 1991 by
**University Press of America®, Inc.**
4720 Boston Way
Lanham, Maryland 20706

3 Henrietta Street
London WC2E 8LU England

British Cataloging in Publication Information Available

**Library of Congress Cataloging-in-Publication Data**

Stephenson, Peter H.
The Hutterian people : ritual and rebirth in the evolution
of communal life / by Peter H. Stephenson.
p. cm.
Includes bibliographical references and index.
1. Hutterian Brethren. 2. Anabaptists. I. Title.
BX8129.B64S74 1990 305.6'87—dc20 90–44901 CIP

ISBN 0–8191–7986–8 (alk. paper)

 The paper used in this publication meets the minimum requirements of
American National Standard for Information Sciences—Permanence
of Paper for Printed Library Materials, ANSI Z39.48–1984.

*for my family*

## ACKNOWLEDGEMENTS

My thanks must first be extended to those persons among the Hutterian Brethren with whom I worked over a period of many years. They and the colonies that they live in remain anonymous here as a protection against unnecessary external prying and, in some cases, the possibility of internal censure.

I was first introduced to the Hutterites in the classroom by Hermann K. Bleibtreu whose research and teaching have served as an inspiration for my own. John Bennett introduced me to fieldwork among the Brethren and over the past decade has been a valued source of criticism and support for my work. Even when we have not agreed I have found our differences stimulating, and have been forced to refine my thinking as a result of his critique of this manuscript. I have also benefited from discussions with V.C. Serl whose work during the early 1960s remains a milestone in Hutterian ethnology. Brief exchanges and discussions with Peter Clark, James Frideres, Paul Gross, Marlene Mackie, John Hostetler, and Paul Diener have also proved helpful.

I also wish to thank Tom McFeat, Stuart B. Philpott, Frances Burton, V.H. Kobrinsky, Ross D.E. MacPhee, Chris Koch, David Counts, Janet Bavelas, W. Kenneth Little, Roy Wagner, Michael Lambek, Michael Korovkin, and Leland Donald for their suggestions over the years on the various themes of this book. Special thanks are also extended to Margaret Edwards for her extensive typing and retyping of the manuscript; to Maureen Stephenson for her work on the graphics; and to Liza McGuinness and N. Ross Crumrine for help with the tables and formatting.

The research reported on here began in the summers of 1972, and 1973 under funds liberated for me by John Bennett from the Saskatchewan Cultural Ecology Research Programme (which was supported by the Wenner Gren Foundation and Washington University Graduate School) and a University of Calgary Intersession Bursary Award. Research for 14 months was also conducted from June 1975 through July 1976 with support from a Canada Council Doctoral Fellowship. During a two-month break in the winter of 1976 I taught at *Muskwaches* Cultural College at the Hobbema Cree Reserve. Subsequently, I have visited colonies of Hutterites casually to see friends, or to meet with people who sometimes contact me by mail asking for copies of papers, or to discuss letters I have written to newspapers defending the Hutterite's right to be different. The last visit was in 1985. I wish to thank all of these institutions and individuals for their generous support. The students at *Muskwaches* and director Bob Silverthorn gave me an especially valuable and interesting perspective on the lives of the ranchers, farmers and Hutterites who inhabit the region around them. I thank them for it and the encouragement that they gave me in studying a non-Indian group — something which perforce they do almost daily.

I wholeheartedly endorse Mead's (1972) remarks in her discussion of methodology in anthropology to the effect that it is not an ethnographer's business to test formal hypotheses on people. My principal tasks here are descriptive and interpretive, not predictive. Because the description is especially sensitive to translations used to mount it, I wish to make explicit my choices of textual material.

I have chosen to use the King James version of the English Bible. While the English translation of the Lutheran Bible may sometimes come closer to the semantics of the Hutterite use of the German Lutheran Bible, and while I admire the clarity of the New English bible too, (and accordingly have used it for references to the *Apocrypha* because readers are *not* likely to be familiar with its content) neither are appropriately evocative of Hutterite sentiments concerning the actual use of language. The Hutterians use high German at church and comment that something of "strength" is lost when their services are occasionally conducted in English for the benefit of visitors. It is the slightly antiquated German which differs from *Hütterischen* dialect which adds an aura of eternal truth to the service — not

vi

the use of German *per se*. Since this work is intended for English readers, I feel that the same feeling can be best engendered by using English of the same "vintage" quality. Marcel Proust (1971:63, originally, 1906), in his essay "Sur la Lecture," makes similar reference to the language used in the tragedies of Racine and books of Saint-Simon:

> For they contain all the beautiful outdated forms of language which preserve the memory of usages and ways of feeling that no longer exist, persistent traces of the past which nothing in the present resembles, and of which time alone, passing over them, has still been able to embellish the coloring.

The standard German translations of the Hutterian chronicles are Zieglschmid (1943) and Zieglschmid (1947). These are printed in Gothic figures because they are preferred by the Hutterians. The earliest printing of a limited number (1943) were in modern script but were rejected by the Brethren. Working with the chronicles is greatly facilitated by finding one of these rare modern editions. A partial translation of the Chronicles exists (Horsch, 1931), but the great bulk are untranslated. I have employed modern German to facilitate reader comprehension — few of us know Gothic script.

I was first introduced to the word "cybernetics," and the concept of regulatory control, at the age of 13 in the context of a discussion of "governors" on steam locomotives. The concept has fascinated me ever since, and so this work is respectfully dedicated to inventors George and Robert Stephenson who went on to apply the concept we now call "feedback" to miner's lamps, bridges, and even alarm clocks, as well as to those current members of my family who have devoted their scientific and artistic lives to documenting and understanding "control" and "runaway" growth in Oncology, Physiology, and Human affairs in general: Dr. Richard B. Stephenson, Dr. Richard C. Stephenson, Dr. John L. Stephenson, Dr. Elizabeth Stephenson, Dale Stephenson, David Stephenson, and J. Scott Stephenson.

# CONTENTS

# PROLOGUE

... it is precisely the function of tragic myth to convince us that even the ugly and unharmonious is an artistic game which the will plays with itself in the eternal fullness of its joy . . . (F. Nietzsche)

... any fool could devise a more consistent social system than exists, but even a despot rarely can institute one. (A.L. Kroeber)

The Hutterian Brethren [*Hutterischen Brüder*] are the most successful example of communal society historically known. Although their numbers have fluctuated widely mainly due to persecution and migration over the past 465 years, with the exception of several brief lapses into collective apostasy, they have sustained a communal existence throughout that period.

By contrast with such durability, only four of the 130 communal societies listed by Williams (1939:15) existed for over 100 years.[1] Besides the Hutterites, whose numbers are now pushing towards 30,000, the others were the Seventh-Day Baptists of Ephrata (173 years) and the Harmonists (100 years) both of which are groups now extinct. Williams (1939) and Hostetler (1968:331) both state that the Shakers are also extinct, having expired after 162 years. This is not quite the case, however, for there were until at least the early 1980s still nine (three men, six women) Shakers known to the author to be living communally at the Sabbath-Day-Lake commune in central Maine (see also Starbird 1977:742-745). Although the Shakers still cling to a slim existence, the likelihood of the members, who are now in their 70s and 80s, attracting converts is minimal. In order for the Shakers (who practice absolute celibacy) to continue, a steady influx of converts would be necessary. In any case, the vitality and longevity of the Hutterites contrast markedly with the vast majority of utopian ventures.

Exactly how the Brethren have accomplished such a rare feat

is partly the subject matter of the work in hand. The durable nature of Hutterian communalism has resulted in a large number of studies framed within the theoretical parameters of change and persistence. Previous studies have isolated and emphasized particular sectors of Hutterian society thought to be key variables with respect to change and persistence. Thus, for example, Hostetler and Huntington (1967, 1968) and Hostetler (1970, 1974:285-289), have dealt mostly with the socialization process and Kaplan and Plaut (1956) and Eaton and Weil (1955) with those personality factors which derive from socialization. While research on stability has emphasized the acquisition of Hutterite culture and its psychological concomitants (personality), other researchers interested in the study of processes of change through an examination of adaptation within a highly stable social system have emphasized ecology and economy in terms of cultural evolution (Bennett 1967, Diener 1975), group decision making (Bennett 1969), social structure and historical processes (Peters 1965, Peter 1975), and social organization and networks (Deets 1939, Serl 1960, 1964). Flint (1975) emphasizes the role which external pressure in the form of prejudice has played in producing Hutterite solidarity and recently Karl Peter (1987) has re-emphasized the role of demographic vitality as a force propelling Hutterite society.

Kanter (1968, 1972, 1973) has examined communal societies which existed during 19th century America in an attempt to determine which elements of social life might be critical to the success or failure of communes. From a sample of 30 societies for which sufficient information existed, Kanter found that only nine were "successful," that is, they persisted for over two or more sociological generations, whereas 21 failed. The critical feature often shared by the nine successful communal societies and often conspicuously absent from the 21 failures was ritual. Kanter (1972) suggests that ritual is critical to the persistence of communes because it produces solidarity by fostering what she terms "commitment" in individuals. However, since no anthropological, sociological, or psychological studies or ritual within communes has been attempted, little is known about the specifics of "commitment" and it remains a loose, descriptive concept. "Commitment" also seems insufficient as an explanation of persistence even where it is found in both the prevailing attitudes and beliefs of a people, for it is little more than a repetition of the older functionalist equilibration of ritual and "integrative effect." Indeed, if persons were not already committed they would probably not perform rituals. This is not to say that ritual does not foster commitment or have certain integrative functions – it clearly does – it is simply an inadequate portrait of ritual which requires an ontology as well as a function, a history as well as a present.

The Hutterites arose from one of a large number of sects practicing adult baptism [*Beigiessungstäufe*] during the radical reformation period of the early 16th century. In the past such groups have been called "Anabaptists" (rebaptizers). Since these people thought the baptism of infants to be at once both ineffectual and an abomination, the concept was and remains *Anathema Maranatha* for them and the term Anabaptist is therefore a pejorative misnomer. It is customary in anthropology to call a people by the name they choose for themselves so I have used the word *Täufer* for those groups heretofore called Anabaptists. *Täufer* literally means "baptizers" and until the death of their leader, Jacob Hutter, the Hutterites called themselves *Täufer*, or *Täufergemeinschaften*. The ritual of baptism has always been central to the Hutterians' conception of themselves both as a group and as individuals. However, the absence of a description and analysis of ritual both in the history and contemporary life of the Hutterites constitutes a serious gap in our understanding of them. With the exception of a very short paper in Friedmann's (1961:89-90) compendium, there is no important description or analysis of *Beigiessungstäufe*. Information on other Hutterite rituals is also scant, although brief sketches of most may be found in Hostetler (1974). The primary sources for an understanding of Hutterian ritual are still the writings of early Hutterite leaders such as Peter Riedemann's *Confession of Faith* which was originally published in 1545.

In a far reaching review of research on the Hutterian Brethren, Bennett (1976b) noted that to date nearly all studies have been concerned with description while theoretically-oriented studies have been neglected. He proposes six theoretical orientations which future Hutterite studies might fruitfully pursue. These are: the colony as a nucleated agricultural village; Hutterian management as a conflict-resolution system; Hutterite personality as a problem or relationship between repression and aggression; intercolony relationships as cooperative exchange; Hutterian agriculture as a resource-conservationist system; and Hutterian history as a homeostatic [read "cybernetic"] system (1967b:23).

While I agree, I would, however, add to this list the investigation of Hutterite beliefs through attention to rituals, symbols, music, texts, stories, and their use of the Bible. These are an interwoven fabric of meaning which has emerged from experience in the past and which constitutes experience in the present. Bennett (1976b:38) states that Hostetler's recent work *Hutterite Society* (1974), "provides a base of operations: for the first time the task of general description, which all students of Hutterian society have been engaged in for the past quarter-century, can be considered concluded." While Hostetler's book, as Bennett indicates, does go a long way, I disagree with the implication that the historical emergence of contemporary Hutterite beliefs as revealed in their ritual life has been adequately described. Most Hutterite sermons have yet to be transliterated from script let alone translated into English, and major themes (some of which appear in them) such as the Trinity, Angelic visitation, belief in demons, "evil eye," and the rebirth of Christ's very body in the form of the Hutterian people, have gone thus far untranslated, uninterpreted, and unanalyzed. This lack of overall description stems in part from the lack of an analytical perspective on Hutterite history. Hutterite values and symbols grow out of historical context as a developing ideology and gain import, inertia, and validation today in both the everyday events and ritual celebrations of individual lives. The Hutterite experience of today is always seen against the backdrop of the group's history which is in turn associated with the lives of the apostles as told in the Bible. In Bloch's (1977:279) apt phrase, "the present cannot be understood apart from the past in that it answers it." The approach to ritual here will be as a multimedia event involving communication via all sense modalities and levels of consciousness. I am especially drawn to the use of silence and space in my interpretations of Hutterite rituals. The approach is similar to that advocated by Tambiah (1985).

While I agree with Bennett that we need an analytical perspective on Hutterite history drawn from the domain of general systems theory, I would also emphasize that such a study must include both a description and analysis of Hutterian ideology via its primary symbols. Bennett (1976b:38) suggests that:

> What the analysis of Hutterian Society by cybernetic models does suggest is that the fit of an existent system to those mechanical principles may be largely dependant on the degree of authority exerted over the social system by its members. That is, strong authority and conformity is required in order to regularize the movements, and render the outcomes as predictable as possible.

The Hutterites, in other words, must to a large degree be conscious of the results of their acts, their social system is not wholly a *sub rosa* thing but must also be, *sub voce*, a part of their spoken and enacted beliefs. To exert control over such a social system the representation of the system itself must find expression in symbol and through metaphor. One yardstick for the evolution of Hutterite society is then the development of its symbols and its primary metaphor for itself as a communal social entity. Thus, this work attempts to include in the systems approach to Hutterite history, the development and refinement of Hutterite symbology as a measure of emergent "consciousness."

One primary arena for the analysis of symbols is also ritual and, moreover, ritual is a focal point of the cybernetic perspective on the evolution of human culture. Rappaport (1967, 1968, 1971a, 1971b) has employed a well-known negative-feedback model to the incidence of ritual during war/peace cycles which occur among the *Tsembaga* (a *Maring* people) of New Guinea.

Briefly, warfare seems to last for ten- to 15-year intervals among the *Maring* peoples and is followed by roughly equivalent periods of quiescence broken only by episodic occurrences of relatively petty feuding (see Vayda 1971). Although one could theoretically enter this circular pattern at any point, it is convenient to take as a starting point the end of warfare.

After the cessation of fighting, a shrub (the *rumbin*), is planted symbolizing the attachment of the *Tsembaga* to the land. Pigs are then slaughtered in thanks to the *Tsembaga's* ancestors for success in warfare. Yet, this ritual alone does not adequately recompense the ancestors for their assistance in war, and the *Tsembaga* cannot initiate new fighting while still indebted to them: more pigs must be slaughtered in ritual propitiation to accomplish this.

As a consequence of the debt to ancestors, pigs are allowed to multiply until about 36% of the land under cultivation is devoted to their sustenance. At this point acreage must expand rapidly, burdening the women who work the fields and care for the pigs. Pigs also increasingly cause disputes by ravaging the gardens. The complaints of women finally reach a plateau where consensus is reached by the men and the pigs are slaughtered; feasts are held for a period of a year, and the ancestors are finally repaid. Those neighboring *Maring* who come "to dance" with the *Tsembaga* are also said to come "to fight." Thus, the distribution of pork includes allies whose participation in ritual constitutes an affirmation of their alliance to the *Tsembaga* and announces their intention "to fight" alongside them.

Following this, the *Rumbin* is uprooted and warfare ensues for a period of 10-15 years during which a shift in the land the group occupies is possible. The cycle then hypothetically repeats itself. Rappaport's earlier works (1967, 1968) are mostly concerned with the ecological balancing which occurs in this pattern and ritual is considered to be a control factor operating much like a thermostat on a furnace. In fact, Rappaport (1968:229) terms ritual "a homeostat" or "information transducer." In summarizing this control aspect of ritual, Rappaport (1967:28-29) states that

> The operation of ritual among the Tsembaga and other Maring helps to maintain an undergraded environment, limits fighting to frequencies which do not endanger the existence of the regional population, adjusts man-land ratios, facilitates trade, distributes local surpluses of pigs throughout the regional population in the form of pork, and assures people of high-quality protein when they are most in need of it.

In his later work Rappaport (1971a, 1971b) has emphasized ritual to greater extent, and also developed a hypothesis in which the "sacred" aspect of ritual stems from the effective regulatory function it performs and the analogic context in which information is communicated in ritual. Basically this means that digital information of an "either/or" nature ("yes, I will fight with you"/"no, I won't fight with you") concerning human relationships (alliances) is validated by being part of a ritual. In this particular ritual stylized fighting in the form of "epideictic display" (threat-trading to assess aggressive potential and intent) takes place. Basic to this hypothesis is the idea that falsification in the analogic (gestural) mode is very difficult because behavior has no opposite (see Bateson 1966, 1968). Therefore, inherently falsifiable information (the promise of alliance – "yes, I will fight with you") imbedded in a highly-analogic frame (ritual) is accepted on faith. In Rappaport's scheme "sacred" ritual then serves the purpose of controlling a complex system which is beyond the awareness of the unquestioning participants in it.

Rappaport has been criticized for not connecting his analysis to his own enormous quantity of data and for dealing only with what his data imply (Bennett 1976a: 178-186). Yet the difficult of performing such an analysis almost certainly stems from the length of time spent in the field (one year) and the much longer duration of the putative cycle (up to 60 years for one whole repetition). My own criticism is simply that sometimes the work seems mostly about pigs and not about the *Tsembaga* who appear largely as a contingency of the other species in the ethnography. One also wonders how such a system might have evolved. However, the *Maring* have no easily-accessible history so this probably cannot be determined.

Nonetheless, Rappaport's thesis, and its later "spin-offs" (especially Rappaport's revised 1984 edition of *Pigs for the Ancestors*) are grounded in systems theory and have far-reaching implications for the study of cyclical phenomena in demography and land-use studies, and for the study of ritual in that context. Before I went to the field for the second time, I had become aware of a similar pattern among the Hutterites and began to wonder whether Rappaport's ritual-control model might not have some application to the Hutterites. I also thought the model might be better refined in a society with some accessible history.

Because women cannot hold managerial positions, and birth rates are exceedingly high (almost half of the population is under 15 years old), there is a very high ratio of productive workers to dependants among the Hutterites. The labor pool is made up of males between 16 and retirement age, or about 25% of the population. Within the male work force only about 14% are over 25 and are likely to be baptized, able to vote, hold managerial positions and marry. Hutterite colonies have minimum and maximum population sizes within which the operation of the farm enterprise is efficient and safe, beyond these parameters, however, cultural disintegration can easily occur. There is an absolute minimum of ten necessary managerial positions and so the minimum effective operational size is about 65-70 persons; below this figure colonies begin to resemble extended-family-operated farms where job promotion (and baptism) can become nepotistic. There is also a maximum size of approximately 140 people because above this figure the pressure of an increased male labor pool for new occupations and marital eligibility increases the likelihood of disputes, and raises the coefficient of inequality in promotion to jobs because kin groups begin to manoeuvre to facilitate promotions of their relatives (see Clark 1974a). At the peak of growth, colonies must divide, that is, they split down through the age pyramid and two smaller colonies are created with all managerial positions filled from the available labor pool. The decision to baptize and the decision to divide are both in the hands of those who can vote (the baptized). Both of these highly-political decisions are muted by making the decisions sacred; votes are thought to be manifestations of the will of God and baptisms are clearly sacred events. I suggested in my research proposal that prior to colony fission requests for baptism would increase and that some disputes might break out, although the religions ("sacred") significance of the ritual itself would serve to keep disputes at a minimum, or perhaps even keep people completely unaware of the operation of the larger system of which they were a part. Finally, I hypothesized

. . . that the system of Hutterian rituals focusing around adult baptism has served as a homeostatic device in a cybernetic system which has sustained ideology, sorted occupation, ordered politics, expansion, growth of population *vis-a-vis* land use and has also served as a device which maintains an unusually high degree of 'commitment' necessary to deal with the outside world without being co-opted by it (Stephenson 1975:6).

Beyond this grand level of generalization I really was unsure about *how* ritual fitted into the whole colony fission procedure but I thought it wise to frame my proposed investigation with Rappaport's important study in mind. Finally, it was clear that the Hutterians had not always practiced colony fission. Therefore, in tracing the evolution of Hutterite symbols and metaphors of self-reference through history, there would also be an opportunity to see how a complex practice like colony fission had come into being. Thus, the systems perspective which Bennett (1976b) has called for in the analysis of Hutterite history might be effectively fused to the cybernetics perspective on contemporary ritual practice and the fission cycle.

My first task was to learn everything I could about Hutterite history from a Hutterian perspective. To that end, I did my first eight months of fieldwork under the tutelage of several Hutterians interested in their own history to an extraordinary degree. My guided readings emphasized the Bible (including the *Apocrypha*), Hutterian *Codeces*, hymns, proverbs, children's songs, and the works of some selected Mennonite historians. The first three chapters represent part of the fruits of this labor in as succinct a form as I believe possible. The third chapter is an attempt at merging the history of the Brethren as seen (for the most part) by themselves with the structure of their major symbols of rebirth. These are, in turn, linked in the analysis to existential universals. The third chapter also contains a suggestion of how the Hutterites of the 16th century may have created new colonies in the absence of today's fission pattern. I also wanted to find out how conscious the Hutterites are about the operation of the system they are part of. Salisbury (1975:130-131) and Bennett (1976a:62-206) have been critical of Rappaport's implication that much of the control of the Maring cycle was an uncognized process. Rappaport attempted to answer this criticism (1984:320-330) by stating that the decisions made by the Maring are conscious and pragmatic forms of management just as his critics suggest they must be, but that because their rituals regulate much more than pig populations, the significance of the latter as phenomena imbedded within the sphere of ritual practice is "subsumed" by the wider and essentially religious issues. (Rappaport 1984:322, 324). Rappaport's response notwithstanding, the issue of how individual acts constitute the reproduction of social patterns which may lie not only outside of awareness, but are also of longer duration than the individual lives which comprise them, takes us into the heart of critical theory itself. We need to know how the mystification of cyclical events is itself reproduced, and a theory which models this process must be both psychological and social. We need to know how the ritual and its creation as a "sacred" event developed, and any theory which purports to explain this must be evolutionary and its data historical. Is there a multiple and historically variable form of consciousness whereby events of a mundane sort when "subsumed" by a wider sacred context become "decognized" (rather than uncognized) for some participants but not for others? Moreover, what do the participants say when asked if they see the pattern which the analyst thinks he has detected? Are the members of one culture (or one historical period) more aware of how their society is "controlled" than the members of another culture or time? Clearly, there seems to be much to learn by studying Hutterian ritual practice while keeping in mind the kinds of questions his critics have exacted of Rappaport's description of the Maring ritual cycle. To answer these questions necessitates a fairly detailed recounting of Hutterian history and the first chapters are an attempt to give the reader a good grasp of the unfolding of Hutterian historical consciousness. The word "consciousness" is used here as a rough functional equivalent to "self-awareness" but I have employed it instead because it appeals to the social and historical interpretations we make of human life, as opposed to the contemporary psychological judgements implicit within the term "self-awareness." This also goes to the root of the problem of "cognized" as opposed to "uncognized" decisions as well as the relationship between individuals and groups, and the legitimacy of our studies of the past as opposed to the present. Without revealing too early the finer points of the conclusion — which depend to an extent on a reader who is not overburdened with a knowledge of the outcome — I should suggest here that within a cybernetic perspective learning is not merely an individual thing, it is a group process as well. Moreover, consciousness is not restricted to forms of verbal and statistical discourse employed by analysts as direct measures of performance. There are heightened states of consciousness where individual and group blur into synergistic activity and I think that rituals serve to focus just such kinds of collective intent. I also think this is the case whether one is discussing the use of hallucinogens by groups of Amazonian hunters or dances in the highlands of New Guinea, as well as the baptism of adults in the colonies of Hutterites. The dramatic particulars may vary from one culture to another, but ritual is a universal human experience.

Learning and cultural evolution are also joined in the form of ritual activity itself because rituals not only convey information within feedback loops; they become new information as well. Almost four decades ago, Wiener put this succinctly:

> ...feedback is a method of controlling a system by reinserting into it the results of its past performance. If these results are merely used as numerical data for the criticism of the system and its regulation, we have the simple feedback of the control engineers. If, however, the information which proceeds backward from the performance is able to change the general method and pattern of performance, we have a process which may well be called learning (1950:84).

Ritual is an avenue through which cultures code and represent collective learning. Seen this way cultures are themselves a form of mind with primitive memory mechanisms which make decisions. In the concluding epilogue this topic will re-emerge in a discussion of Hutterian social history as an example of the evolution of a self-simplifying system. I have abbreviated my discussion here in order that the reader's experience match, in some respects, the learning which the Hutterians have collectively experienced over nearly five centuries. Previously unknown outcomes are the gist of learning and the nesting place of decisions within evolution. Discovery is also the hallmark of understanding and so I hope that I have gone no further here than a clear indication of my intent in these prefatory remarks. A clear intent is also the basis with which the earliest *Täufer* began their movement. Theirs was an awareness that could not yet encompass the outcome of a whole people — the Hutterian People — at least partly because many among them thought the end of the world was at hand. Indeed, for many who were martyred, just such was the case. And yet, it was to be from their sad fates that the wisdom of a people was formed. Hopefully, through this book, something of what the Hutterian People have learned may be passed on outside the borders of their own society and experience. To have created and tenaciously preserved an essentially egalitarian and pacifist culture out of near oblivion is no mean accomplishment. Perhaps the hope such a rare event can inspire may lead to real insight into the rebirth which many of the darkened corners and persecuted peoples of our world have despaired of ever finding.

## NOTES

1   The number of communes which have been established are assuredly much greater now than when Williams wrote, but their total is not at present relevant to the criterion of longevity.

# CHAPTER I

# THE BIRTH AND REBIRTH OF THE *TÄUFER*

"Look for new heavens and a new earth" (II *Peter* 3:13)

On January 21, 1525 around 12 men gathered together during the evening at the house of Felix Manz to worship, study scripture, and to discuss recent setbacks which they had suffered at a disputation heard before the city council of Zürich concerning the baptism of infants. The men were probably frustrated. They had lost the disputation partly because Ulrich Zwingli, who had originally been their leader and teacher, and who had served as the catalyst for the Reformation in Zürich from as early as 1517, had acquiesced to the wishes of the council members. Zwingli had introduced young humanist scholars such as Conrad Grebel and George Blaurock, who now met in defeat, to Erasmus and the Greek New Testament. However, by late January of 1525 Zwingli and his former students had come to occupy quite different philosophical and political positions. Zwingli had repeatedly capitulated to the city council and had resigned to them the right to decide on issues such as a proposal to abandon mass in favor of an annual celebration of the Lord's supper, and adoption of adult baptism. Although Zwingli had originally favored both proposals he demurred in the face of council opposition. Several of the young radicals, Simon Stumpf and Conrad Grebel in particular, had objected to Zwingli's capitulation to secular authorities on what they considered to be strictly religious matters (see Estep 1963:7-19).

The schism that developed between Zwingli and his former

pupils, especially Conrad Grebel, had profound implications for it marked the beginning of a movement for absolute separation of church and state, which in much of the world would eventually become known as freedom of religion.

> The decision of Conrad Grebel to refuse to accept the jurisdiction of the Zürich council over the Zürich church is one of the high moments of history, for however obscure it was, it marked the beginning of the modern 'free church' movement (Bender 1950:99-100).

The meeting at the house of Felix Manz on a winter night in 1525 was to have other profound results, for it also marked the beginning of the *Täufer* movement of the radical element of the Reformation itself. Conrad Grebel and his associates were the original Swiss Brethren; spiritual antecedents of the Mennonite, Hutterite and Amish peoples of today.[1]

An account of the events of the evening of January 21, 1525 still exists in *Die älteste Chronik der Hutterischen Brüder* and appears to have been written by an eyewitness – perhaps, as Estep (1963:9) suggests, by George Blaurock himself.[2]

> And it came to pass that they were together until anxiety [*Angst*] came upon them, yes, they were so pressed within their hearts. Thereupon they began to bow their knees to the most High [*Hochstenn*] God in heaven and called upon him as the Informer of Hearts [*Hertzenkundiger*], and they prayed that he would give to them his divine [*göttlichen*] will and that he would show his mercy unto them. For flesh and blood and human forwardness did not drive them, since they well knew what they would have to suffer on account of it.
>   After the prayer, George of the House of Jacob stood up and besought [*gebeten*] Conrad Grebel for God's sake to baptize him with the true [*recht*] Christian baptism upon his faith and knowledge [*erkanntnis*]. And when he knelt down with such a request and desire, Conrad baptized him, since at that time there was no ordained minister [*Dienner*] to perform such work (Estep 1963:9-10).

Following Blaurock's baptism at the hands of Grebel, the former proceeded to baptize all others present.

The validity of infant baptism had been discussed and called into serious question by a number of reform-oriented pastors and priests including Ulrich Zwingli and even implied by Martin Luther himself.[3] The first person to actually preach against infant baptism among the Swiss Brethren appears to have been Wilhelm Reublin, a pastor at Wytikon, a village not far from

Zürich. In the same year (1524) at Zollikon, three fathers withheld their children from baptism and were supported in their actions by Johannes Brötli, their pastor.

Response by the authorities was swift and Reublin was imprisoned in August and later expelled from Zürich. The disputation of January 1525 at Zürich had been precipitated by the insistence of Reublin, Brötli, and Grebel, among others, for baptism based upon professed belief — something which they held infants to be incapable of (Estep 1963:13, also Bender 1950). The baptism of Christ as an adult by John in scripture was at obvious odds with the practice of infant baptism. Since a literal interpretation of the Bible was at the root of many Reformation disputes, it is not surprising that infant baptism should become a Reformation issue too. For Grebel and the other Swiss Brethren, to be a Christian was to live a life modeled upon Christ's life and this meant adult baptism. The rationale for this interpretation derived further from I *Peter* 3:21, which in Luther's translation reads; "Baptism is a covenant [*Bund*] of a good conscience with God."[4] Another biblical passage cited from Luther's translation is *Titus* 3:5; "Baptism is the bath of regeneration." In his Petition of Protest and Defense before the Zürich authorities, Grebel had stressed that the regenerative qualities of baptism derived from a free choice based upon knowledge and understanding:

> It is clearly seen what baptism is and to whom baptism should be applied, namely, to one who has been converted by the Word of God, has changed his heart, and henceforth desires to walk in newness of life. . . . From this I have clearly learned and know assuredly that baptism means nothing else than a dying of the old man, and a putting on of the new, and that Christ commanded to baptize those who had been taught (Bender 1938:47).

Grebel and the other radicals, by their actions on the evening of January 21, 1525, had separated themselves from secular authority and legitimate reform elements of early 16th Century Swiss society. Zwingli, despite his own objections to infant baptism, had capitulated to secular authority and abandoned his former colleagues, who had chosen to put their faith in "the word of God" above secular power and interpretation.

Both the tone and content of the passage cited above from the *älteste Chronik der Hutterischen Brüder* are ample testimony to the trepidation with which the Swiss Brethren acted for they knew very well that the full power of the state would be brought to bear upon them, as indeed it was.

While several elements of the Reformation from Zwingli to the Zwickau prophets as early as 1521, had questioned the validity of infant baptism, only the Swiss Brethren actually put their beliefs into practice, despite opposition from the state.[5] The Swiss Brethren had dared to appeal to a higher moral authority than the state; their personal belief in the "Word of God" as revealed in the Bible. The response of the state to the religiously-rationalized personal civil disobedience of the Brethren — during a time when much of the European social order was in chaos, and social movements such as the Peasant's Revolt (1524-1525) were afoot — was brutally repressive.

**The Early Persecutions**

The first of the *Täufer* known to have been executed for practicing what had become known as "Believers' Baptism" [*Beigiessungstäufe*] was a preacher, Eberli Bolt, who was burned at the stake in Schwyz, Switzerland, May 29, 1525 by Roman Catholic authorities, only five months after the first baptism at the home of Felix Manz. As early as March 1, 1526 — within a year of Bolt's martyrdom — Zürich had introduced the death penalty for all *Täufer*, and Zwingli had completely disowned his former colleagues. He appears to have renounced his earlier beliefs as well, for he became a formidable polemicist whose published tracts were aimed primarily at Grebel. Zwingli eventually even sanctioned the arrest and execution of the *Täufer*.[6] By December 1526, the death penalty was extended and was prescribed for anyone attending *Täufer* meetings. By the beginning of 1528 Charles V declared that the *Täufer* should be "exterminated by fire and sword" (Peters 1965:11-12). The persecution was so severe that extermination was nearly the result. According to the Hutterite chronicles alone, over 2,173 persons were drowned, burned at the stake, or put to the sword, often after long imprisonments and incredibly cruel tortures (Horsch 1931:39).[7]

Conrad Grebel lived only slightly more than a year following the institution of "believers' baptism" and much of that time he was either extremely ill or imprisoned. Grebel was arrested October 8, 1525, along with George Blaurock, and tried after more than a month's imprisonment. Three weeks after their arrest, Grebel and Blaurock were joined by Manz and all three were condemned to an indeterminate term in prison, in isolation, with only a bread and water diet (November 18, 1525). After five months of imprisonment, Grebel, who had utilized his time well, asked to have a manuscript published which he had composed while confined. The authorities were incensed by Grebel's request which closely followed a second trial, held on the 5th and 6th of May, 1525. The 7th of May all three men were condemned to prison for life. The same day an edict prescribing death for all *Täufer* was passed in that jurisdiction. Fourteen days later all three prisoners, with the help of confederates, escaped. However, Grebel, who was never physically strong, and who was by then in a much weakened state, succumbed to the omnipresent plague, probably in August of 1526 (Estep 1963:27-28, Bender 1950, Kessler 1902:142, 148, 314).

Felix Manz was condemned to death January 5, 1527 and was the first to perish under the March edict of Zürich passed the year previous. Manz was drowned in lake Zürich and it was reported that as his limbs were bound he shouted out in a loud voice: "*In Manus tuas, Domine, commendo spiritum meam* [into your hands, Lord, I commend my spirit] (Estep 1963:30).

Although he never wrote copiously, as Grebel had done, among the several works left by Manz is a hymn which is still preserved in the *Ausbund* (literally, "embodiment" a book of 16th Century hymns) of the early *Täufer*, and is still sung by modern Amish, Mennonites and Hutterites

*Mit Lust so will ich Singen,*
*Mein Herz, freut sich in Gott*
*Der mir viel Kunst Thut bringen,*
*Dasz ich entrinn dem Tod*

*Der ewiglich nimmet kein End.*
*Ich preiz dich Christ von Himmel,*
*Der mir mein Kummer wend (Ausbund 1955:41).*

With gladness will I sing now,
   My heart delights in God,
Who showed me such forbearance
   That I from death was saved,
Which never hath an end.
   I praise thee, Christ in heaven,
Who all my sorrow changed (trans. Raymaker 1929:114).

George Blaurock was beaten with rods on the day Manz was executed, but he continued to preach for two and a half more years until he was captured in the Tyrol, and there burned at the stake. Because of his powerful physique, aggressive behavior, and the duration of his ministry, he was nicknamed *der Starke Jörg* [strong George] (Estep 1963:31, also Moore 1955). Blaurock's last works were a prison epistle, a brief sermon, and two hymns. The epistle is styled like a psalm for his fellow prisoners and emphasizes eternal life:

> I will therefore sing praises in my heart to thy holy name, and forever proclaim the grace I have experienced, I entreat thee, O God! in behalf of all thy children, preserve all for ever from all the enemies of souls; I will not build upon flesh, for it passes away, and is of no duration, but I will place my trust in thy word; . . . Our latter end is at hand. Blessed Lord! enable us to bear the cross to the destined place; and incline thyself to us in mercy, that we may commit our spirits into thy hand (Braght 1837:358).

In his final sermon Blaurock, knowing he faced death, understandably wrote of regeneration and salvation through baptism in the face of eternity. Blaurock's final hymns are both instructive and testimonial in nature. One of the hymns is soteriological and puts forth the conditions for salvation, the second is a personal expression of faith. An excerpt of four lines from the second hymn follows: "Lord God, how do I praise thee/from hence and evermore/that thou real faith didst give me/by which I thee may know" (trans. Raymaker 1929:115-116).

The persecution of the *Täufer* persisted in varying degrees through three centuries and permeated virtually every major European state from Italy to the lowlands and stretched through Austria and Hungary into the Ukraine.

## Existential Christianity and the Early Persecutions

The *Täufer* theology has been described as being essentially "existential" or "concrete" by Friedmann (1973:27-35). Friedmann suggests that no formal theology was produced by the early *Täufer* because such a system of logical thought is antithetical to a people who made Søren Kierkegaard's "leap of faith" to subjective belief as "truth."[8]

> God is known to us foremost in this state of subjectivity. Otherwise – in the form of objectivity – God could easily become an idol. Existential certainty is then the direct opposite of speculative thought. Since the latter presents itself usually in the form of a 'system,' Kierkegaard comes to the profoundly convincing conclusion that an *existential system is impossible* [italics in original] (Friedmann 1973:31).

The public statements and last acts of condemned *Täufer* leaders are replete with references to the certitude of their belief in final salvation. The equanimity with which nearly all of the accused met their deaths, and the paucity of persons who abandoned their beliefs, are both strong indications of the sway which absolute faith adopted through "believers' baptism" held over its practitioners. Also of special significance to later Hutterites is the inspirational nature of these writings: they are replete with instructional value in the face of life and death situations. Of specific interest to the whole issue of sanctity and consciousness is the fusion of an obvious awareness that *Täufer* leaders had of the consequences of their acts with the metaphysical world. They were going to die as a consequence of their belief that they were reborn to eternal life through baptism and this set a precedent for later *Täufer*, and eventually Hutterites, which became incorporated into the very structure of their society. Given the number of executions, the statements of the executed understandably are voluminous and although the statements of early leaders are sometimes instructional in character, the final testimony of less well-known persons is also of great analytical importance. The absence of virtually all complex theology in them is all the more startling for their brevity and single-minded emphasis on faith and action. The last public statement of George (Jörg) Wagner at the execution place itself is exemplar:

> It would be a bad thing that I should suffer death from something which I had confessed by mouth and not also in my heart. I certainly believe what I have confessed. My treasure is Christ whom I love, and to Him also belongs my heart, as He speaks: where your treasure is there is your heart also. And this treasure no man will ever pull out of my heart, nor shall any suffering or pain make me turn away from Him. For I have known it well beforehand that I shall have to carry the cross when I follow Him. No idol will possess my heart, and it is the dwelling place of my Lord (Friedmann 1973:30).

Friedmann (1973:30) indicates that Wagner's statement is quite typical

> . . . whoever studies the records meets similar testimonies on nearly every page. What is so extraordinary about these testimonies is the matter-of-factness of their words. No tragic pose, no big words, simply the admission that it was to be expected that the world would contradict the way of faithful discipleship at all times.

The *Täufer* were not only willing to give a vocal "account of the hope that is in you" (I *Peter* 3:15) their actions often bespoke their faith as eloquently as their words. In 1527, after a trial of several days, Michael Sattler was executed. The trial itself is well described (see Estep 1963:37-47) by numerous sources and Sattler's serenity in the face of arrogance and hostility appears to have been its hallmark. Sattler's quiet dignity only infuriated his captors further and his execution was particularly grisly. The account of Sattler's death which follows derives from eyewitness accounts.

> The torture, a prelude to the execution, began at the market place where a piece was cut from Sattler's tongue. Pieces of flesh were torn from his body twice with red-hot tongs. He was then forced to a cart. On the way the scene of the execution the tongs were applied five times again. In the market place and at the site of the execution, still able to speak, the unshakable Sattler prayed for his persecutors. After being bound to a ladder with ropes and pushed into the fire, he admonished the people, the judges, and the mayor to repent and be converted. Then he prayed, 'Almighty, eternal God, Thou art the way and the truth; because I have not been shown to be in error, I will with Thy help to this day testify to the truth and seal it with my blood.'
> As soon as the ropes on his wrists were burned, Sattler raised his two forefingers of his hands giving the promised signal to the brethren

that a martyr's death was bearable. Then the assembled crowd heard coming from his seared lips, 'Father, I commend my spirit into Thy hands' (Estep 1963:44, also Bossert 1951).

An account of Sattler's martyrdom was written by Wilhelm Reublin and circulated widely throughout Germany, Austria and Switzerland. The martyrdom of Sattler was greatly revered by the *Täufer* and the account of it proved influential in obtaining converts (see Bossert 1951).[9] Many accounts of the executions of *Täufer* are brief and the names of many of the victims are often unknown, as the following quote illustrates. "Wolfgang Uliman . . . was burnt at Waltzen, together with his brother and seven others, all testifying to their faith with their death, A.D. 1528" (Braght 1837:360). Mass executions were often held; "Wolfgang Brand-Huber, Hans Niedermaier, and about seventy others, A.D. 1529" (Braght 1837:360). At one point, in Swabia, first 400 and later 1,000 special police were hired to hunt for and execute immediately all *Täufer* wherever they were found. In summarizing the persecution of the *Täufer* the primary difficulty is dealing with the vast numbers of persons who were executed for what we might regard as a trivial ritual distinction. Perhaps the best summary possible is that of a Hutterite Chronicler around the end of the 16th Century who expressed his own astonishment when he wrote the following lengthy entry.[10]

> These all were executed with all sorts of torture and death, a new cloud of witnesses which surrounds us, a pillar of fire by night to go before us, confessors of the faith and Christian heroes of the truth of God, men and women, youths and maidens, old and young, teachers and hearers, by which we see that God has poured out his grace and power in these latter days as well as in the former time.
>
> Some were tortured terribly on the rack, so that they were torn apart and died.
>
> Some were burned to ashes and powder as heretics.
>
> Some were roasted on beams.
>
> Some were torn with red-hot irons.
>
> Some were penned up in houses and all burned together.
>
> Some were hung on trees.
>
> Some were killed with the sword and their bodies chopped to pieces.

Many had gags put into their mouths, and their tongues tied, so that they could not testify to their faith, and were thus led to the stake or scaffold.

What they confessed with their lips, they testified with their blood.

Often they were led to death in groups, like lambs to the slaughter, murdered. Thus the devil works who is a murderer from the beginning.

Many women were cast into the water and then taken out again and asked if they would recant and save their lives. Seeing that they were steadfast, the executioners cast them again into the water and drowned them. So terribly Satan raged through his children.

Others were starved to death in dark towers where they were deprived of the light of day.

Some were cast into deep, noisome dungeons where they lay among bats and vermin.

Many were tortured with hunger and only given insufficient bread and water before they were executed. Many who were adjudged too young to be slain, were bound and beaten miserably with rods, as happened to brother Hans Mandel when he was arrested at Sterzing as a boy. The same happened to Aendel Tuchmacher in the Tyrol as a lass of 16 years.

In spite of all they remained faithful with joyfulness. Nothing could move them from their faith or from the love of Christ Jesus our Lord. In them was the word of Christ truly fulfilled when he said: 'Ye must be hated by all men.' Likewise: 'They will put you out of the synagogue, yea, and the time will come when those who slay you will think that they do God a service thereby.'

Many were promised great gifts and riches should they recant. Others were asked to utter only one expression of swearing and they would be released, yea only a slight profanity. This was proposed to Brother Christian in the Mermesser district in Bavaria, but he would rather suffer bitter death, and was thereupon executed.

Many were talked to in wonderful ways, often day and night argued with, with great cunning and cleverness, with many sweet and smooth words, by monks and priests, by doctors of theology, with much false witness and testimony, with threats and insults and mockery, yea with lies and grievous slanders, against the Brotherhood, but none of these things moved them or made them falter.

Some sang praises to God while they lay in heavy imprisonment, as though they were in great joy. Some did the same as they were being led to the place of execution and death, as though they were going to meet the bridegroom at a wedding, singing joyfully with uplifted voice that it rang out loudly. Others stepped to the place of death with a smile on their lips, praising God that they were accounted worthy to die the death of the Christian hero, and would not have preferred even to die a natural death in bed.

Others very earnestly admonished the crowds who stood about as spectators to repent and be converted. Others, who were imprisoned before they had yet received water-baptism, hastened to receive the baptism or blood, to be baptized therewith on a living faith for the sake of the truth of God.

. . . In some places they literally filled the prisons and dungeons with them, as did the Count Palatine of the Rhine. They thought they could dampen and extinguish the fire of God. But the prisoners sang in their prisons and rejoiced so that the enemies outside (who supposed that the prisoners would be in fears) themselves became more fearful than the prisoners and did not know what to do with them. Many others lay for years in dungeon and prison and endured all sorts of pain and torture. Others had holes burned through their cheeks and were then let free.

The rest, who escaped all this, were driven from one place to another, and even from one land to another. Like owls and bitterns they dared not come out of hiding in daylight. Often they had to hide in rocks and cliffs, in wild forests, caves and holes in the earth to save their lives. They were sought by constables with dogs, hunted like birds of the air. *And yet they all were without guilt, without the least wicked deed; they neither did nor desired to do any one the least harm or injury* (*Geschicht-Buch*:182-187, trans. Horsch 1931:39-43).

The results of such severe persecution upon the numbers of the *Täufer* are difficult to ascertain. In some districts near extermination occurred, however, the manner in which the *Täufer* went to their deaths – often singing and professing their belief to the last – lent encouragement to their brethren, and often brought new converts into the fold. The count of Altzey is reported to have said, "What shall I do, the more I execute, the more they increase?" (Braght 1837:364). When mass executions failed to stem the growth of the *Täufer*, sequestered executions, bounty hunting and dungeon imprisonment were implemented. The *Täufer* were to flee from one country to another in the hope of escaping persecution by all authority – Roman, Lutheran, and Reformed alike. However, it was a vain hope, for nowhere could the *Täufer* escape; "Burning fagots and smoldering stakes marked their trek across Europe" (Estep 1963:46), and even 150 years after the baptism of Blaurock by Grebel, *Täufer* were still being tried in the courts of Bern, Switzerland (Gratz 1953:34-37).

## The Doctrine of Two Worlds

> "Ye are not of the world, but I have chosen
> ye out of the world *(John* 15:19)

The long and antagonistic relationship between the *Täufer* and establishment throughout Europe served to amplify the fundamental dualism of the New Testament as it was interpreted by them: "that is, an uncompromising ontological dualism in which Christian values are held in sharp contrast to the values of the 'world' in its corrupt state" (Friedmann 1973:38, Friedmann 1957:105-118, 1961:92-102). The following quote is from the *älteste Chronik der Hutterischen Brüder* and is illustrative of the separation from "the world" which the *Täufer* both experienced and espoused.

Between the Christian and the world there exists a vast difference like that between heaven and earth. The world is the world, always remains the world, behaves like the world and all the world is nothing but world. The Christian, on the other hand, has been called away from the world. He has been called never to conform to the world, never to be a consort, never to run along with the crowd of the world and never to pull its yoke. The world lives according to the flesh and is dominated by the flesh. Those in the world think that no one sees what they are doing; hence the world needs the sword [of the authorities]. The Christians live according to the Spirit and are governed by the Spirit. They think that the Spirit sees what they are doing and that the Lord watches them. Hence they do not need and do not use the sword among themselves. The victory of the Christians is the faith that overcometh the world (I *John* 5:4), while the victory of the world is the sword by which they overcome [whatever is in their way]. To Christians an inner joy is given; it is the joy in their hearts that maintains the unity of the Spirit in the bond of peace *(Ephesians* 4:3). The world knows no true peace; therefore it has to maintain peace by the sword and force alone. The Christian is patient, as the apostle writes (I *Peter* 4:1): 'As Christ hath suffered . . . arm yourself likewise with the same mind.' The world arms itself for the sake of vengeance and [accordingly] strikes out with the sword. Among Christians he is the most genuine who is willing to suffer for the sake of God. The world, on the contrary, thinks him the most honorable who knows how to defend himself with the sword.
    To sum up: friendship with the world is enmity with God. Whosoever, therefore, wishes to be a friend of the world makes himself an enemy of God *(James* 4:4). If to be a Christian would reside alone in words and an empty name, and if Christianity could be arranged as it pleases the world; if, furthermore, Christ would permit what is agreeable to the world, and the cross would have to be carried by a sword only . . . then both authorities and subjects – in fact, all the world – would be Christians. Inasmuch, however, as a man must be born anew *(John* 3:7), must die in baptism to his old life, and must

rise again with Christ unto a new life and Christian conduct, such a thing cannot and shall not be: 'It is easier,' says Christ, 'for a camel to go through the eye of a needle than for a rich man (by whom is meant the authorities in particular) to enter the kingdom of God or true Christianity' *(Matthew* 19:24) (trans. Friedmann 1973:39-40).

The essential duality proclaimed as Christ/World is often phrased in terms of "kingdoms"; the kingdom of heaven and the kingdom of darkness. Christ's own words, as cited in *Matthew 24*; *Mark 13*; or *Luke 21*: "The Kingdom is immanent. But only the pure will enter into it, while the rest will perish," serve as the basis for the *Täufer's* existential, free will eschatology. The possibility of attaining the kingdom of heaven was immediate and within one, and not solely a statement of life after death. Willingness to die a martyr's death as a statement of absolute faith despite the logical contradictions of the world was understood by the *Täufer* to be a way to gain the kingdom of heaven while on earth. Baptism was regarded by the *Täufer* as an analogous death and rebirth itself and they epitomized choice and free will by their restriction of it to adults. The *Täufer* believed that life was a constant struggle against the negative aspects of human nature which derive from "original sin." The struggle with human nature rendered the true Christian a "child of God." The metaphorical expression "Child of God" was commonly used and, according to Friedmann (1973:42), was central to the self-understanding of the *Täufer*. Wenger (1947:18-22) makes the same point: "Considering themselves as such children of God, they willingly accepted all subsequent hardships in the world in childlike obedience." Peter Riedemann, an early Hutterite leader, called the situation in which the *Täufer* found themselves "a covenant of childlike freedom" (Riedemann [or Rideman] 1950 edition:68).

**Metanoia and the Baptized Life**

Although brief in their duration, the "ministries" of the earliest Swiss Brethren were intense. Blaurock's energetic preaching was the longest and he gained a number of converts, particularly in the Tyrol, however, his writings do not yield to analysis much in the way of abstract statements. The devotional nature of the earliest *Täufer* writings evidenced the deeply existential nature of the movement and it was left to later writers to rationalize *Täufer* thought against their brief but intense history of suffering.

Foremost among *Täufer* apologists who followed were Balthasar Hubmaier, Menno Simons, Pilgrim Marpeck, and Peter Riedemann. Somewhat more peripheral, but nonetheless important, were Hans Hut, Hans Denk, Melchior Hoffman, and Thomas Müntzer.[11]

A thorough comparative study of all of these thinkers would of necessity be a work of enormous scope in itself, so I shall deal with the basic themes which emerge from their collective writings over time and which eventually articulated to form the ideological bases of today's *Täufer* peoples – particularly the Hutterites.[12]

The most central concept and act of the *Täufer*, as is implied by their very name (*Täufer*="baptizers"), was baptism itself. The baptism of adults rather than of children was a dramatic departure from the practices of all the established churches where one's membership in church began in infancy, just as one's membership in society began at birth. For the *Täufer* infant baptism was simply irrelevant. Membership in the church group *[Gemeinde]* was membership in the body of Christ *[corpus Christi]* and stemmed from a voluntary act based upon knowledge and understanding *[erkanntnis]* of moral issues. Just as one made a choice of free will by asking for baptism, one must continue to make such choices throughout life and be responsible for one's acts. Children were regarded as innocent but inclined toward sin *[Sünde]* because they had a proclivity for it which derived from their selfish *[selbstsüchtig]* nature. Selfishness, as manifested by Adam's eating of forbidden fruit was "original sin" and epitomized human nature which had to be overcome by leading a Christian or Christlike *[Christlichen]* life. To live a Christlike life, one had to adopt or aspire to a condition which was antithetical to selfishness *[selbstsüchtig]* which was called *gelassenheit* [literally, a "giving-up-ness" or self-possessed calm; resigned composure; deliberate patience]. The state of *gelassenheit* allowed humanity a chance to enter a bit of God's kingdom on earth [*Nachfolge*, literally, "succession"]. The condition of doubt or temptation [*anfechtung*] was the only impediment to *Nachfolge*. The *Täufer* understood that children were capable of doing evil but inasmuch as they were not capable of distinguishing between moral absolutes their salvation and absolution were assured. Only after the realization of conscious free choice which was manifested by baptism, could a person be held responsible for his acts. It was the freedom to choose (as Adam had done) which was linked to original sin, not the acts of children. Children were regarded as gifts of God and came from him – not from Adam. Pilgrim Marpeck's statements on these matters are particularly clear:

> Since however the guilt of sin consists in knowledge, Christ Jesus took away the whole world's sins through his blood, the sins of the ignorant through his world of promise, the sins of those who know through faith in him. To be sure one root of sin is in the lack of knowledge or ignorance yet it is not the essence of sin (trans. Klassen 1965:29).

> Children have before the use of their reason no sin, for the proclivity to sin (*erbbresten*) is the only thing they have, and this does not harm their salvation until it actually breaks out into open sin. Therefore baptism is not instituted for them (trans. Klassen 1965:3).

Simply put, the atonement of Christ covered the mistakes of children and was their salvation. Through the rebirth of baptism *Täufer* adults were reborn as children of God, and also represented their salvation against their impending doom and wider vision of the apocalypse. Baptism was the seal of their salvation against that day and brought them a part of it [*Nachfolge*] during the present.[13] According to Armour (1966:140), the all-encompassing character of *Täufer* baptism stemmed from the textual source of I *John* 5:6-8 which speaks of a tripartite baptism of spirit, water, and blood. The first baptism was that of spirit, which renewed a person from within. The awareness of this spirit was the source of some difference of opinion; Hubmaier believed it to be instantaneous but most writers thought it to be a more gradual awakening of conscience (Hut, Hoffman, and Marpeck took this position; see Armour 1966:141). The latter, more popular, view fitted early *Täufer* and later Hutterite and Mennonite child-rearing practices better and probably represents the difference between the early use of baptism as a ritual of conversion and the later incorporation of the rite into the socialization process (see Harada 1968). Baptism of the spirit was the essence of salvation itself because it was the inner revelation of free choice. The appearance of the baptism of the spirit as the first in the baptismal triad in the life of the individual is also consonant with its historical appearance. The earliest theological discussions of the baptism of adults were concerned with the spirit, not the act of water baptism itself. This concern with spirit spawned what historians call the spiritualist sects (see Friedmann 1973:117). The baptism of the spirit was also associated with the holy spirit of the trinity itself.

The second baptism was the baptism by water which was bestowed by the group upon the individual and was explicitly a recognition of his or her membership in the *Gemeinde*, which was also the "body of Christ" [*corpus Christi*]. Water baptism was essentially a social recognition of the inner revelation worked by the Holy Spirit. Water was also understood by some as a harbinger or mark of suffering for it was antecedent to and associated with that condition throughout the Bible (see Armour 1966). The appearance of water baptism is also consonant with this historical context: following theological discussion of spiritual revelation adult baptism was actually practiced, just as within individuals water baptism was felt to proceed from group recognition of the inner revelation of individuals. Water baptism is also the most obviously holistic manifestation of the trinity and is associated with God the Father as the unity of three.

The final baptism of blood is also consonant within historical context for it was a product of the persecution which followed closely upon the first water baptisms of adults. The *Täufer* claimed that true disciples of Christ would suffer just as their exemplar had. The suffering of Christ could be both an inner suffering of doubt and despair [*anfechtung*] and corporeal suffering. Christ's crucifixion brought both aspects of suffering together when out of his pain he was reputed to have said "Father why hast thou forsaken me?"

. . . if the consciences of some may not have been sensitive enough to have created the expected trials within, the officials of the civic order were certain to create trials without. The anabaptists [sic Täufer] expected both. And thus, they experienced the baptism of blood on two sides; the baptism of the mystics on the one side, and the baptism of the martyrs on the other (Armour 1966:141).

The primary linkage of blood baptism is with the Son of the trinity. The baptism of blood was martyrdom, which was directly the result of living a Christlike [Christlichen] life. When regarded as a baptism or rebirth, blood-martyrdom was not death but the essence of life itself. "Thus from the initial reception of the Spirit to the final death and resurrection of the body, the whole Christian life was a series of 'baptisms'" (Armour 1966:14).

I will deal with the more formal structural analysis of the equation of the tripartite baptism with the trinity conception of God and the symbols of birth, life and death in Chapter III. However, in concluding this chapter on the origins of the Täufer movement as drawn from the statements, biblicism, and reported acts of the Täufer themselves, it should be evident that Täufer cosmology was the embodiment of a growing aggregate of ideas forged together by the experience of persecution. The concern with baptism was an existential issue of the mind, forged by experience itself, and regarded as a triumph of the free will over death. Rebirth represented an answer of eternal life to the existential question posed by living under a constant threat of death. The fullest conception of the tripartite baptisms of spirit, water, and blood derives from the experiences of the Täufer over time and is consistent with their history of persecution. As we shall see, the calm of gelassenheit has come to pervade Hutterite history as well as contemporary ritual practice and has much to do with the kind of "cognized" process that baptism has become. It would be folly to suggest that people who must be prepared to die for their beliefs do not know what they are doing. In the most profound sense they must know the consequence of their act better than we can ever conceive of it.

The pervasive theme which emerges from the origin of the Täufer movement, or its "birth" as understood by themselves, is metanoia, that is, new life. However, theirs was not only the "rebirth" of individuals through baptism, since the reinstitution of the believers' baptism for adults was also regarded by them as a "rebirth" of the church of God itself, or Body of Christ as a group of believers alienated from the world. The awakening of the spirit within individual *Täufer* marked a rekindling of Christianity itself, as they understood it.

The events of nearly five centuries ago in which the torture of one segment of society by established religious and political authorities may seem remote to us now but one has only to think of contemporary events and issues in human rights struggles around the world to connect our experiences to those of both the *Täufer* and their persecutors. Seen from the vantage point of those who chose adult baptism, the baptism of infants and children was invalid because they could not make moral choices. From the point of view of those who identified with the position of the established church, to deny children the sacrament of baptism was to deny them salvation. Given the mortality rates of the period, even surviving childhood was a grim possibility and so the debate raged and overflowed into violence because the meaning of existence turned on the issue of baptism for both groups. Heady notions of free-will, choice, predestination, and God's will were intrinsic to the debate on baptism and are also raised today in the extreme acrimony of our own debate over abortion. In the early 16th century the gulf widened quickly and the possibility of violence turned to certainty within a year as the *Täufer* and their opposition both pursued what each felt was a moral imperative.

## NOTES

1 The Amish, Mennonites, and Hutterites all trace their origins to Switzerland and the Swiss Brethren and although the three groups differ in social organization and ideology, they can be understood to comprise a special branch of Christianity based on adult baptism and varying degrees of alienation from their host societies. All three groups are characterized by varying degrees of collective production, great resistance to change, and a very wary approach to material goods. The descendants of the Swiss Brethren in Switzerland itself still exist although they are usually called Mennonites, and are barely distinguishable from them.
2 For the original German see Zieglschmid (1943). Beck (1883:19-21) gives virtually an identical account. For English translations see Wenger (1947:24-25); Bender (1950:37); Williams and Mergal (1957:41-46). The

Hutterite chronicles have only been translated piecemeal – there is no comprehensive translation.

3 Luther's position is largely implicit in his own translation of the Bible. See Armour (1966:114-116, 118), Estep (1963:7-20, 126-145).

4 Denck was probably the first to point out this passage, but the translation was always suspect. The Greek word in the passage translates better as "pledge" or "promise" (but not "oath"). The Zürich Bible utilizes *Kundschaft* (literally, "clientele, or information"), and so Hubmaier explicitly denied the "covenental" theology of baptism. Marpeck was puzzled by the translation but eventually used *Bund* for clarity. See Friedmann (1973:134, 155fn.).

5 For the positions of the Zwickau prophets and other related movements which preceded the *Täufer* see especially Newman (1896) and Williams and Mergal (1957).

6 Zwingli's abandonment of the persons he had begun the Reformation in Zürich with is poorly understood, but appears to have been no less than a lapse in faith itself for his later acts and statements are directly contradictory to his earlier statements. The *Täufer* felt betrayed by Zwingli and among contemporary Hutterites he has taken on the dimensions of a "Judas" character.

7 For a systematic examination of the records and their varying degrees of reliability, along with regional distributions, see Clasen (1973).

8 Kierkegaard's discussion of existence, actuality, objectivity, subjectivity, faith, etc., occurs in his most significant essay, *Concluding Unscientific Postscript*, written in 1848.

9 At least four accounts of this martyrdom still exist, Reublin's account is reprinted in Schmid (1952), an account written by Klaus von Graveneck remains in the Wolfenbuttel library, a third account can be found in Köhler (1908), and the fourth is from *Die alteste Chronik der Hutteriscshen Brüder* itself.

10 I have abridged the entry as marked (. . .).

11 Thomas Müntzer's relationship to the *Täufer* movement has been the source of considerable debate for many years. Müntzer was involved in the Peasants' War (1524-1525), and later in the capture of the city of Munster by revolutionaries with *Täufer* affiliations. The tyranny which was established at Münster included a forced adoption of adult baptism and polygamy, which were condemned by Swiss Brethren, but Reformed, Roman, and Lutheran groups used the *Täufer* connection to condemn the entire movement. Müntzer's theological writings have recently been reexamined by Stoesz (1964) and fall for the most part within the *Täufer* tradition. Müntzer's main divergence was his insistence upon the doctrine of the sword (violent revolution) as a means to re-establish the Church of God in what he felt to be the last days of the world. Müntzer was sure that the world would end within several years and his chiliastic vision of the apocalypse found a ready adherent in Hans Hut and definitely influenced Hans Denck as well (Stoesz 1964). For a review of Müntzer's relationship to Luther see especially Hinrichs (1952), and for a discussion of the Peasants' War (or revolt), see Dirrim (1959:41-93).

12 For reviews of the baptismal theologies of Hubmaier, Hut, Hoffman, and Marpeck see Armour (1966), and for Menno Simons, Estep (1963:104-126). The emergence of Marpeck as a *Täufer* spokesman in the Strasbourg area is well documented by Krahn (1969). Riedemann's own works are available in translation (1950) and speak eloquently for themselves, however, for analysis see especially Heimann (1952).

13 The eschatological notion of the "seal" against the last day of judgment implies that the baptized will be an "elect" at the apocalypse. This conception of baptism is isomorphic with the ordinance of circumcision.

Both ordinances were "seals" (sigilla) in which *vis justificandi* were confirmed. See especially Armour (1966:36) for discussion. For a review of suffering as attainment of "grace" in martyrdom see Stephenson (1981a).

# CHAPTER II

# COMMUNAL LIFE AND THE HUTTERITES

"And all that believed were together, and
had all things common"
*Acts* 2:44

Amidst the general persecution of the *Täufer* people throughout Europe several islands of temporary sanctuary appeared. These areas of religious toleration were in Moravia, East Friesland, and the United Provinces (The Netherlands). In these places the *Täufer* organized themselves and established patterns of community life which allowed them to continue their existence through the following four centuries and into the present. Given temporary respite, *Täufer* refugees in scattered sanctuaries developed into the Amish, Mennonite, and Hutterite peoples. The Amish and Russian Mennonite groups underwent several transformations after the Reformation era and do not live in the same manner now as then. The rest of the European and American Mennonites have adapted to their host societies and are not easily distinguished from other sectarian church groups of the evangelical type. Only the Hutterites developed a pattern of life which has persisted from the Reformation era to the present (Harada 1968:88).

## Nikolsburg and the Liechtenstein Estates

In 1526 a *Täufer* community was established on the Liechtenstein estates in Moravia, in the Nikolsburg area. The early leader of the Nikolsburg group was another of the Swiss Brethren, Balthasar Hubmaier, and most of his followers were converts from Austrian and Tyrolean Hapsburg lands. Many of the Nikolsburg *Täufer* had been converted by George Blaurock, and later by a man named Jacob Hutter – a "hatter" by trade. The Nikolsburg *Täufer* community practiced believers' baptism in a manner which Hubmaier had established for them.

One aspect of Hubmaier's conception of baptism was that the spirit came instantaneously upon a person. This notion of instant revelation may have served well in converting persons but it did not correspond well to the socialization needs of a developing community with children. Friction over this issue was compounded by the arrival of increasing numbers of refugees from the Hapsburg lands whose mettle had recently been tested by "the diviner's fire" of persecution, whose conversions were in the past, and whose needs for material assistance were immediate. A schism developed between the older and indigenous *Täufer*, who had Hubmaier as their leader, and some of the recent arrivals, who had Jacob Wiedeman as their leader. Many of Wiedeman's group were widows and orphans who lived in abject poverty and who had recently seen close relatives die martyrs' deaths. The latter group believed in a doctrine of non-resistance when physical force threatened; martyrdoms equivalent to Christ's and their own lost family members' could not be accomplished otherwise.

Wiedeman's group needed much material assistance and greatly strained the resources of the fledgling community. The needs of the always increasing numbers of refugees resulted in a grudgingly instituted sharing of wealth. Wiedeman began to advocate the adoption of a total community of goods [*gemeinschaft der Güter*, or *Gütergemeinschaft*] modeled after the first church of Jerusalem as indicated in *Acts* 2:44: "and all that believed were together, and had all things common." Eventually, the faction led by Hubmaier lost their leadership following his arrest and Hans Spitalmaier was left to defend and expand upon the political and economic positions of that group. The intensity of Wiedeman's demands increased in Hubmaier's absence and the two groups began to worship separately. The indigenous and more entrenched people of Spitalmaier's faction began to espouse the use of the sword for self-defense and they became known as *Schwertler* (people of the sword), while Wiedeman and his followers chose the route of non-resistance and were called *Stabler* (people of the staff).

During the Reformation era the unity of church and state was thought to yield a resultant social stability because diversity was conceived of as a harbinger of generalized instability and administrative chaos. Dissension in the ranks of their subjects could potentially threaten the power relationships among lords of estates and so were undesirable from their perspective. According to one account (Smith 1950:56), Lord Liechtenstein, in the midst of this discussion of the uses of violence, gave Wiedeman a choice of conforming to the majority view or of leaving his lands altogether. A second version of the schism is that the Lord Liechtenstein was put under pressure to tax the *Täufer* of Nikolsburg for a war chest needed by the Hapsburgs to protect themselves from invading Turks. If Liechtenstein refused their demands, the Hapsburgs threatened to march on him with an Imperial army. Lord Liechtenstein's reply was that force would be met with force. Wiedeman's response to the situation was to state, "since you threaten to protect us with the use of force we cannot stay" (Hostetler 1974:15). The latter version is given general credence by contemporary Hutterites. Whatever social forces dictated events, it is certain that two factions developed over a dispute concerning the proper redistribution of scarce resources and the use of arms in the face of impending warfare. The two groups came to an impasse and Wiedeman's group decided to leave Nikolsburg altogether. According to Estep (1966:85), many of Wiedeman's group were widows and orphans who had "little food, fewer clothes, and less money." The departure of the *Stabler* from Nikolsburg and the adoption of *gütergemeinschaft* are described in *Die alteste Chronik der Hutterischen Brüder* as follows:

> Therefore they sought to sell their possessions. Some sold, but others simply abandoned them and they departed with one another from thence. Whatever remained of theirs the lords of Liechtenstein sent after them. And so from Nikolsburg, Bergen and thereabouts there gathered about two hundred persons without [counting] the children before the town [Nikolsburg]. Certain persons came out . . . and wept from great compassion with them, but others argued . . . . Then they got themselves up, and went out and pitched camp . . . in a desolate village (Bogenitz) and abode there one day and one night, taking

counsel together in the Lord concerning their present necessity, and appointed ministers for their temporal necessities . . . . At that time these men spread out a cloak before the people, and every man laid his substance upon it, with a willing heart and without constraint, for the sustenance of those in necessity, according to the teaching of the prophets and apostles *Isaiah* 23:18; *Acts* 2, 4, and 6.

## Austerlitz and Auspitz on the Estate of the Lords von Kaunitz

Wiedeman's group reached an agreement with the Lords von Kaunitz concerning the nonpayment of war tax and the doctrine of nonresistance and were allowed to settle at Austerlitz after three weeks of travel and living in the open. The Lords von Kaunitz had long tolerated a diversity of religious groups on their lands including other *Täufer* and the *Picards* (Hussites).

The persecution of the *Täufer* throughout the rest of Europe continued unabated and by 1530 at least 1,000 persons had been executed for their professed belief in adult baptism (see Clasen 1973). Due to intense persecution the influx of refugees onto the estates of the Lords von Kaunitz steadily increased until by 1529 at least 2,000 persons were living in an emergency state of *Gütergemeinschaft* in several *Brüderhofes* (communes) (Friedmann 1958). These early settlements can be thought of as little more than crowded and rather poor refugee camps.

The entire collection of *Brüderhofes* was presided over by one leader [*Vorsteher*] named Gabriel Ascherman. Ascherman's poor leadership meant that the *Brüderhofes* were disorganized and by the time Wilhelm Reublin joined the *Brüderhof* at Austerlitz in 1530 he found conditions there to be intolerable. Wiedeman's leadership was despotic and included inequities such as forced marriages between nonconsenting young people (see Harada 1968). Reublin eventually accused Wiedeman of an unequal distribution of wealth and on January 8 Reublin left Austerlitz for Auspitz with a following of 250 adults and many children. In addition 40 persons too ill to travel or work were lodged together in a cottage until the Brethren could establish themselves at Auspitz. However, large-scale internal dissension also plagued Reublin's *Brüderhof* at Auspitz and his attempt at revitalization failed.[1]

Finally, Jacob Hutter, the *Täufer*'s most successful evangelist in the Tyrol, was forced to flee to Moravia. Hutter had previously stayed at Austerlitz but his sympathies were now with the people at Auspitz and so he joined them on August 11, 1533 (Estep 1963:86).

Hutter thought that he had been called upon by God to organize the fragmented Moravian groups into one elect people and he began to reorganize the *Brüderhof* at Auspitz almost immediately. An announcement was made during Hutter's first sermon which described the chaotic state of the *Brüderhof* and advocated the immediate institution of reforms. After much diligent work Hutter was elected *Vorsteher*, but the other leaders whom he had displaced decided that his reforms were too harsh and constituted an usurpation of their elected authority and so eventually they broke away from Hutter's group at Auspitz. The egotism of the previous leaders was manifest in the names chosen for their respective *Brüderhofes*: Gabriel Ascherman's followers became known as Gabrielites, and Philip Plener's as Philipites during their own lifetimes.[2]

Hutter's initial attempts at obtaining the leadership of the Moravian *Brüderhofes* were blocked by Schutzinger, Plener and Ascherman. Hutter had insisted that a complete severance of all contact with the "world" was necessary for converts. Hutter insisted that they give up all material wealth and family contact. These, Hutter preached, were necessary forms of *gelassenheit*. When several recent converts were discovered to be hoarding private funds, Hutter boldly accused Schutzinger's wife of being a "Sapphira" who also possessed forbidden private wealth. The people of the *Brüderhof* were upset by Hutter's accusations but they eventually searched Schutzinger's room, there discovering four Bernese pounds. Schutzinger was deposed and Ascherman and Plener also, for having supported him in the dispute (Hostetler 1974:19-20, Friedmann 1964).

Hutter was elected *Vorsteher* following this episode and immediately instituted broadly-based reform measures. Hutter's relationship to his following was charismatic and after several years he had the Moravian *Brüderhofes* operating efficiently (see

Miller and Stephenson 1980).

For many years (since 1528) King Ferdinand of Austria had demanded that the *Täufer* be expelled from Moravia, however he had met with little success. In 1535, following the bloody capture and rule of the city of Münster by a group with *Täufer* connections, Ferdinand appeared in person before the Moravian nobles to renew his demands, promising war if they would not accede. Thereupon, all *Täufer* were driven from their villages and forced to wander in small groups through the forests. Some groups actually lived in caves during the Moravian persecution. Bounty hunting for *Täufer* was widespread. Hutter left the Moravian groups at their request that he go into hiding in the Tyrol — a condition and district with which he was familiar. Hutter hid until he was discovered November 29, 1535 in St. Andrews, Austria. He was immediately imprisoned with Hans Stener (who had hidden him) and his own wife. Hutter was taken to Innsbruck for trial and execution. Hutter's captors tried to elicit information about his confederates and followers by torturing him. He was whipped, put on the rack, and held alternately in freezing water and then made to stand in an overheated room. His captors publicly poured brandy over his wounds and lit it on fire. He was burned at the stake February 25, 1536 after three months of torture (Hostetler 1974:23). After hearing of Hutter's demonstration of courage and faith throughout excruciating tortures, his followers took his last name and openly called themselves the Hutterian Brethren [*Hutterischen Brüder*].

**The Golden Period in Moravia**

Following the martyrdom of Jacob Hutter, the persecution in Moravia subsided and lesser lords began to allow *Täufer* people — including the group now calling themselves Hutterians, or Hutterites — to settle on their lands. There is every evidence that Hutterite (indeed all *Täufer*) settlements were economically advantageous to the nobility who needed skilled craftsmen, and so the lords of lesser estates had a great deal to gain by encouraging resettlement on their lands. On the smaller estates the Hutterites were also initially less visible (Klassen 1962:169-

190). The resettlement of Moravia by the Hutterites accelerated, partly driven by their initial acceptance by lesser lords. As a consequence they were even accepted by the nobility on major estates whose political and economic positions were to a degree threatened by the newfound Hutterite-based solvency of the smaller estates. The Hutterite chronicles describe this efflorescence as a movement from a "good" period (1554-1565) to a "golden period" (1565-1592). During the intervening years (1529-1621) 102 *Brüderhofes* were begun and inhabited by 20-30,000 people.[3]

## Social Organization of the Moravian Brüderhofs

The size of the *Brüderhofes* varied from between 100-400 people during the Moravian "golden period" but communes of around 300 appear to have been common (Hostetler 1974:52). The populations of the *Brüderhofes* were not only subject to natural increase but were swelled by the efforts of Hutterian missionaries at work throughout Europe – particularly in the Tyrol. The occupational backgrounds of Hutterian converts were diverse. Klassen's (1962:126-154) study of court records indicates that converts came from virtually every social class and from most occupational groups. However, a sizable portion were peasants and craftsmen and many of the leaders were from urban, professional backgrounds, or came directly from the clergy. The relatively large size of the *Brüderhofes* was partly an accommodation to the volume of converts and to the wide diversity of their occupational backgrounds.

Among the most common trades practiced in the *Brüderhofes* were agriculture, bookbinding, brewing, carpentry, carriage- and wagon-making, cutlery manufacture, lantern-making, leatherworking, harness- and saddle-making, masonry, milling, nursing, pharmacy, rope-making, shoemaking, tanning, pottery-making and glazing, tailoring, watchmaking, dyeing, weaving, warping, caring for vineyards, medicine, coppersmithing, tinsmithing, locksmithing, roof thatching, scythe-making, and wheel-making (wheelwrights) (Hostetler 1974:42). The crafts were governed by sets of rules [*Ordnungen*] which were used to standardize the products and their quality through their manner of production. For example, ornate pottery designs and glazes were not allowed, nor were tailors allowed to fabricate elaborate clothing styles. Some enterprises were forbidden altogether such as merchandising, arms manufacture, and selling drinks (innkeeping). The pottery industry of the Hutterites stimulated the development of an indigenous ceramics industry which persisted long after they had abandoned Moravia, and the earliest examples of *Haban* pottery in the *faience* or *majolica* styles are valuable museum pieces today. (Hostetler 1974:44-52; Krisztinkovich 1962).

The control and organization of economic activities was accomplished by a managerial hierarchy fused to a set of spiritual leaders at an intermediate level, but separated from the latter at the uppermost level of hierarchy. Each trade industry had a foreman [*Furgestellten*] who was responsible for its overall management. Profits from all the industries were turned over by their respective *Furgestellten* to the steward, or householder [*Haushalter*] of the *Brüderhof.* The *Haushalter* converted profit to material goods for distribution; he was the active redistributor of wealth and was responsible for the welfare of the aged, infirm, and children as well. The *Haushalter* sometimes had an assistant *Weinzierl* to help him and to assume his responsibilities in the former's absence. The position of the *Einkaufer* (treasurer, or buyer) involved dealing with the "outside world." The *Einkaufer*'s commission was to take care to neither be cheated nor cheat in dealings with the "world" for supplies and trade. There were two principal managerial positions connected with agriculture and these were *Kellner* (caretaker of vineyards, literally "waiter"), and *Meier* (sometimes called *Kastner*, "caretaker of storage bins"; *Meier* is literally "dairy farmer"). The *Meier* and *Kellner* were responsible for general maintenance of all tools, buildings, roads, and cellars. The positions of *Haushalter, Weinzierl, Einkaufer, Kellner, Meier,* and the *Furgestellten* were collectively called *Diener der Notdurft* (ministers of temporal needs, or "stewards").

The administration of the economic organization was linked to the spiritual leaders at the position of *Haushalter.* The *Haushalter* cooperated closely in general managerial duties with the preacher (or oldest of two preachers) [*Diener am Wort*], or "minister of the word." The duties of the *Diener am Wort* were described by Michael Sattler as follows

> To read, to admonish and teach, to warn, to discipline, to ban in the church, to lead out in prayer for the advancement of all the brethren and sisters, to lift up the bread when it is broken, and in all things to see to the care of the body of Christ, in order that it may be built up and developed, and the mouth of the slanderer stopped (Sattler 1527, trans. by Wenger 1945:250).

All of the collective *Diener am Wort* elected a leader or *Vorsteher* ("elder," "moderator," or less accurately, "bishop") who had the responsibility of converting the word of God to social order by issuing regulations [*Ordnungen*]. The *Vorsteher* also presided over meetings of ordained leaders for the discussion of problems, or election of new *Diener am Wort*. The *Vorsteher* also corresponded with the missionaries [*Sendboten*] (more precisely "apostles") which were sent out from the *Brüderhofes* to preach in foreign and (usually) hostile lands. The *Sendboten* were held in the highest regard by their fellows because they were the most likely to be martyred – approximately 80% were executed (see Hostetler 1974:32-35; Harada 1968:130-134; Friedman 1961:11-114). Die *alteste Chronik der Hutterischen Brüder* is largely an account written by various *Vorsteher* and includes correspondence with the *Sendboten*. The *Vorsteher* was also *Diener am Wort* in his own *Brüderhof*.

As is implied in the official name of the Hutterites [*Hutterischen Brüder*], the Hutterian Brethren were (and are) a patriarchal society; women were not allowed to vote, or hold managerial positions. Women were organized into task-oriented small groups whose membership varied according to the vagaries of postmarital residence (patrilocality was practiced) and the exigencies of pregnancy and motherhood. The tasks of women were cooking, spinning, sewing, childcare, and laundry. Contemporary Hutterite social organization resembles that of the Moravian "golden" period, but differs in that contemporary Hutterites do not practice trades for commercial purposes, and neither are there *Sendboten* to missionize on behalf of "the word of God." During the Reformation era there was a generalized belief among radicals – including the *Täufer, Schwenckfelders,*

*Münsterites*, and leaders of the Peasants' Revolt – that the return of Christ was imminent and that the end of the world was drawing near. This chiliastic vision was partly responsible for the missionary zeal which permeated the Hutterite communes of Moravia. The harsh reality of the *Täufer*'s persecution fostered a generally apocalyptic world view, and their response was simultaneously an attempt to convert and save as many others as possible, and a protective withdrawal from "the world" in quotidian affairs. Many persons felt "called" to missionize and, as previously indicated, the *Sendboten* were held in high esteem by their contemporaries. Each *Sendboten* was given handwritten tracts to carry and territories to cover. Commemorative hymns were written to honor their departure and their (somewhat rarer) return. The letters and hymns written by captured *Sendboten* form a large part of the Hutterite Chronicles, various codices and their *Ausbund* hymnody (see Martens 1969).

**The Second Moravian Persecution**

During the latter stages of the 16th Century, Europe was plunged into war and the Counter Reformation. One area which was central to both sources of turmoil was Moravia. The Hutterites were subjected to demands for war taxes by landlords hard pressed by Emperor Rudolph II to support repulsion of the invading Turks. The Hutterites refused to pay war taxes and so livestock and other material goods were confiscated from them. To avoid payment of war taxes Hutterites began to seek refuge on other estates and a pattern of transience quickly emerged. Poorer nobility would occasionally allow Hutterites to settle on their small estates in hopes of enriching the quality of their holdings. Unfortunately for both the poorer nobles and the Hutterites, increases in the equity of their holdings meant greater visibility and increased pressure from the Emperor for more tax revenues – which the nobility would in turn attempt to extract from the frustrated Hutterites. Once the exploitation cycle had been completed, the Hutterites would either be expelled from the estate or leave of their own free will.

The Counter Reformation also resulted in intolerance in

Moravia. In 1575 Nikolsburg became Roman Catholic when the Dietrichstein family inherited the estate. The anti-Hutterian polemics initiated at this time increased to a virtual crescendo of hate after 1599 and were orchestrated largely by Christoph Fischer, a Roman Catholic priest. Fischer's tracts such as *Fifty-four Important Reasons Why the Hutterites Should Not be Tolerated in the Land*,[4] stirred the envious and impoverished local peasantry to acts of open hostility towards the Brethren. Eventually, 16 of the *Brüderhofes* were sacked by the Turks and many of their inhabitants killed; still more were enslaved and transported to Turkey (Friedmann 1943). Following the Hapsburg-Turkish wars (1593-1606), and before the Hutterites could regroup, the Thirty-Years' War broke out (1618). During this time the Catholic and Protestant states fought one another and the Hutterian pacifists were again caught in the middle. Of the remaining 40 *Brüderhofes*, 29 were destroyed or plundered by Roman Catholic troops in 1619. In 1620 the Polish Army killed or wounded 116 people at the Pribitz *Brüderhof*. The Hutterite Chronicle contains the following descriptive passage of that event:

> It is impossible to write or tell of all the great and inhuman cruelties which came upon us and others in this ungodly, accursed and devilish war at the hands of the . . . imperial forces. . . . Women with child and mothers in childbed as well as virgins were shamelessly attacked. The men were burned with glowing iron and red-hot pans; their feet were held in the fire until the toes were burned off; wounds were cut into which powder was poured and then set afire; fingers and ears were cut off; eyes forced out by inhuman tortures on the wheel; men were hung up by the neck like thieves; all sorts of such brutality and unheard of godlessness were committed, half of which is not be written for shame (trans. by Horsch 1931:55).

During the 15th and 16th Centuries the aftermath of brutal war was often just as terrifying as actual conflict due to the ravages of disease. Following the beginning of the Thirty-Years War plagues further devastated the Brethren. In one year alone (1621), approximately one-third of the Brethren succumbed to disease (Hostetler 1974:66-67).

**The Persecution/Migration Sequence**

After the second Moravian Persecution, there followed a sequence of starts at communal life which were always met with destruction by outside forces and which resulted in the abandonment of an old locale and migration to a new one. This pattern is described in great detail by Hostetler (1974:61-18) and summarized by Stephenson (1978:55-63). Here I am concerned mainly with the cultural themes imbedded in the patterns of migration and so (with the exception of the appearance of a major visionary in their midst) we can begin to move away from a close-up view of Hutterite history in favour of a broader historical perspective.

There are a number of interesting precedents set during the course of Hutterite history thus far described which later developed into an institutionalized form of community growth and fission. The first of these precedents is that migration settled disputes which were incurred by unequal assess to material wealth and abuses of power by various leaders. *Gütergemeinschaft* was in fact born of such a dispute and was first practiced while actually *en route* to a new locale. This solution to poverty among refugees was both biblical in rationale and practical in nature. Furthermore, it was precipitated by a collective act of conscience in the face of violent persecution. *The baptism of adults, in other words, had obvious consequences for the group, not just for individuals.*

A second precedent is that the successful radiation of the *Brüderhofes* depended in part on the loss to the commune of some of its most energetic young men who, if they were lucky enough to survive their tenure as a *Sendbote*, could return to take up important leadership positions. While some of the population was leaving (*Sendboten*), others were arriving, and this booming population drove the spread of *Brüderhofes* across the countryside.

The repetition of persecution/migration sequence which subsumes these two precedents, entails nine major migrations until the exhausted remnants of the Hutterites arrived at a settlement named Radichev on the banks of the Desna in Russia. This sequence is summarized below and graphically demonstrates the enormous difficulties the Hutterian people encountered for over three centuries (see Figure 2.1).

## MIGRATION/PERSECUTION

| | | |
|---|---|---|
| Zurich (1525) | to | Nicholsburgh (1526) |
| Nicholsburgh (1528) | to | Austerlitz (1528) |
| Austerlitz (1530) | to | Auspitz (1530) |
| Auspitz (1535) | dispersal | Sabatisch founded (1546) |
| Sabatisch (1547) | to | Moravia (until 1605) |
| Moravia (1621) | to | Alwinz, Transylvania (1621) |
| Transylvania (1767) | to | Wallachia (1767) |
| Wallachia (1770) | to | Vishenka, Ukraine (1770) |
| Vishenka (1802) | to | Radichev (dissolution, 1819) |

**Figure 2.1**

When they were not being crushed by armies, having their books burned by priests, their children taken from them, burying the dead and searching for a new home while the old one smoldered; they encountered severe problems in maintaining communal life anyway. In a sense the problems of persecution and the constant need to migrate solved the principal difficulties of continued communal life before they could arise. These difficulties finally emerged in Russia where a surplus of manpower could not be deployed in new settlements and disputes over land ownership arose. The community fragmented and seemed on the verge of being assimilated into groups of nearby Mennonites when an important visionary appeared. A Hutterite leader named Michael Waldner, who had long been troubled by the collapse of communal life, had a vision while in a trance state. In the vision an angel appeared and showed him both heaven and hell. Heaven, he described as "a multitude of angels who praised God with indescribable songs." Hell "was a terrible picture to behold, with anguish and pain, which no mortal can imagine." Waldner then asked the angel what his own fate would be. The angel posed a question in response: "Can you tell me whether any person was saved from the great flood besides those in the ark? Now you know your place. The ark is the *Gemeinschaft* of the holy spirit to which you no longer belong." Waldner wept and was told to return to his Brethren and to re-establish a *Gemeinschaft* "after the pattern of Jesus and his disciples." Waldner then described flying through the air after his guiding angel left him. He awoke to find his family surrounding him, weeping, and thinking he had died. His first words were, "Don't you hear the angels sing?" (Friedmann 1966:149). From that day Waldner described himself as a "new man" and began to pray and meditate with his friend Jacob Hofer. One day the two agreed that whichever of them finished their prayer first would incorporate the other into a new *Gemeinschaft*. Hofer finished first and laid his hands upon Waldner, who in turn laid hands upon the other. Both men then included their wives, and began to exhort others to join them. The *Gemeinschaft* grew as each day more persons underwent incorporation into it. The renewal of *Gütergemeinschaft* took place at one end of the village of Hutterdorf in 1859. One year later Darius Walter established *Gütergemeinschaft* at the opposite end of the village.[5]

Michael Waldner was a blacksmith and was called *Schmied-Michael* after his occupation. His group became known as the *Schmiedeleut* ("Smith-group"), Darius Walter's followers took his first name and were called *Dariusleut* (Darius-group). The two groups lived communally for 15 and 14 years respectively and then, after resisting pressure from the Russian government to accept Russian schooling and conscription yet again, they migrated. This time, however, like so many others they went west to North America – arriving in North Dakota in 1874 after having survived three and a half centuries of persecution for daring to put an act of individual conscience and the simple ideas of shared wealth and pacifism before their duty to the state. The European crucible molded Hutterian consciousness which took shape in the relative calm and open spaces of North America. Their relationship to "the world" is still problematic and imprisonment and even death have been encountered in America. However, the storm of strife and suffering has abated and a new culture has emerged from the chaos. In describing the Hutterian people our first step is to try and understand the sort of symbolization which their history has yielded and to see how these symbols now fuse individuals to the group through ritual expression.

## NOTES

1 Reublin represents an important link to the origins of the *Täufer* movement in Switzerland where he was among the first to advocate adult baptism (see Chapter I). Reublin's own tenure as a *Brüderhof* leader was shortened when he was accused of hoarding private wealth (being an "Ananias") and deposed.
2 After becoming disillusioned with their leader the Gabrielites eventually reunited with the Hutterites following a brief inhabitation of Silesia. Most of the Philipites left Moravia but were imprisoned at the castle at Passau. The few remaining Philipites rejoined the Hutterites after being visited by Peter Riedemann (Hostetler 1974:23). Hutter's version of the schism can be found in Friedmann (1964).
3 Estimates vary widely (between 20 and 70 thousand) but the lower range appears less prone to the exaggerations of polemicists. See especially Clasen (1972:244) and Hostetler (1974:29fn.).
4 Fischer's entire career seems to have been devoted to ridding the world of what he was convinced was the work of the devil – the Hutterites. He authored many tracts containing half-truths and blatant lies about life in the *Brüderhofes* – logical reasoning does not appear to have been his forte (see, for example, *Der Hutterischen Widertäuffer Taubenkobel* (Ingolstad, 1607), Hostetler (1974:27, 37-38, 50, 56, 62). For many years Fischer's importance and reliability were vastly overestimated by historians and led to an inaccurate representation of the *Täufer* in most Reformation histories.
5 Waldner's experiences were originally related by his son but were unknown outside Hutterite society until 1964 when Hostetler found the original document in an Alberta Hutterite colony. For an edited translation see Friedmann (1966).

# CHAPTER III

## TOWARDS A STRUCTURAL ANALYSIS OF HUTTERITE HISTORY AND SYMBOLS OF REBIRTH

> . . . man becomes *himself* only after having solved a series of
> desperately difficult and even dangerous situations
> (Eliade 1958:128)

Contemporary Hutterite society cannot be properly understood through a conventional synchronic ethnological mode of investigation. Because Hutterite social organization and beliefs derive from the interpretation of sacred texts (the Bible and Hutterian Chronicles), which are thought to contain both history and eternal truths, continuity through time is an essential aspect of Hutterite life.

> The . . . Hutterites are not a 'community' or a 'tribe', but a people or nation, with a written history and with historical precedents for their social system. They cannot be studied apart from their history; the classic ethnological style of accepting a single living community as the totality of human experience simply won't work. The everyday behavior of Hutterites is saturated with precedents and guidelines derived from historical experience. They study their history books and sermons, their epistolary literature consisting mainly of pathetic letters written in sixteenth- and seventeenth-century jails, and above all, the Bible (Bennett 1975:448).

In this chapter I shall attempt an analysis of Hutterite history which relates phenomenal factors (demography, poverty, persecution, etc.) to their emergent existential and communal ideational system. The important consideration here is the relationship between the symbols which encode meaning and the history which serves as the source of that meaning and of those symbols. This is the first step to an understanding of Hutterite consciousness and its relationship to ritual praxis.

## The Reformation and the Täufer

The Lutheran Reformation occurred within the context of changing economies which radically altered traditional medieval social patterns and transformed many previously rural populations and areas into urbanized ones. To finance burgeoning urban government, high rents, taxes, and church tithes were implemented, but were greatly resented by the common tradesmen they pauperized. The influx of large numbers of people to the cities left many rural estates with labor shortages which in turn resulted in the passage of harsh laws designed to keep the peasantry on the land and at fixed incomes. Consequently the turmoil among the rural peasantry matched that of the angry tradesmen in the cities. Increased urbanism also corresponded with a general rise in literacy, and the translation of the Bible into the vernacular of the common people had given them both a spiritual guide and a court of last appeal when church-rationalized and state-instituted economic reforms became burdensome.

The Roman Catholic church was the sole legitimate vehicle of religious expression in the medieval tradition and since the Roman Catholic church was state affiliated from monarch down to cleric, its position on state political and economic affairs was generally one of *status quo*. In accordance with the church's political affiliation to "divine right" monarchies, the dominant cosmological theme of Roman Catholic theology was determinism in the guise of "predestination."

The Lutheran Reformation carried within itself the seeds of its own eventual fragmentation simply because by reinterpreting the Bible, and by basing their separation from Rome on that new interpretation, the Lutherans legitimized the same technique among dissidents within their own ranks. After affiliating with the governments of those states where the Roman authority had been deposed, the Lutheran church itself began to espouse a deterministic view of the universe known as "works righteousness," and became less sensitive to the aspirations of the common people, and more interested in the princes who ruled them.

Luther's reforms had destroyed the relationship of the priest as mediator between the laity and God. "But once the layman began to feel that he himself stood face to face with God and to rely for guidance on his individual conscience, it was inevitable that some laymen would claim divine promptings which ran as much counter to the new as to the old orthodoxy" (Cohn 1970:252).

The authority system of the Catholic ecclesiastical organization had fostered a dependency situation with respect to the entirety of European society. The monarchies were dependent for legitimation upon the church and many government functions were carried out by the clerics in the name of both God and the reigning monarch. The Roman Catholic church had performed these and many other normative functions in medieval Europe and its departure left a serious power vacuum which threatened the monarchies themselves and which confused the common people. The Lutherans quickly filled some aspects of the vacuum — particularly those relating to the monarchies — but they were unable to quell all the anxieties which they had released in the people (Cohn 1970:253). Social unrest reached a climax in the German-speaking lands with the Peasants' War (1524-1525) which was brief but extremely bloody. The *Täufer* originated at the peak of the unrest and their spread coincided with the peasant uprisings. The *Täufer* movement was never centrally organized and approximately 40 sects developed, each with its own leader who claimed to be a divinely-inspired prophet. The dominant cosmological theme of all the *Täufer* sects was that of the "free spirit" and in their adherence to that notion they were united. In most instances the *Täufer* were perfectly willing to obey the laws of the state as long as they did not conflict with religious belief. The issue which catalyzed the anti-establishment potential of the *Täufer* into open civil disobedience was one which was central to their religious beliefs and which encapsulated both the free-will and determinism epistemologies. Baptism was the most sensitive arena for the discussion of the competing cosmologies because it involved demands made upon adult individuals by the state (the baptism of their infants) and the religious convictions of some individuals that incorporation into the state and the church were separate matters. Furthermore, if membership in the former was one of choice, implicitly so, then, was membership in the latter. For the *Täufer* the baptism of adults upon petition and professed belief epitomized the workings of a "free spirit" and the machinations of the "Holy Spirit." From the perspective of either of the state-affiliated religions, the dogma of child baptism meshed with their *status-quo* oriented politics and their deterministic theologies. To both sides the "believers' baptism" of the *Täufer* represented a symbolic repudiation of the state and its religion because the *Täufer* had been born again to membership in a wholly different state – an unassailable state of mind. Finally, when the state moved to prohibit "believers' baptism" the *Täufer* fulfilled the worst expectations of the state and the best expectations of themselves by defying the law; the choice of adult baptism was thereafter equivalent with choosing against the state. Eventually accusations of Anabaptist heresy – membership in *Täufer* groups – became punishable independent of actual baptism and, finally, non-*Täufer* people were accused by their political enemies of being "Anabaptists." The *Täufer* were used as an object lesson to all those who would violate the laws of the state and accusations of "Anabaptism" were used to control the general turmoil – even where the *Täufer* did not exist.[1]

### Revitalization, Metanoia, and Existential Symbolism

Attempts to reformulate entire cultural systems have been discussed under terms such as "nativistic movement" (Linton 1943), "Millenarian movement" (Worsley 1957), or are more generally described as "religious revivals," "sect formations," and "cargo cults." Wallace (1956) has examined the underlying processes common to examples of large-scale cultural reformulation, which he calls "revitalization movements." Ramsayer (1970) has demonstrated how Wallace's theory of revitalization process fits the *Täufer* movement and Koenigsberger (1965) has discussed social revolution in the Reformation. Without going into great detail it is nonetheless apparent that the *Täufer* movement grew almost inevitably out of the general turmoil of the Reformation itself. The economic collapse of many of the estates of the ecclesiastical princes, increasing urbanization, transience, literacy, the new translation of the Bible, and rising but suppressed expectations of the peasantry and tradesmen combined to form a fertile matrix for the seeds of new cultural syntheses (See Miller and Stephenson, 1980).

The founders of the *Täufer* movement were young urban intellectuals who had grown up in the midst of social turmoil, had travelled widely, studied abroad, and whose rejection of established social order often coincided with their personal rejection of their own fathers. Conrad Grebel, for instance, was educated in Basel, Vienna, and Paris. Grebel's father was a member of the council of Zürich which eventually condemned him to life imprisonment. Grebel married against his father's wishes and was financially estranged from him as well. Felix Manz was actually the son of a canon of the Grössmunster church. Extensive cross-cultural survey has shown that the pattern of foreign travel, education, alienated youth, and father rejection are all common antecedents of charismatic leadership and to the production of a new cultural synthesis or message of prophecy (see Cell 1974:255-306).

The symbolism of the *Täufer* revitalization movement was explicitly regenerative and tied to ritual intended to foster both "hysterical conversion" and what Wallace (1956) terms "mazeway resynthesis." The symbolism stemmed from the naive discovery of the Bible by a populace freed from the interpretations of priestly mediators, and was drawn directly from the primitive Christian church itself. Early Christian baptism had ushered the convert into a new religious community and made the convert worthy of eternal life in the face of almost certain persecution. The *Täufer* baptism was structurally similar and bolstered the already popular chiliastic world view of the times.

Between 150 B.C. and A.D. 300 there were numerous baptism movements in Palestine and Syria among both Jewish and later Christian groups.[2] For the Christians, the rite became a sacrament because it was implemented by Christ (Gaster 1956). However, by the 4th Century the Christian sacraments and their meanings were hidden from the uninitiated under the doctrine of *arcana disciplina.* The transformation of the early sacraments into mysteries coincided with the absorption of Greek scholasticism and the southern Mediterranean adoption of Christianity as a state religion. As a result of the investiture of the sacraments with arcane symbols and their withdrawal from public domain, the Eucharist was elevated into a richly-symbolic act, but the shift to baptism of infants neutralized its significance for the initiate while maximizing its importance to parents and to the state.

The baptismal sacrament became the focus for the regeneration of Christianity itself among the *Täufer*, who equated their own literal interpretation of the act and performance of the ritual with pre-4th century biblical times. The passages from the Hutterite Chronicles quoted in Chapters I and II manifest an obvious biblical style and the interpretation of events such as the flight from Moravia are consistently compared to biblical descriptions of similar events (in the case of migration, with the flight from Egypt of the Israelites). We are told by one chronicler that in the martyrdom of the *Täufer* "we see that God has poured out his grace in these latter days as well as in the former time" (Horsch 1931:39, *Geschicht-Buch*:182).

## Baptismal Symbols

The development of the tripartite baptism of spirit, water, and blood, is consistent with Hutterite history, and is also structurally isomorphic with the trinity concept of God. The first discussion of adult baptism was by the spiritualist sects (Zwickau prophets, etc.) and its later performance was implemented by the Swiss Brethren who used water to mark the spiritual awakening. Finally, the blood baptism of martyrdom was to be suffered by all who had the "seal" of water baptism. The "seal" of baptism by water was the harbinger of suffering for all who had it would likely suffer death for it. Through the collective martyrdom of the *Täufer*, the "seal" took on eschatological proportions. If the *Täufer* were to die for the practice of "rebirth," that death would be conceived of as another rebirth, one denied to all who did not have the "seal" and who persecuted them.

A large number of concepts are condensed within the *Täufer* baptism. *Beigiessungstäufe* is often glossed as "believers' baptism" but it is derived from a number of words including *Täufe* (baptism) and *Beigiessung* (poured on, or sprinkled with), and implies that the baptism of a true believer involves the symbolic use of water rather than total immersion. *Glaubenstäufe* (*Glauben* = belief) is actually the correct word for "Believers' Baptism," although Hutterites rarely use the latter of the two words. Baptism was first performed upon the Son of the Trinity, who was the first to arise from the dead following his own execution, to join his "Father" and thereafter to judge the souls of all the dead. Only those who had been baptized and reborn following his example would be granted eternal life in heaven. For the *Täufer* to be baptized as adults and then martyred was actually leading the most "Christ-like" [*Christlichen*] lives possible, and meant eternal salvation.

The symbolism of the tripartite baptism is equated with the Trinity and the life of the martyred savior but is also consistent with the experiences of both individual *Täufer* and the historical experience of the entire movement. The power of the symbols of spirit, water and blood also accrues from their relation to the natural event of birth itself. The existential cast of the entire *Täufer* movement is fused to the universal existential experiences of birth and death. The symbolism of life and death reveals a concern with the meaning of life which permeated the confusing times of the Reformation era.

The first sign of pregnancy is the cessation of menses (an absence of blood), and with gestation an increasing awareness arises that a new being or "spirit" is entering the world. The first physical sign that the being is taking its place among the living is "breaking water." The issue of amniotic fluid or "water" from the womb is followed by the birth, which is in turn followed by the placenta, or "after birth," which is obviously characterized by the presence of blood. If delivery is successful, eventually ovulation and menstrual cycles return. Although childbirth is a relatively safe experience now, it was certainly not always so. In medieval European times, one of the most salient aspects of childbirth was the frequent death of either or both the newborn and mother, and the notion that death was life's companion was accordingly made obvious (Stephenson 1978b:434-435).

The physical properties of "spirit," "blood" and "water" are such that water synthesizes the triad by incorporating mutually-exclusive aspects of "blood" and "spirit," just as the "Father" incorporates mutually-exclusive aspects of the Holy Ghost ("spirit") and Jesus (the corporeal Son). "Spirit" has no physical form but can be witnessed in the acts of persons and when given physical description is usually associated with light, fire, or with the wind. The spirit has no solid or liquid form, and is not visible itself, although its effects may be noted by the observer. The "spirit" has the qualities of something in a gaseous state. Water is a liquid, which if left to stand evaporates to a gaseous, invisible state and which reappears as rainfall, condensation, etc. Of course, water can also be solidified but it eventually returns to a liquid state. Blood is a substance which − like water − in its normal state is liquid, but which if left to stand, solidifies rather than evaporates (Stephenson 1978b).

Structurally, the trinity concept of God, which incorporates one son born of a union of spirit and flesh, the natural symbols of birth, and the existential nature of the *Täufer* movement and its historical trajectory are all isomorphic. The changes in phenomenal attributes of the existential symbols of birth derive from transformations of the substances over time just as the experiences of Christ during his putative lifetime, and of the *Täufer* during their individual lives and collective history, transpired over time. The content of the symbols of the tripartite baptism is a condensation of the life experiences of Hutterite individuals, the history of their group, and the acts of their God.

Leach (1965:242) has pointed out that human notions of time seem to derive from the observations that a) certain natural phenomena are repetitive, and that b) life change is irreversible. Much of religious practice seems directed at denying the uncomfortable notion of irreversible time through artificial or symbolic repetitions of life events in ritual − particularly life crisis events such as birth and death which occur as single instances in individual lives though they are observed many times collectively. Leach (1965:242) continues by reasoning that:

Religions of course vary greatly in the manner by which they purport to repudiate the 'reality' of death; one of the commonest devices is simply to assert that death and birth are the same thing – that birth follows death, just as death follows birth. This seems to deny the second aspect of time by equating it with the first.

Symbolically, the equation of irreversible events with cyclically recurrent events is accomplished by associating the reversible transformations of the symbolic substances with the irreversible course of both personal and collective history. The historicity of the existential symbols is part of their current synchronic arrangement in a structure. History, as Levi-Strauss (1967-262) points out,

> proves to be indispensable for cataloguing the elements of any structure whatever, human or non-human, in their entirety. It is therefore far from being the case that the search for intelligibility comes to an end in history as though this were its terminus. Rather, it is history that serves as the point of departure in any quest for intelligibility.

History leads to everything on the condition that after it has been imbedded in symbols it can then be simultaneously left behind while being projected into the future. The structure of *Täufer* regenerative symbols and the diachronic matrix from which they emerged are represented in Figure 3.1.

| {-} ◄─────────────────► | {-/+} ◄─────────────────► | {+} |
|---|---|---|
| [gaseous] | [evaporative liquid] | [liquid coagulant] |
| [spirit] | [water] | [blood] |
| [Holy Spirit] | [Father] | [Son] |
| | ─── (time) ─── | |
| (conception, | (gestation) | (infant & placenta) |
| (birth) | (life) | (death) |
| (revelation) | (baptism) | (martyrdom) |
| (Spiritualists) | (Swiss Brethren) | (Hutterians) |

(After Stephenson, 1978:436)

**Figure 3.1**
Structure of Täufer Symbols of Baptism

Given the severe persecution of those who practiced "believers' baptism," the power of the ritual to neutralize the threat of death must have been great indeed. Since performance of the act of adult baptism was also the rationale for persecution, the salvation of the initiate and his acceptance by society were mutually exclusive.

The very act which implied salvation also guaranteed persecution which in turn might lead to martyrdom which guaranteed eternal life — death meant life and life meant death both in practice and religious belief.

By placing, or re-enacting birth in adulthood, death was displaced — in the Christian conception — to a time outside existence altogether, and since for the *Täufer* that time which followed birth was childhood, placing rebirth in adulthood rendered them children of God whose salvation (like that of children) was assured. The Christian conception of rebirth differs from reincarnation theories because the cycle only occurs once and never repeats itself; death is final but if one has been reborn in baptism previous to death, then death becomes a birth to eternal life.

There are numerous quotes wherein early *Täufer* describe baptism as "a dying of the old and a putting on of the new man" (see Chapter I), but in the writings of Hans Hut and Thomas Muntzer the entire linkage between death, rebirth, and leading the *Christlichen* life is elaborated as the following summary quote from Stoesz (1964:295-297) illustrates:

> One's faith is tested [*probiert*] as silver or gold in a fire and one becomes 'purified in spirit' [*gerainigt im Geist*]. This must take place in the members of Christ's body as it occurred in its head, Christ himself. One is related to the head by the following [*Nachfolge*] of Christ in his suffering.
> In this process there is a good bit of uncertainty [*Ungestimigkeit*] which may be compared to the waves of a sea. God leads his purificatory waters through the soul. This water of all tribulation [*Wasser aller Truebsal*] is the true baptism, however. One will feel forsaken in spirit in the midst of this, but this feeling is a sign of being not forsaken. One passes through hell as this happens, but God raises one up out of it again when one has learned to rely on one's self. The Holy Spirit finally brings comfort, and the result is the word of God being born and becoming flesh within one, as was the case also with the Virgin Mary.

The *Täufer* movement sprang from times of change and

confusion in which the meaning of life was increasingly questioned. In the midst of wars, revolts, plagues, economic collapse, and the collapse of the Roman Catholic church, one small group sought to invest their lives with meaning through the revitalized use of a traditional ritual which emphasized eternal life. Violent death, which was likely in such troubled times anyway, was virtually assured by practice of the ritual which meant salvation to the practitioner: baptism meant a meaningful death in a troubled time. Membership in the *Täufer* was a transformation into a sacred mode of being through baptism which symbolized the transformation in terms of death and rebirth, and which led to the outcomes of persecution and salvation. "If we can say that initiation constitutes a specific dimension of human existence, this is true above all because it is only in initiation that death is given positive value. Death prepares the new, purely spiritual birth access to a mode of being not subject to the destroying action of time" (Eliade 1958:136). The baptism of adults created an elect membership in the Christian church called the body of Christ or *corpus christi*. The murdered savior was reborn in the rebirths of the body's members (parts). *Metanoia* as a collective experience was also a kind of rebirth — a metaphorical and spiritual second coming of Christ which allowed the members of the body immediate salvation. Christ's body was reconstituted by His followers who had undergone sacred initiation: He lived in them, and they in Him.

Eventually, the Eucharist was abandoned by the *Täufer* and replaced by an annual celebration of the Lord's Supper. Grebel had advocated such action from the beginning of the movement, but not all *Täufer* had immediately responded to his argumentation. Daily, and even weekly, celebration of the sacrament probably lapsed under the pressure of persecution as much as from the preachings of persons wishing to return to a celebration of the commemorative feast. Eventually, the Lord's Supper was held once a year and participation limited to the baptized persons of the community for only the initiated could partake of spiritual reunion of Christ's body. Marriage was also restricted to the baptized members: one could not bear children until one had been "reborn" oneself. Membership in Christ's body was established at *Beigiessungstäufe*, and renewed at the Lord's Supper, but the matter of how the members of the body should live together was to be determined by later events.

## The Re-establishment of Communal Life: The Rebirth and Growth of the Body of Christ

A number of ideas which had been part of the *Täufer* movement from its inception acted as ideological constraints upon the type of communal social organization which the Hutterites were eventually to adopt. The notion of a nonviolent Christian Brotherhood living in harmony had broad currency throughout the Reformation era (see Cohn 1970). The doctrine of two worlds set the Christian apart from the "world" and the idea of *Nachfolge* implied social as well as spiritual separation. The concept of *gelassenheit*, and the importance of the Holy Spirit, implied that material wealth should be unimportant to the individual.

The implications of early *Täufer* cosmology were given phenomenal expression following their persecution because the few islands of sanctuary which existed for them were virtually refugee camps. Population was dense, and resources were scarce at Nickolsburg where two factions developed – one constituted of recent arrivals who pressed for total adoption of communal life and a second indigenous and entrenched group which resisted complete sharing of their meagre wealth. Given the scarcity of material resources, the former faction could only gain economically by adopting communal life, while the latter faction perceived that it would lose. Within the parameters of the discussion of material goods, and under conditions of impending warfare during which their defense might prove necessary, the issue of nonresistance surfaced and provided the moral basis for a schism which finally drove the two factions to separate worship services. The poorer pacifist faction (the *Stabler*) who eventually left Nickolsburg altogether was comprised of orphans, widows, widowers, solitary people, and fragments of families which banded together to share what little they had as if they were one family. This pathetic group, seeing themselves as latter-day apostles, adopted communal life perhaps as much from material necessity as from spiritual conviction after the pattern of the acts of the apostles.

Early attempts at communal living were fraught with difficulties which stemmed from poor leadership, differential redistribution of wealth, and the hoarding of private wealth in the event of emergencies (persecution). Hutter's reorganization of the Moravian *Brüderhofes* ended marriage by arrangement or lottery, redistributive inequities were solved, and missionary activity (the *Sendboten*) appears to have replaced the divisive use of banning to drive the zealots as well as the lazy from the *Brüderhofes*. The cosmology of "believers' baptism" had been loosely tied to *Gütergemeinschaft* by Hutter, because only a baptized person could vote, hold office, or marry. The proper organization for the body of Christ was felt to be peaceful, and egalitarian, rendering the integration of its parts harmonious. For successful communal life Hutter stressed that the attitude of *gelassenheit* should be adopted by the parts of the body at baptism. The relationship between *Gütergemeinschaft* and *gelassenheit* is exemplified well in the old Hutterite proverb:

> *Die Gemeinschaft war nicht schwer*
> *Wenn der Eigennutz nich war!*
>
> Communal life would not be so hard,
> if there were not such self-regard!

The Moravian *Brüderhofes* flourished after Hutter's death, which probably served posthumously to magnify his charismatic influence. The social stability and orderly expansion of the *Brüderhofes* seems to have derived from the relationship of the *Sendboten* and converts to the social organization which both sent and received them. The *Sendboten* were the most zealous of the *Brüderhof* constituency; they were usually young men who, if they remained in the *Brüderhof* would have produced families, and who constituted a serious political threat to established patterns of leadership. The departure of the *Sendboten* doubtless contributed to the peaceful internal character of the Moravian *Brüderhofes*. The converts obtained by the *Sendboten* increased the populations of the *Brüderhofes* but they were incorporated by eventually building their own new *Brüderhof*. The Moravian communes produced *Sendboten* from their indigenous population and received grateful refugees in return, and these refugees provided for orderly expansion. The number of schismatic disputes during the Moravian "Golden Period" appears to have been greatly reduced and expansion facilitated by the *sendboten*-convert exchange. Exactly how this process has evolved into the contemporary practice of expansion is the subject of later chapters. For now, however, it is sufficient to recognize that the cyclical pattern of migration and persecution was similar to the structure of birth and rebirth itself.

When lapsed communal life was re-adopted based upon Michael Waldner's vision, the key synthesis of the vision was its equation of communal life itself with salvation. Just as baptism had previously been equated with salvation, now the "ark" of *Gütergemeinschaft* had become the vehicle of rebirth following disaster. Waldner equated his vision with rebirth, thereafter describing himself as a new man. The re-establishment of communal life became regarded as the rebirth of Christ's body. The communal social organization then migrated to North America prior to either severe persecution or overpopulation — indeed they migrated to avoid further persecution but also sidestepped the troublesome effects of overpopulation on limited employment. By the time of their arrival in North America, the Hutterites had begun to integrate the idea of rebirth into the systematic expansion of Hutterite society itself — *metanoia* was increasingly becoming the central theme of their culture.

Upon finding itself in North America, the movement of the reborn was itself reborn. This new rebirth — *metanoia* — has served the Hutterian people rather better than the passage of time has served their old persecutors. While in Zürich several years ago I walked into the old city from the lakeside, where over 450 years ago the ancestors of today's Hutterites were being drowned. Entering the twisting narrow lanes I came to Martin Zwingli Platz, so marked by a rust-streaked old sign. Underneath the sign bearing Zwingli's once illustrious name several prostitutes were plying their trade, speaking quietly to passing men. The "Platz," my companions informed me, was their "regular" place. Zwingli, I could not help but think, had found his place as well.

## NOTES

1 See Estep (1964), Chapters I, II, and III especially, for a review of *Täufer* origins which includes letters from high officials to regional and local officials warning them to beware of persecuting those persons who were not actually *Täufer*. The practice of accusing unpopular persons of being *Täufer*, or merely associating with the *Täufer*, appears to have been commonplace. Since torture was the usual means of extracting confessions from taciturn prisoners, it is unlikely that unintended mistakes were ever detected. For detailed regional studies of the efflorescence of the *Täufer* in Hessian lands see Dirrim (1959), and for analysis of the conflict between reformed authorities and the *Täufer* in Strasbourg see Krahm (1969:vols. 1 and 2).

# CHAPTER IV

## HUTTERITE LIFE IN NORTH AMERICA

There may be those who see in these pulsing events only a meaningless play of capricious fortuitousness; but there will be others to whom they reveal a glimpse of a great and inspiring inevitability which rises as far above the accidents of personality as the march of the heavens transcends the wavering contacts of random footprints on clouds of earth.

(A. L. Kroeber 1917, 1952:44)

Just a mile or so outside one of the Alberta *Dariusleut* colonies and plainly visible from the road, seasoned by blizzards and bleached by draught, there stands an old "buckboard" type of dray such as was in common use nearly a century ago. Having seen these still in limited use in several colonies in Saskatchewan, and after reflecting on the frugal nature of the Hutterian people I knew, I once asked the "field boss" at that colony why they "just left that old wagon out there on the hill to rot." His answer was instructive in many ways. "Oh it still serves a purpose," he quickly replied, "it reminds us all that someday we'll have to leave in just as big a hurry as we got here."

This comment reflects the view Hutterites have of themselves as a people involved in a kind of Gentile diaspora much like those that affected the Jews and the Gypsies long before them, and which affects the Palestinian Arabs today. The Hutterians are a migrating people and their symbols of themselves are creations which grow out of their movement: they are created out of the barest material entities — abandoned wagons and the like, or out of virtually nothing at all, save the space that they live in. I will have more to say about this in later chapters but for now I only seek to enliven my description of colony life with a few apt examples of how their history saturates everyday life for the Hutterian people of today.

The North American history of the Hutterites has not been as tumultuous as their European experience, but nonetheless has involved some persecution as they spread from the United States into Canada.[1]

The Hutterites were just one of the many German groups recruited from the Ukraine by land and travel agents to settle in the Dakota Territory under Lincoln's "Homestead Act" of 1862.[2] Lured by the prospect of new land and freedom from governmental interference with their lives, the first Hutterite immigrants arrived in the port of New York aboard the *Harmonia* (out of Hamburg) in the summer of 1874. More than a third of the passengers bore Hutterite names, their number totalling 365 (Hostetler 1974:116 fn.). Not all of the settlers lived communally after their arrival in the Dakota Territory. The first *Schmiedeleut* settlement was at Bon Homme, on the banks of the Missouri, and held a population of 123 as of April 1, 1875: 61 men and 62 women. The *Dariusleut* settled just 40 miles north at Wolf Creek in 1875, after a temporary settlement on Government land at Silver Lake. Those migrants who did not settle in the *Brüderhofes*, or "colonies" as they became known in America, were called *Prairieleute* by the communal Hutterians. At first some marriage into and out of the colonies was allowed but was ended after the colonies became established in a matter of several years. In the earliest years some of the *Prairieleute* were organized by a school teacher named Jacob Wipf, and adopted *Gütergemeinschaft* in 1877. The group led by Wipf adopted the term for his profession (*Lehrer*=teacher), calling themselves the *Lehrerleut*, and built their first colony at Elm Spring, several miles from the *Dariusleut* colony at Wolf Creek. The Hutterites prospered in South Dakota and attracted very little attention from the outside world until World War I.

There were no provisions other than noncombatant status in the military service itself for conscientious objectors during World War I and so the Hutterite men, who refused to wear uniforms or contribute to the war effort in any way, were imprisoned. As German-speaking pacifists they were cruelly abused in army guardhouses and American federal penitentiaries (see Unruh 1969, and Hostetler 1974:126-133).

One elderly Hutterite gentleman whom I knew, had been

incarcerated throughout the first World War but still managed to
keep a diary of much of what transpired, carefully coding parts
of it and writing it all in archaic script in the hope that it
would not be destroyed. Probably because I had come to Canada
as a pacifist during the war in Vietnam, he talked to me at
length on several occasions. Although he was old and frail his
voice gained strength as he spoke about what he had endured...

>...the guards used to like to dunk my head in a bucket of water 'til I
couldn't hold my breath no more...then they'd pull me up for air...
'soon as I stopped chokin', well they'd put my head under
again...wouldn't take long an I'd just pass right out. When I come to,
I'd be naked in my cell and shakin' from the cold – an there'd be a
uniform there, an Army uniform, for me to put on if I wanted t' be
warm. I used t' wrap the pants 'round my shoulders like an old woman
with a shawl. There was no military marks on the pants so I used
'em...'till they come for me again. But I guess I was lucky compared
to some...I knew those other Hofer boys who died.

The abusive treatment of the Hutterites culminated in the
deaths of two young men after they were tortured at Alcatraz
and at Leavenworth. Four Hutterites, Jacob Wipf, and three
brothers; Michael, David and Joseph Hofer, were kept in a
guardhouse for two months, after which all four were condemned
to 37 years' imprisonment and sent to Alcatraz. At Alcatraz each
of the men was put in solitary confinement in their underclothing
and a uniform was placed in the cells with each. The men were
never fed and were allowed only a half-glass of water per day.
Along with being forced to live in their own filth, the men were
beaten with clubs, tied with their arms crossed to the ceiling,
and denied access to any other clothing. The men slept on cold,
wet, concrete floors for five days, after which they were taken
from solitary confinement, fed, and allowed one hour of exercise
every Sunday. According to Hostetler (1974:129), the men's wrists
were so swollen from insect bites and skin eruptions that they
could not even don their own jackets. After four months of
confinement at Alcatraz the men were manacled and shipped
under guard to Leavenworth penitentiary where, after being
marched through town at bayonet point, they were stripped and
forced to stand, dripping with sweat, for several hours waiting
for their prison garb. By the time the men received their prison

clothing they were suffering from chills, yet they were made to stand outside through the entire night. By early morning Michael and Joseph had collapsed and were hospitalized, but the remaining two were put into solitary confinement, placed on a starvation diet, and made to stand for nine hours a day with their feet just brushing the floor and their hands tied high on the wall. After Michael and Joseph became ill, Wipf had managed to telegram their wives, who boarded a train — accompanied by a prison attendant — to plead with the prison officials at Leavenworth on their husbands' behalves. The women were misdirected by officials and sent to Fort Riley instead of to Leavenworth. The wives arrived at Leavenworth near midnight, a day late, to find their husbands near death. During the night Joseph Hofer died and, incredibly, his wife was denied permission by the guards to see his body. After much pleading, a colonel finally led Maria Hofer to the casket, where she discovered the obscenity of her husband's body dressed for burial in the very military uniform which he had refused to wear in life. Within two days Michael Hofer also died. The bodies were returned to the Rockport colony by the men's wives and relatives, and a large funeral was held which "seared Hutterite minds with the price of true apostolic faith" (Hostetler, 1974:131).

Following the funeral of the Hofer brothers, enormous quantities of livestock were stolen from the Jamesville colony and sent to Chicago for slaughter. The "patriots" who stole the stock intended their sale to make up a local deficit in war bonds (which the Hutterites had refused to buy) and, although several hundred cattle and about a thousand sheep were taken, the thieves were never tried. The Chicago stockyards refused to accept the stolen stock and they had to be sold at enormous losses. It had become clear to the Hutterites that their situation in the United States was worsening and, fearing more deaths, they loaded up their wagons and departed for western Canada, where they had been promised, once again, the freedom to remain pacifists during wartime. In 1918, 15 colonies were founded in Canada. Eventually, only Bon Homme colony remained populated in the United States. The *Dariusleut* and *Lehrerleut* moved to Alberta, while the *Schmiedeleut* went to Manitoba. After

1920 the *Schmiedeleut* began to reoccupy the South Dakota sites and, according to Hostetler (1974:132), all but three have been repossessed.[3]

During World War II the Hutterites were again extremely unpopular throughout both countries, but they were not subjected to the violent and even lethal abuses typical during World War I. In 1942, Alberta passed the "Land Sales Prohibition Act" which prohibited the sale of land to enemy aliens, Hutterites or Doukhobors.[4] After the War, the act was amended to cover only enemy aliens, but further legal restrictions on expansion were devised and persisted in Alberta until the repeal of the "Communal Properties Act" in 1972.[5] During the years of land restriction in Alberta the *Dariusleut* and *Lehrerleut* expanded into Saskatchewan and Montana partly to avoid the restrictions. A pattern of consultation and cooperation between the governments of all of the prairie provinces and the Hutterites now exists and formal laws restricting land purchase have been avoided. Even if such laws were passed, they would likely have to be repealed for violating various Provincial civil rights acts and the Canadian Charter of Rights and Freedoms. It is important to realize, however, that the wanderings of the Hutterian people are not understood by them to be over, nor did their persecution end entirely with their migration to North America.

**Contemporary Social Organization: Kinship**

Contemporary Hutterites live communally by holding very nearly all wealth collectively and investing that collective capital in the commune's farm enterprise and the process of expansion, while practicing personal austerity at the level of individual consumption. Hutterite colonies are often million-dollar farm enterprises today, and the managers of the various segments of the colony farm enterprises (hogs, chickens, cattle, dairy, etc.) may preside over highly profitable and productive operations. However, the same middle-aged man may have amassed no more than $50-worth of personal belongings during his entire life. Most of the personal possessions which individual Hutterites own are items such as house slippers, western-style hats (men), flashlights, etc., which are often owned by the majority of the other people in the colony too. A large proportion of the personal belongings of individual Hutterites are either gifts or items which were found — such as old magazines, books, or abandoned pieces of "interesting" furniture, such as church pews, old benches from deserted railroad stations, etc. Homemade items such as hatracks and wallets are also commonplace. A young woman might typically own a brush and comb set, an inexpensive drugstore perfume and cosmetic kit, a tiny mirror, a bar of scented soap, a "liquid embroidery" kit, decorative stationery, and slippers. Personal possessions are usually kept locked away in cabinets out of the reach of children and reference is rarely made to them in conversation, for they are not supposed to exist at all. The purchases of small luxury items by Hutterites are made possible by the small monthly allowance (*Zehrgeld*) which they are given by the colony. The *Zehrgeld* is generally no more than several dollars, and items such as candies for the children are also purchased from it.

When a Hutterite dies the small personal possessions which he or she may have accumulated over a lifetime may be distributed among the close surviving relatives by the spouse or eldest son but, since no power of office is hereditary, no land or stock is inherited and there is no formal rule of inheritance for personal belongings, one cannot speak of a lineage system of kinship among the Hutterites. However, inasmuch as patrilocality is practiced and only men may have the right to vote after baptism, or hold elective office (other than the head cook — who the men elect) a system of patrifiliation may be said to exist. Postmarital residence is patrilocal and the majority of marriages are to persons outside the colony of residence thereby producing a normative pattern of colony exogamy. Colony exogamy is a product of both a factor of incest avoidance (in most colonies the great majority of age equivalent persons are first cousins and siblings) and a feeling even where potential spouses exist, that they are nearly family. Although kinship is reckoned bilaterally after standard German usage, there is a tendency for children to extend the terms of "uncle" and "aunt" [*Onkel* and *Basel* respectively] to all men and women of their mother's and father's generation – whether in fact they are such kin or not. Persons of one's own generation are often called "cousin" [*Vetter*, or *Base*] by children and later in life *Vetter* is reserved for both kin and nonkin as an honorific term. For example, the preacher in a colony is often called by both his sister's children and his sister's husband's brother's children *Peter-Vetter*. The same man, who is from a *Dariusleut* colony, once conducted a church service in a *Schmiedeleut* colony which he was visiting, after being requested to do so as a visitor from a distant group. The *Darius* people typically sing hymns somewhat more slowly than the *Schmieden* do and, after the service an elderly woman approached the preacher and said, in very long and drawn out syllables, "Vetter, we don't sing so slowly in the *Schmieden colonies* . . ." The use of the honorific [*Vetter*] in combination with a statement of difference in which the statement was exemplified by the very manner in which the phrase was rendered, constituted a humorous, teasing, yet effective way in which to instruct a fellow Hutterite about *Leut* diversity.

The three Hutterite *Leute* are all endogamous units. *Leut*-endogamy has been broken several times, but life for the couple has usually been difficult. Although to the outsider the differences between the *Leute* appear superficial – hooks and eyes rather than buttons, et cetera – to the Hutterites, who are used to the redundant uniformity of dress, the uniform tempo of hymns, a particular number of hours of kindergarten, traditional recipes, etc., even small differences break the homogeneity of experience which they feel to be necessary for the smooth maintenance of *Gütergemeinschaft*. When rigid *Leut* patterns are broken out of ignorance rather than on purpose, the rule-breaker (who would be a woman due to the patrilocality of postmarital residence) would be subjected to disciplinary actions reserved for children, who act out of ignorance rather than malice. A woman who had acquired the requisite skills in sewing, cooking, and a particular style of hymn-singing, would have to alter patterns of behavior which had been honed over the years to match those of her own *Gemeinde* and *Leut*. Accordingly, inter-*Leut* marriages are exceedingly rare, and are problematical when they do occur.

Marriages are for life among the Hutterites – there is no

divorce – and both spinsterhood and bachelorhood are rare. It is common practice for siblings to marry other sets of siblings in both of the patterns indicated in Figure 4.1:

A

B

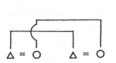

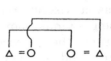

Sibling Set Marriage
(Usually Colony Coresident)

Sibling Exchange Marriage
(Often Colony-separate Residence)

**Figure 4.1**
Sibling Set and Sibling Exchange Marriages

Marriages between sibling groups are not always between persons of equivalent ages; a set of brothers may be separated by as much 18 years and yet still marry a set of sisters. Occasionally, sibling set marriages take place on the same day, however, the opportunity for meeting and courting future spouses often arises at weddings themselves, so the contemporaneous wedding between sibling sets does not always take place. Multiple weddings are nonetheless commonplace: at one colony five couples were married at the same service. Occasionally, a sibling pair will marry either an aunt and niece, or uncle and nephew pair. The Hutterites do not practice widespread birth control for religious reasons and so the resultant large family size facilitates avuncular-sibling marriage sets and what might be termed an intragenerational avuncular unit in which uncle and nephew (or aunt and niece) are in the same age set but siblings are not. Figure 4.2 contains both sibling set and avuncular unit marriages, in which one and eleven are of the same age, but one and nine (brothers) are separated by 19 years.

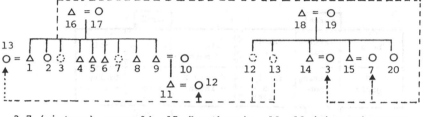

3,7 (sisters) marry 14, 15 (brothers);   12, 13 (sisters) marry
1, 11 (age mate uncle and nephew)

**Figure 4.2**
Sibling Set and Avuncular Unit Marriages

The intragenerational avunculate is indicative of the high
degree of homogeneity that exists in Hutterite social structure.
An uncle and nephew of the same age usually belong to the
same or adjacent baptismal cohorts, which crosscut not only
families, but the generational structure as well.

The Hutterites regard the nuclear family as the basic social
unit, but its functions are restricted to domestic arrangements
for sleeping, most bathing, and the socialization of children up
to the age of three when they are sent to join the colony
kindergarten. Nuclear families are assigned apartment quarters
in communal longhouses dependent upon family size and the
amount of room available. The nuclear family is associated with
the apartment unit and is referred to as the "home," the term
"family" is preserved for the larger extended kin group (Bennett
1967:118). See Figure 4.3 for a diagram of a typical Hutterite
longhouse.

The pattern of interaction between colonies is largely a product
of their geographical proximity, *Leut* affiliation, and the degree to
which colonies have exchanged brides. There is a strong tendency
for marital exchanges between colonies to continue once begun

due to the inertia created by the practice of courting at weddings
and at "shivarees," or *hulbas* (parties held prior to the wedding
to celebrate the event).[6]

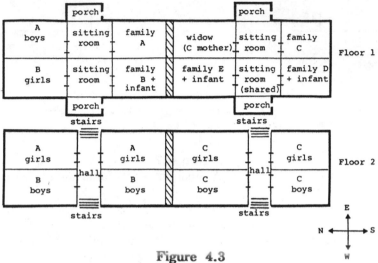

**Figure 4.3**
Hutterite Longhouse Plan

Once a marriage has taken place, visits by the bride's relatives
to her new colony allow courting to take place. Equipment loans
and sharing of information or labor also tend to follow marriage
networks. Over several years I interviewed 28 Hutterite men
from five different colonies and 15 (more than half) said that
they had met their spouses at the weddings of kin, or during
"shivarees." Of the remaining 13, most (5) grew up with their
spouses but were sometimes separated from them by the process
of colony division (see Chapter 5); some met their wives visiting,
or being visited by, relatives (4); several while operating heavy
equipment or repairing it while on loan as labor to distant
colonies (2); or met their spouses at funerals (2).

## Contemporary Social Organization: Formal Structure

Contemporary Hutterite colonies have forsaken the crafts industries of the Moravian *Brüderhofes* and now practice mixed commercial farming. Each colony has at least one preacher [*Praediger*] (a second is selected when the colony becomes large), and an administrative supervisor, or "bursar" [*Wirt*] who is responsible for all economic matters and for the general management of the colony. Additionally, there are a German school teacher (often the assistant preacher), a gardener, "field" or farm manager, and managers for each of the various production enterprises (hogs, chickens, dairy, cattle). Some specialist occupations have become increasingly important in recent years (notably, electrician, mechanic, and carpenter), particularly in large colonies, although in smaller collectives they are still the part-time responsibilities of the *Praediger*, *Wirt* and "field boss."

The *Praediger*, *Wirt*, *Gros Schul* teacher [*Lehrer*], farm manager, and several of the older and most responsible production managers, comprise the executive council of a colony. Membership in the colony executive, or "elders," [*Aufsehern*], as they are usually called, is for life and is by election. All of the baptized males may vote in the general assembly and issues of importance are put before the assembly for their consideration. Routine matters of administration and discipline are carried out by the council of elders. Majority votes are thought by the Hutterites to be a manifestation of the will of God, who communicates his desires to the voters in the contemplation of prayer prior to voting. Persons voting in the minority are thought to be "out of touch" with the divine will, so consensus votes are commonplace. Since every issue is well discussed and everyone voices an opinion prior to the vote, the outcome is usually predictable and the minority will often acquiesce, resulting in a consensus-vote outcome.

All positions except that of preacher are filled by the direct vote of the baptized men of a colony. The preacher is selected partly by vote and partly by the machinations of the "divine will" in the form of a lottery. Several nominations are made by the members of the colony, and several by a group of visiting preachers. A vote is held and each person receiving five or more ballots has his name placed in a hat. It is thought that God guides the selection of the proper man's name from the hat, and so the choice is that of divine will, not of man. If only one name receives more than five votes, then the manifestation of God's will is inherent in the unanimity of the choice. Because Jacob Hutter was Jacob "the hatter," the choice of a leader is also a living commemorative act (see Miller and Stephenson, 1980).

Boys and girls over the age of 15 constitute a floating labor pool which receives work assignments from the "field boss." Young men usually begin to apprentice themselves to various enterprises by the age of 17 but can be called upon to perform many tasks because each has a considerable repertoire of skills learned from working in the many facets of production in a colony.

The head cook is a woman, and each of the colony women spends some time working on the kitchen crew. Several older women run the kindergarten with the assistance of some of the younger women. Women often care for the geese and ducks in a colony, and sometimes slaughter and prepare them. Women and young girls usually tend the garden under the direction of the gardener, and often wrap and package produce for marketing. Women sew all of the clothing, make down quilts, and care for the flood of children who populate all of the colonies. Women are usually responsible for painting the colony buildings and waxing the floors, for general cleaning, and in recent years, with the advent of lawns, women have also been wielding the lawnmowers. Women are not allowed to vote, hold elective office (other than the head cook), or drive heavy equipment or automobiles. The significance of women's labour as a resource which helps to underwrite the competitive edge the colonies maintain over most other farms should not be underestimated. Given the sizeable population of Hutterite colonies, the cost of the food they raise and prepare alone would be considerable if it had to be bought. Add to this bedding, clothing, cleaning and childcare and one can easily see that women's labour is at least as significant as men's labour in undercutting the overhead of other farmers who pay for a higher percentage of these services than Hutterites do.

The formal organization of a typical *Dariusleut* colony — fictitiously called "Darius-Dorf" — is diagramatically represented in Figure 4.4. The absolute division of labor between the sexes is also manifest in Figure 4.4. The only woman whose position is regarded as sufficiently important to be effected by a vote is that of head cook. The head cook is elected by the council, but men carefully consider their wives' opinions on the matter, and usually vote accordingly. The head cook is sometimes the wife of the *Pradeiger*, more rarely of the gardener, but in my experience she is usually the wife of the *Wirt*. Cooperation on the financial aspects of the kitchen is greatly facilitated by such an arrangement. The head cook usually has an assistant to take her place should she become ill, or leave the colony to visit relatives, or enter the hospital for childbirth. The cooks associate with the kindergarten teachers regularly because kindergarten children usually receive their meals at school. In some colonies — particularly older ones — there is a "summer kitchen" where light meals which require less preparation are made by the assistant cook and young girls learning culinary skills. The kindergarten teachers themselves are usually not directly involved in cooking, but they are normally present at the children's meals and utilize the occasion for teaching prayers, proper table manners, and discipline. There is some discussion between the teacher and the cooks about what might be served — particularly when overly zealous young girls try to be innovative or experimental with their cuisine.

The duck and goose operation is often tended by an older (55-65) woman in colonies where those fowl are not raised for commercial purposes but are instead intended for colony consumption. The tender of geese and ducks cooperates with the cooks in determining the numbers of fowl required for slaughter. The slaughter of domestic fowl usually involves some women's work, whereas the slaughter of mammals or fowl for sale is generally the province of men. Young boys are sometimes instructed by the "field boss" to assist in the loading and

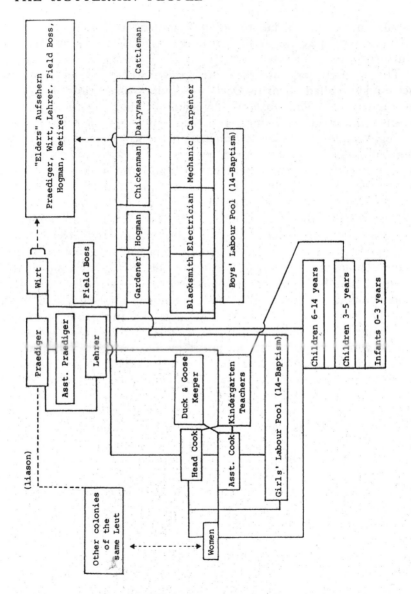

**Figure 4.4**
The Formal Organization of "Dariusdorf" Colony

unloading of fowl for slaughter. A young man is obtained to drive the truck from ponds to the slaughterhouse, but the actual butchering and plucking are conducted by women in most circumstances. The duck and goose operation is a man's administrative responsibility in colonies where it is a commercial as well as an indigenous supply enterprise.

Young women are supervised in their work on the colony garden by a man (the gardener), who controls the girls' labor pool with the exceptions of those persons required by the head cook for work on the kitchen crew, or those who are needed by the kindergarten teachers for assistance there. Membership on the kitchen crew is based on a revolving schedule and kindergarten work is only part time. However, all of the girls and most of the women spend time working in the gardens. Garden labor is diminished by motherhood and becomes voluntary in middle age — old women rarely work in the garden but instead spend their time sewing, knitting, visiting, baby sitting for short periods, or simply cluster around the kitchen where they can spend time with other people and gossip. Other than the supervision of women by the gardener, or the occasional supervision of young boys by the goose keeper during the selection of fowl for slaughter, and consultations between the *Wirt* and production managers with the cooks, women and men do not normally engage in common work. The labor cooperation of men and women is symbiotic but quite rigidly separated. (See Looney 1986, or Mackenzie 1978 for analyses of women's labour).

**Contemporary Social Organization:**
**The Relationship between Kinship and Formal Structure**

The relationship between a patriarchal kinship system and the practice of communal life might be expected to produce some strains between competing demands made upon individuals by the group and the nuclear family. Indeed, these occasions do arise but they are rare (see Chapter V). Adult Hutterites do not use kin terms when the frame of reference is the colony, or the social context is one which refers to the group (Bennett 1967:130). The use of the honorific term "Vetter" which means "male cousin," by adults, and the extension of kin terms like *Vetter, Base, Basel* and *Onkel* to all members of the colony by children are also evidence of the degree to which the demands of the colony organization supersede those of the family. There is a marked tendency for men to name their first sons after themselves, but there is no strong tendency for sons to succeed their fathers in job-roles. Hutterites regard the promotion of kin to positions previously occupied by close kin as potentially disruptive and carefully scrutinize such promotions to ensure that they are not nepotistically motivated, but are based instead on skill. The kinship of an entire colony is represented in Figure 4.5, and is indicative of a number of patterns discussed in the first section of this chapter. Sibling set, and sibling exchange marriages are in evidence and a number of other social patterns commonly found are also present. The tendency for the *Praediger* and *Wirt* to come from separate kindreds is apparent. It is not uncommon for the preacher in a colony to belong to a minority kindred, which frees him from the power block of brothers which is prone to develop, and allows him to better control the potentially excessive use of political power by the majority. Indeed, all of the family whose members are represented by the blackened symbols on the chart are the descendants of one man, a *Praediger* who settled in the colony when it was founded during the move from the United States to Canada. The man's wife was a member of one of the kindreds who established the colony, and they asked him to join them as preacher. The *Praediger* and *Wirt* cooperate closely and this is facilitated by the marriage of one's sister to the other (see Figure 4.6). The same woman was in turn elected as head cook. The election of the *Wirt*'s spouse and *Praediger*'s sister as head cook satisfied the desires of both groups that an indigenous woman be the cook. Food cooked by women from other colonies is sometimes suspect, and favorite recipes endure if the cook has learned her skills in the same colony for which she cooks. The assistant preacher of the colony is from a different kindred than the elder *Praediger* yet has married into the *Praediger*'s kindred, thereby reversing the pattern of the previous generation (see Figure 4.7). The assistant preacher's wife has become an important member of the kitchen

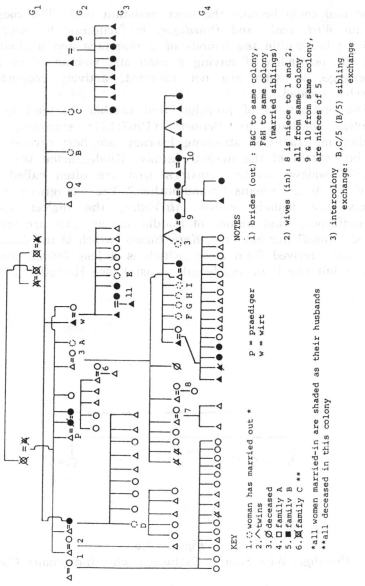

**Figure 4.5**
Kin Diagram of "Dariusdorf" Colony

crew and could become the next assistant cook. The cooperation of the *Wirt*, cook, and *Praediger*, is facilitated by keeping the entire triad within the bounds of a marriage and a sibling pair, and the possibility of having a man and woman of no common parentage, or who are not married, actively cooperating is thereby avoided.

The occupations of preacher and teacher do tend to run in families, perhaps as Bennett (1967:131) suggests, because intellectual traditions stressing literacy are best carried forward in the context of the nuclear family. Kindergarten teachers are usually widows and/or spinsters who are often called *Ankela*, which in dialect means "grandmother." The old retired men in a colony are usually called *Alt-Vetter*, the dialect term for "grandfather," and women of middle age or older are sometimes called "*Basel*" (for example, *Katie-Basel*), which is the dialect term for aunt (derived from *Base*, which is a less formal term than *Kusine* but like it means female cousin) (see Hostetler 1974:243).

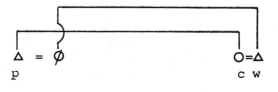

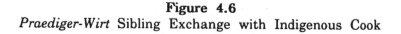

**Figure 4.6**
*Praediger-Wirt* Sibling Exchange with Indigenous Cook

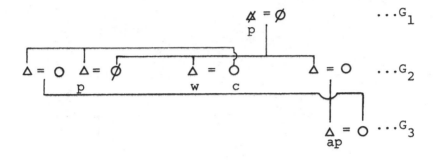

**Figure 4.7**
*Praediger-Wirt* Family and Marriage
Affiliations over Three Generations

Key to Figures 4.6 and 4.7:    c = cook    p = *Praediger*
                               w = *Wirt*    ap - assistant
                               preacher

The relationship of kin position to formal occupation in the colony represented in Figure 4.5 is clarified in Figure 4.8.

Certain relatives are characteristically utilized by the Hutterites when help is needed for the performance of job roles or in emergencies. Bennett (1967:131-132) found that if men needed assistance, they would first ask a brother to help, and if that was not possible due to factors such as a brother's absence, or participation of all available siblings in a critical activity such as harvest, anyone else in the colony would be asked. In periods of stress (harvest, planting) to the general labor pool, the need for assistance is often reported to the field boss who then arranges for help. The pattern among women is similar, with sisters being frequently asked for assistance in the performance of short term emergency tasks (See MacKenzie, 1978). The most formalized

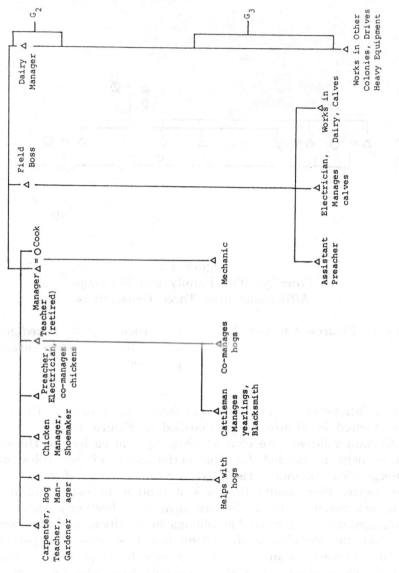

**Figure 4.8**
Occupation-Kinship Index of "Dariusdorf"
For comparison with a Lehrer colony see Bennett (1967:120).

pattern of assistance which I witnessed occurs among women and involves a woman in need of assistance with children. This occurs when a woman's children become ill, or most often when a mother goes to visit her own daughter following the daughter's return from the hospital with a new baby. Mothers usually spend several weeks with their daughter and the newborn, and require someone to care for their own children during this time. If a woman has a niece of marriageable age, asking her assistance is virtually obligatory, and given the enormous size of Hutterite families, there is always a niece of marriageable age to be found somewhere. The visiting-niece pattern often culminates in the marriage of aunt-niece units to avuncular units, or to age distant brothers. Because of the large number of sibling-set marriages, it is very possible for a niece to have more than one aunt in a single colony, and of course aunts may ask for assistance from more than one niece. The *Basel-Nichte* (aunt-niece) assistance pattern is probably responsible for a great deal of the courtship opportunities and ultimately the colony intermarriage patterns among the Hutterites. Although only two of the men I interviewed actually met their spouses as visiting nieces, the pattern gives Hutterites a chance to get to know one another, and is probably more important for its role in courtship than it is for the introduction of potential mates to one another. The visiting niece may also be keenly observed by others in the new colony and her potential as a wife and mother is assessed during her visit. Large Hutterite family size, long fertility range, and fairly uniform birth intervals result in a fairly homogeneous job succession pattern through the generations of single colonies. In Figure 4.8, only one person (a woman) from generation one $(G_1)$ is still living, and so it is excluded; the oldest man of generation two $(G_2)$ is retired, all men of that generation manage major colony production units, and all of the *Aufsehern* (elders) are drawn from that generation as well. In $G_3$ the three oldest men have the major positions; one (the eldest) is a manager himself, and is a contemporary of the youngest man in $G_2$; another is a secondary manager of the colony's largest commercial enterprise — the hog operation; the third is the assistant preacher. The remainder of $G_3$ who actually have assigned positions are engaged in service jobs and maintenance (electrician and mechanic), or labor for major enterprises as apprentices (dairy, hog barn). One man drives heavy equipment and also teaches and employs that skill at other colonies, which have temporary labor shortages. The remainder of the males in $G_3$ are simply members of the labor pool or are still in school. In small colonies the labor-management generational succession can become disjointed due to early promotion.[7] In such cases a $G_2$ who is very young and who usually associates with $G_3$ contemporaries might be promoted to a position like "field boss" which automatically includes membership in the *Aufsehern* (see Bennett 1967:134-135). In larger colonies succession to the managerial positions and *Aufsehern* occurs at an older age and so all positions are usually filled from mature members of $G_2$.

### Daily Life

The austere walls and polished floors, whitewashed buildings and simple garb of the Hutterian Brethren form a pleasant backdrop to life in the colonies. The absence of any embellishment is a soothing aesthetic of absence, in fact an apotheosis of absence (Stephenson 1978), which lends spiritual qualities to the commonplace activities of everyday life with all its tensions and little dramas. It takes great patience and humor to live communally as well as a talent for cooperating with others while still demonstrating responsibility as an individual. Hostetler (1970), and Hostetler and Huntington (1967, 1968) have done detailed summaries of the socialization practices which culminate in adults who are usually able to live and work effectively with others in this communal society, and I have detailed elsewhere (Stephenson 1979) some of the attendant costs and contradictions inherent in that same socialization process.[8] Here, instead of a summary of personality profiles, is a brief description of daily life which is meant to enflesh the rather dry and abstract skeleton of social life and kinship which forms the interior of this chapter on what the Hutterites would term "the body of Christ reborn" — the living colony.

We began with some "real life" examples of Hutterites

commenting on the forces of recent history which have worked a kind of fatalism into the way meaning is sometimes molded in their 'community of goods.' However, Hutterite life is not simply a grim reminder of courage in the face of terrifying persecution, it is also full of warmth and humour (for more detail see Stephenson 1986).

There is a sprinkler system in "Dariusdorf" in which the pump is driven by an old 4-cylinder tractor engine. The sprinklers keep the scraggly lawns in the residence area of the colony alive during the hot dry months of July and August. The lawns are not very old and were sodded in response to complaints from the women about constantly mopping muddy floors when there were clearly better things to do. So now, as mentioned earlier, the women mow the lawns, and sprinklers even had to be installed to keep them growing. The engine sputters and chugs along on every hot afternoon in late summer, pumping water through the pipes that run up from the stream where it flows by the duck and goose enclosure. Everytime it starts up or shuts off, "Chris" chuckles to himself. One day on our way down to change the oil and start up the engine, I asked him why the sound of the irrigation system made him laugh. "Oh," he said, "It ain't really so funny... I can just remember when that engine was new, that's all." He paused for some time in smiling memory, and concluded, "Me and my brother Frank and little Susannah that lives over to Rosebush colony, well, that was the first tractor we ever saw, an' one evenin' we took it for a ride down in the coulee. It was new and shiny and red as a good apple you know, but we crashed and it rolled on its side in the mud — crazy kids! We had t' pull it back up here with a team and 'cuz I was the oldest and responsible, I had t' clean it and fix it...took me days...it's funny...I'm still working on that little engine... I think it'll outlive me, that old Ford."

Even the sounds of an old engine play a part in the personal — and collective — history of the colony. Chris isn't the only person who remembers the incident with the tractor from his youth, and, although it certainly wasn't a common topic of conversation, there was another instance when it came up.

There is a kind of skirmishing between little Hutterite boys and the geese on every colony I have ever been to and this occasionally breaks out into a virtual war when someone gets nipped. This. happened one day to one of Chris and Mary's young daughters who was watching a group of boys throwing rocks at the geese. Outraged, her older brother (then about seven or eight) and several of his young friends, decided to take revenge on the gander responsible by carting it off behind a nearby hill, dispatching and cooking it. Unfortunately, none of the boys knew anything about cooking, so when they were finally found, amidst a few chewed up bones and a lot of feathers and half-raw meat, they all had terrible stomach aches. Goose is rather greasy and consequently needs boiling and long roasting; a short boil in a kettle just won't do. Aching bellies seemed enough punishment for the boys in their engagement with the goose, but as we bumped our way back to the colony in an old pickup truck — the boys in the back along with the salvageable remains of the goose — the smiling driver gently poked Chris in the ribs and in a low voice said, "Well, he's your boy all right — but at least he didn't try to drive off in one of them combines and wind up in the river!"

Hutterite children are not held responsible for their actions by God until after baptism when they become adults. Thus they form a ready reminder both of what adults should act like in order to serve both as effective models for children, and as a source of reminiscence concerning one's own childhood. Inasmuch as adults are thought to be merely "the children of God," this metaphor is actually less a claim for divine paternity than a plea for toleration and patience. Children are regarded as exempt from the original sin of knowledge although they are inclined toward evil through their selfish and "carnal" acts (Harada 1968, Schwartz 1971). The inclination of children to do the wrong things means that they have to be patiently taught the correct way to behave and so the Hutterians attempt to contravene their own idea of "human nature" during the socialization of their young. The Hutterites formed perhaps the earliest "kindergartens" (indeed, it is one of their words) and established the principle of universal education among themselves long before the "world" was prepared to accept such a radical notion. Their intent is still essentially a tolerant one today.

In 1568 the "Hutterite School Discipline" was outlined by Peter Scherer and in it are elaborated the organizational principles, objectives, techniques, and rationale of the contemporary Hutterite school system. The chief objective of the entire socialization process is still to "break" the "self-will" of a child. The selfishness of children is quintessentially human nature, however, it is antithetical to the concept of resignation, or "giving-up-ness" [*gelassenheit*], which the Hutterites conceive of as necessary for leading a *Christlichen* life in *Gütergemeinschaft*. The "self-will" must be broken so that after baptism and its attendant moral accountability has been adopted, a person may enter the state of *Nachfolge*. Hutterite socialization practices attempt to inculcate a sense that the "self" is secondary to the interests of the group and are remarkably successful in that respect. Small "house children" are cared for by the mother and grandmother during the first four months of life and the child is almost never alone during this period. The grandmother cares for the mother and performs many of her normal tasks during the first four postpartum weeks, thereby freeing the mother to devote herself totally to the nurturance and care of her child. Usually after four weeks the mother begins to eat with the colony and perform some of her usual routine, but still devotes most of her time to the infant itself. After six weeks there is usually a small party to introduce the newborn to the husband's family and friends and to which the guests bring small, utilitarian presents for the child. In some colonies the woman's final reintroduction to colony routine is marked after six weeks by having her plan and guide the preparation of an evening meal. After the mother has returned to colony routine she is assisted by one of her older children, a sibling, or a visiting niece when she cannot be with the child herself.

The complex forms of mutual assistance I have been describing and which adults typically offer each other are thought to stem from "selflessness," which is the characteristic sought by adults in their dealings with children as well. Ideally, no adult should punish a miscreant child in anger or from a sense of being personally wronged. In such a state the adult is supposed to hand a child over to another adult and explain what he or she has done and it is then the non-involved adult who administers the prescribed punishment: usually a mild spanking. The attitude of *gelassenheit* means that adults should be calm and kind in their relations with other adults and also with children. "Breaking the "self-will" of a child is really a gradual, almost subversive process — like taming a small wild animal.

There is an essential contradiction which needs to be grasped here. It is precisely the tolerance and patience of adults required by their life "in community" with one another, which grants children their license to act quite freely (in some rather outrageous ways) and which in turn simultaneously reproduces the contradictory keystone beliefs that human beings are inclined towards evil but also have the divine spark of free will. Children are a kind of living representation of that which every Hutterite must subdue within themselves to behave responsibly. They function as a kind of externalized homunculous and because of the high birthrate they are everywhere in the colonies. They constitute a kind of miniature and rambunctious majority within which relatively few adults move in a quiet and often bemused state. The patience needed to deal with the flood of children in most colonies is a prototype for the same kind of love that adults should attempt to employ in their relations with one another, even in the most mundane tasks.

The machine shop at "Dariusdorf" is a busy place, full of the flashes of welding torches and the sounds of drills and hammers. It is a place that small children are drawn towards but where they are normally forbidden entry because of the dangers which some of the equipment represents. But, occasionally a young boy will be allowed to watch a group of men and adolescents at work so that the names for tools and the manner of working can be learned. On one such occasion two men were installing a new master cylinder in the brake system of a colony van and a small boy was standing by the doorway. The following is the entry in my field notes:

...we had the cap off the fluid chamber and Chris was leaning over the engine...Jacob, who had been depressing the brake pedal while we bled the lines continued to do so and squirted Chris in the eye by doing so.

I could see Chris became angry initially but this subsided quickly and he joked about the matter. His response was, 'BY GEE...pause..."I guess that'll clean my eyes out!" (smile)/(I don't believe my presence had too much to do with this...I was out of sight and the exchange was so fast that Chris – who's attention was on his own eyes probably hadn't the time to think about me. There was no mistaking the initial response, Chris's tone was one of anger but was quickly controlled and an attempt at humor followed.)

In retrospect, it may have been the presence of a child which helped to extinguish the anger felt by Chris in this situation – or it may just have been the subdued child within. At any rate, flashes of anger are quickly passed over in a Hutterite colony; they would in fact be a drawn-out act of role playing which is not intrinsic to colony life. Indeed, such performances are probably not common to European peasant village life either. John Berger's observations concerning that form of life are to the point and also suit the Hutterian instance well:

In a village, the difference between what is known about a person and what is unknown is slight. There may be a number of well-guarded secrets but, in general, deceit is rare because impossible. Thus there is little inquisitiveness – in the prying sense of the term, for there is no great need for it. Inquisitiveness is the trait of the city *concierge* who can gain a little power or recognition by telling X what he doesn't know about Y. In the village X already knows it. And thus too there is little performing: peasants do not *play roles* as urban characters do.

This is not because they are 'simple' or more honest or without guile, it is simply because the space between what is unknown about a person and what is generally known – and this is the space for all performance – is too small. When peasants play, they play practical jokes. (1985:17).

. . . It is late on a Friday afternoon and "Joe" and I are rapidly winding our way down the back road to the colony to try and make it to church and supper on time. The dust fans out behind us like a jet-trail and hangs suspended in the windless evening heat. Thunderheads are building up over the Rockies. It looks like we'll be in for a soaking if one of them blows over us. We need it too. The rolling sprinklers have been working all month and the 'hoppers are having a "field day" with the crops. As we rumble down towards the stream and the culvert, in the distance we spot a man's clothing draped over a branch extending nearly to the road itself.

Joe cuts the engine and, as we roll by, he swiftly pulls the clothing off the branch and then smiles the incorrigible smile of a boy who has just gotten away with something. "Look for the tag" he whispers as we continue to roll, silently and ever more slowly, towards the colony buildings. "It's "Jacob"!" I tell him, "these belong to Jake Waldner!" I put my hand over my heart, Jacob — "Jake" — Waldner is the name of the colony preacher. Joe smiles and says confidently, "don't worry Peter, these belong to 'little Jake' (his son)." We let the truck continue to roll until it finally stops next to some geese. We get out and walk quietly back to the colony buildings — I'm still holding 'little' Jake's clothes and looking for a place to stash them. Joe says to me, "Just hang them on his peg" (in the schoolhouse/church building where each man daily takes the same peg for his hat). "What was he doing, do you suppose?" I ask...Joe flashes another smile and tells me, "He was likely divin' to clear the branches from the culvert there, the water's low now and it needed doin'... we'd been talkin' 'bout it lately."

The conclusion of this little joke ended with a few glimpses of 'little Jake,' clad only in his hat, furtively making his way behind the farm buildings until he could get one of his small brothers to fetch some clothes for him. He also became known for the remainder of my stay in the area, as the first and only 'Hutterite streaker.'

But the biggest joke was really on me. I was seen with his clothing, and so while Joe's role in the entire affair was tacitly recognized by everyone, I was the person some held to be responsible — I put the clothing on Jacob's peg before church. This occasioned much commentary throughout the colony — (all of it quite humorous). Even many years later I was to feel the effect of this one practical joke.

A decade later, while attending a conference near Banff, Alberta, I borrowed a van and drove 75 miles to meet someone I had been corresponding with at a colony I had never previously visited. It was early Sunday afternoon when I arrived, and so all of the children should have been at Sunday school, while the adults slept away the afternoon in relatively quiet contentment, or took the opportunity to create even more children to send to Sunday School. Knowing that this respite of private time would end in an hour or so, I decided to have a look around and see what kind of equipment the colony had. So I wandered over to the farm buildings and there, behind one of them, I surprised a young boy of about 13 or 14 years, who was reading a contraband copy of *Mad Magazine* and smoking a forbidden cigarette. I asked him in the best German I could muster where the preacher's apartment was. He stayed pretty calm but I could see I was making him nervous. Was I some Hutterite returning from "the world"? Would I turn him in? Finally, he couldn't stand it anymore and he asked me who I was. I told him I was a professor and that I came from Victoria. His face widened into a smile as I stumbled along in my halting German, then in English he blurted out: "Oh! You're the guy who stole Jacob Waldner's clothes!"

The joke, and the stories that they germinate, help the colony to define itself as a collectivity. They are a daily oral history of close events, out of which the larger movement of history has been created. Jacob Hutter celebrating the Lords Supper in the fields of Czechoslovakia at Easter, a man freezing in a prison cell in the United States, are alive and well in the *personae* of men fixing brakes and playing practical jokes on one another. As Berger (1975:16) concludes, it

> ...is also a *living portrait of itself*: a communal portrait, in that everybody is portrayed and everybody portrays; and this is only possible if everybody knows everybody...A village's portrait of itself is constructed, not out of stone, but out of words, spoken and remembered: out of opinions, stories, eyewitness reports, legends, comments and hearsay. And it is a continuous portrait; work on it never stops.

## NOTES

1 The Chronicles which record Hutterian history are comprised of two volumes composed by various *Vorsteher* throughout the course of Hutterite history. The first of the two chronicles, *Die älteste Chronik der Hutterischen Brüder* was begun by Kasper Braitmichel during the Moravian efflorescence as a compilation of diverse documents and letters which describe events in *Täufer* history as early as Conrad Grebel's institution of "believers' baptism." The "Great Article Book," or *Geschictsbuch* as it is called by the Hutterites, also summarizes human history from Genesis to the year 1523. A total of eight Hutterite writers worked on the Great Article Book, which ends in the year 1665. A second chronicle, *Die Klein Geschictsbuch* (small

94  *THE HUTTERIAN PEOPLE*

chronicle) was begun by Johannes Waldner and summarizes events between 1665 and 1802, when Waldner ceased writing (although he lived for 22 more years – dying in 1824). The *Klein Geschitsbuch* was written between 1793 and 1802. The end of *Die alteste Chronik der Hutterischen Brüder* is roughly coterminous with the death, in 1665, of *Vorsteher* Andreas Ehrenpries, who was one of the last of the great sermon and hymn writers. The *Klein Geschictsbuch* ends with the move from Vishenka to Radichev in Russia. The European history of the Hutterites ended with the vision of Michael Waldner and the reinstitution of communal life in Russia, just 15 years prior to migration to the United States.

2  Hutterite historiography in the *Geschictsbuch* tradition has been carried forward to the present and a third volume is now being prepared. Several persons are evidently at work on the new volume but I was unable to contact them since I learned of the project only several weeks before leaving the field. The Hutterites have published a number of pamphlets concerning their beliefs and way of life during their North American history (see Hofer, 1955, Hutterian Brethren of Montana, 1963), and one Hutterite preacher has authored several extremely articulate and revealing works about his people (see P. Gross, 1954, 1959, 1965). The centennial of North American occupation was also celebrated recently and a brief historical text was produced by the brethren. Several colonies now have modest press facilities (bookbindery operations) and the circulation of items such as rare sermons, etc., may be facilitated by this technique. Hutterites still spend much of their time copying old tracts, however, and care is being taken that the scribal medium of Hutterite learning will not be affected deleteriously. The circulation of rare sermons only means that more people may copy them.

3  Brock (1970) contains a general description and analysis of the treatment of pacifists during World War 1. Jacob Waldner was one Hutterite who kept a diary during his incarceration and his account has been published and translated into English (see Schlabach (ed.), Reist and Bender (trans.), 1974). See also Conkin (1964:59-64), Smith (1927:272-293) and Goodhope (1940:1415) for valuable discussion of the Hutterites and prisons during World War I. A number of other diaries probably exist. I know of at least one belonging to a *Darius* man who I interviewed in 1973 when he was 79 years old. The informant, whom I quote in the text, was also incarcerated at Kansas and Alcatraz and his descriptions of many events corroborate Waldner's account. I also heard the story of the Hofer brothers from this man (who was nearly drowned by guards himself), prior to the publication of Waldner's account.

4  The Hutterites are often confused with Doukhobors by the public. In fact, the two groups have very little in common, with the exception of a mutual interest in communal life. For a description of the Doukhobors see Hawthorn (1955, 1956, 1957).

5  For a brief review of restrictions on land use by Hutterites see Hostetler (1974). Valuable discussion of the "Communal Property Act" of Alberta occurs in Griffen (1947), Hostetler (1961), Sanders (1964), Palmer (1971), and the *Report on Communal Property*, by the select committee of the assembly (Edmonton, Alberta). Serl (1964, 1966), discusses relations between the Saskatchewan government and the Hutterites. Peters (1965:51-71) describes the relationship between the *Schmiedeleut* and the Manitoba government.

6  *Hulba* is the dialect word, however, "shivaree" seems to have almost replaced it in some colonies since the word is used when speaking in dialect as well as in English. The word is curiously their own, having long gone out of common parlance among their neighbours. *Hulba* itself is not a word of German origin but seems instead to derive from a Slovak

dialect so the adoption of "shivaree" is not an index of assimilation at all, but stems instead from a Hutterite practice associating secular celebrations with "the world."

7 The largest number of defections from the colonies occurs among adolescent males, and also older men who have been passed over for promotions to managerial roles. Adolescent defection is temporary in nearly all instances, but adult defection is more likely to be permanent or of long duration. Between 1918 and 1950, 113 people, only seven of them women, left the colonies. The differential defection of the sexes is striking and represents in part, the strict division of labor and the different ways in which the two sexes approach self-fulfilment. Only men are allowed to drive and transact business (deliver goods or pick up parts, etc.) in the towns and so their contact with the "outside" world is much greater (as is their facility in English) than that of women. Men must also express responsibility by obtaining a managerial job. Men who fail to do this are regarded as poor specimens of Hutterite manhood ("lazy") and, once defined as such, may become part of a "self-fulfilling" prophesy. Women are supposed to bear children to realize responsibility and this is a talent less constrained by external forces like the availability of managerial jobs. These figures represent a loss rate of less than 2%, a ratio which has climbed recently but certainly not to alarming proportions, see Mange (1963), Eaton and Weil (1953) and Mackie (1965).

8 See also Eaton and Weil (1953), Eaton (1963), Schluderman and Schluderman (1969a, 1969b, 1971a, 1971b, 1971c, and 1973).

# CHAPTER V

# GROWTH AND COLONY FISSION

"Next to knowing when to seize an opportunity,
the most important thing in life
is to know when to forego
an advantage"
(B. Disraeli)

## The Hutterian People as a "Population"

The sheer numbers of the Hutterian people have fluctuated widely due to persecution, migration, and two spectacular episodes of population rebound. Because of their rapid population growth the Hutterians have attracted the attention of many demographers and so, until recently, information about the structure of the Hutterite population has been plentiful and of high quality. During the last two decades, however, national census information in both Canada and the U.S.A. has been collected without additional information on religion, ethnicity, and race. There may be compelling legal arguments for this in terms of civil liberties, but it also means that complete demographic data on subcultures and minorities is unavailable. More recent studies must be content to sample populations in order to estimate population trends. This has been widely done for the Hutterites (See Peter 1987). Unfortunately, as this chapter suggests, without knowledge of the particular stage in colony growth which sample colonies represent, the data collected will be seriously compromised because colony growth rates systematically vary through time, falling from over 7% per annum to less than 2% as a colony grows. Some of the controversy about Hutterite population growth and overestimates of declining fertility (see Peter 1980, and Olsen 1987) probably stem from a lack of intimate knowledge regarding subtle cultural forces at play during the growth and division of Hutterite colonies. This chapter is designed to show how cultural factors (ritual, marriage, etc.) interact with each other to yield population changes — which in turn feedback into the arena of culture, and individual decision-making. In this chapter I have utilized the demographic information collected by other scholars to form a background for my own limited micro-analysis of the relationship between Hutterite population growth and the religious ideology which is both constrained by it, and reproduced by it. To do this, some basic methodological consideration of the concepts of 'population', 'structure,' 'growth,' and 'change' in their most abstract senses, will preface their ethnographic use. This has a twofold purpose: to clarify exactly what kind of change is propelled by growth among the Hutterites; and to ask whether the instance of Hutterian population growth compels us eventually to reconsider some basic ideas about growth itself. This critical dialectic between population concepts and demographic data begins with the conceptualization of 'growth' in simple, mathematical terms.

## Growth, Change, and the Parameters of Persistence

Three levels of abstraction for general principles of growth have been summarized by Boulding (1956) which are hierarchically arranged but which remain functionally interrelated. The lowest grade of classification is termed "simple growth" and involves the increase or decrease (positive or negative growth respectively) of one factor by accretion or deletion within time. Ideally, simple growth occurs at a constant rate and can be measured against time as its exponent. It has long been observed, however, that virtually all known empirical growth curves demonstrate an "ogive" shape, rising to a maximum and eventually approaching zero again as the greatest value of the single variable is reached. The "ogive" curve is expressed in figure 5.1.

The ogive shape of growth curves seems to result from the tendency of single growing variables to exhaust the materials or conditions necessary for continued growth by the very process of growth itself. All growing entities are constrained by the relationship between themselves and an environment – a relationship which by definition is altered as the object grows within a finite universe (see Courtis 1937).[1]

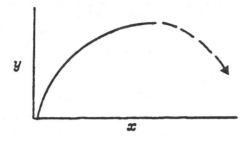

**Figure 5.1**

At a mid-range level of abstraction, where heterogenous rather than homogeneous aggregates are analyzed, algebraic analyses of a detailed and complex nature can be attempted. The analyses of populations, whether they be of persons, artifacts, or capital, are exemplar of mid-range analysis in growth studies. A population is minimally defined as an aggregation of entities of shared definition retained over time which exist for finite intervals (Boulding 1934:650).

The most complex abstraction of growth is widely known as "structural" growth in which an aggregate of interrelated parts grows but whose parts change in their interrelationships in accordance with increases in either negative or positive growth rates. The process of structural growth is fundamental to other related, or potentially identical concepts like "development," "change," or "evolution." For example, natural selection is a theory which purports to explain structural changes over time derivative from population analysis. All levels of abstraction may be applied to the same body of data and do not represent a typology of kinds of growth. Just as natural selection involves structural and population analysis it may also involve simple growth where single taxa are observed through extinction.

Boulding (1956:66) further asserts:

> Similarly, population growth as is the case, say, of a human population, never takes place without changes in the organizational structure of society, that is, in the kinds and the proportions of its 'parts' – its organizations, jobs, roles, and so on. Thus, all actual growth is structural . . .

Boulding's assertion is indicative of the widely-held notion in the social sciences that demographic factors are an irresistible impetus for change. It would be regarded as a truism by most although it is a largely untested assumption which, in Boulding's summary, derives not from the microanalysis of discrete social systems, but stems rather from observations concerning the relationship between shape and size in biology and architecture. D'Arcy Thompson's (1952) theories of morphology and development are particularly well founded, having led to the allometric study of growth, so Boulding (1956:72) relies heavily upon them when he notes the mutual relationship between shape and size such that "growth creates form, but form limits growth." It is a laudable enterprise of general systems theory to compare theoretical formulations in disparate sciences mathematically to ascertain whether or not they share common features or structures. Boulding has not done this, but has rather netted the findings of one discipline with the assumptions of another while dipping into theories of growth. In this chapter (and in this work generally) the assumption that structural growth inevitably emerges from population growth and *de jure* serves as prime mover for structural change – particularly within role relationships – can be examined. Questions turning on the general nature of "growth" are particularly germane to the analysis of Hutterite Culture because the brethren are guided by an essentially unchanging ideology, yet are technologically innovative. Nonetheless, they maintain a rigid division of labor based upon age and sex within a role structure which appears to have changed very little and very slowly during phenomenal surges of growth. The Moravian efflorescence occurred within a period of 50 years, yet the population of the *Brüderhofes* increased during that time from a mere handful to at least

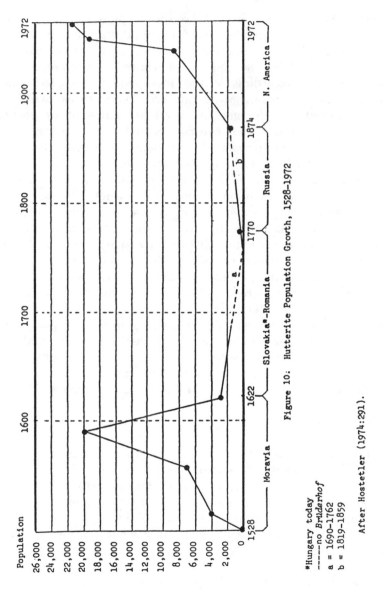

Figure 10: Hutterite Population Growth, 1528-1972

After Hostetler (1974:291).

*Hungary today
---- no *Brüderhof*
a = 1690-1762
b = 1819-1859

**Figure 5.2**
Hutterite Population Growth, 1528-1972

20,000. During the North American period fewer than 500 persons yielded a population of over 20,000 in 100 years (see Figure 5.2). In this chapter I will attempt to elucidate those factors which have served as a control on change within a society which, according to the most widely-accepted canons of contemporary science, grows at prodigious rates which should have augured for changes in social structure of proportionately far-reaching scope. The central ethnological question here is whether the rapid growth of a population necessarily generates structural growth and change, or whether it can be so imbedded within a culture that it may actually serve as a parameter for the persistence of an utopian communal society. Hutterite colonies are by definition founded in opposition to change because they are communal (and utopian) only to the degree that they sustain egalitarian social structure justified by truths felt to be eternal. The institution(s) which transform the demographic vitality of the Hutterites into a parameter of persistence must also be discovered for they are the key to a thorough understanding of Hutterite culture. Much may also be learned in this enterprise about the nature of persistence as a dynamic property of social systems as opposed to a static and circular conceptualization of it as lack of change. Whether, indeed, it is of any particular value to render change and persistence as mutually exclusive by definition, is also a question to be critically considered.

**Basic Demography**

The total population growth of the Hutterites from 443 individuals in 1880 (Friedmann 1970) to the 21,521 reported in 1972 by the Alberta government for its study on communal property represents an increase of approximately 4% per year; doubling at +/- 16 years. The rate of increase appears to have been consistent for the Hutterites as a whole, although departures from the mean have been observed among small subsets of the population (see Figure 5.3). The population pyramid (exhibited by graphic representation of age-specific groups by sex) of the Hutterites remained nearly constant between 1880 and 1950 (Eaton and Mayer 1950).

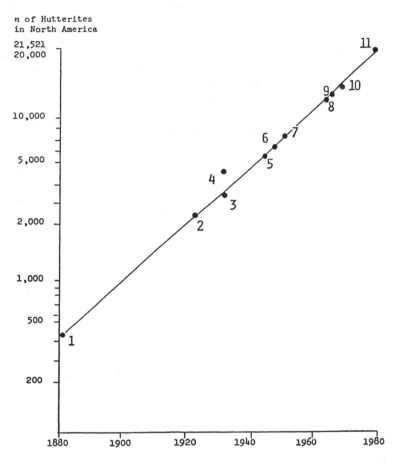

**Figure 5.3**
Population Trajectory of Hutterites
in North America 1880-1972

Sources:    1 Eaton (1954); 2 Clarke (1924); 3 Horsch (1931); 4 Deets
(1939); 5-6 Ziegelschmid (1942, 1947); 7 Eaton (1954); 8 Peters
(1964); 9 Hostetler (1965); 10 Friedmann (1970); 11 Alberta
Government (1972).

After Evans (1973).

The stable population pyramid results in an empirical graph which nearly approximates the statistical model for a stable population wherein the number of persons increases but ratios for their distribution by sex and age do not. In such a population the aged represent a tiny minority and members of one sex do not outlive those of the other. There is actually a slight tendency for Hutterite men to outlive Hutterite women, although the reverse is a nearly universal feature of populations in industrialized countries (Eaton and Mayer 1954; Stephenson 1985; See Figure 5.4).

The growth rate of the Hutterite population is the direct result of an enormous gap between crude birth and death rates. With the exception of social controls on the initiation of reproductive activity (date of marriage does not correspond to the onset of ovulation), the Hutterites approximate the biological maximum for human fertility. In the age groups at the end of the fertility range (40-44) Hutterite women are more fecund than are women from industrialized nations such as the U.S.A. and Sweden during their years (24-29) of greatest fertility (Cook 1968:35) (Table 5.1). In 1953 the median size of a Hutterite family at completion was found by Eaton & Mayer (1953, 1955) to be 10.4 individuals. In 1965, samples of completed family size showed little or no decrease, nor do my own limited data collected between 1972-76 (see Lee and Brattrud 1967, Stephenson, 1978). Evans (1973:35) suggests that a slight decrease in live births during this time may have been offset by decreases in neonatal mortality, thereby vitiating any effect upon actual growth rate. Postpartum infecundity is minimal and mean birth intervals are under two years (Huntington and Hostetler 1966). Peter (1980) suggests that population growth has slowed from 4.12% per year to 2.91% and that the start of this tapering effect began in the mid 1960s coinciding with changes in technology (and consequently labour) which in turn have yielded later age at marriage. I suspect that Peter is correct insofar as his argument that a decline has taken place is concerned and his choice of variables involved is also perceptive. There are, however, a number of factors which might yield a far smaller decline than he suggests.

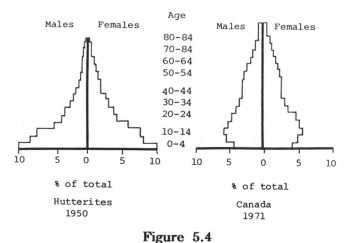

**Figure 5.4**
Age Distribution by Pyramid Graph for Hutterites
and Canada as a Whole

Sources:     Eaton and Mayer (1953); Census of Canada (1971).

**Table 5.1**
Age-specific Birth Rates for the United States and Hutterite Populations,
1926-1950 (per 1,000 Female Population in the Corresponding Age Group)

| Age Group | 1926-30 Hutter-ites | 1926-30 United States | 1936-40 Hutter-ites | 1936-40 United States | 1946-50 Hutter-ites | 1946-50 United States |
|---|---|---|---|---|---|---|
| 15-19 | 19.9 | 50.0 | 13.1 | 47.3 | 12.0 | 74.8 |
| 20-24 | 268.0 | 128.3 | 259.1 | 120.4 | 231.0 | 190.3 |
| 25-29 | 417.4 | 120.9 | 465.6 | 109.8 | 382.7 | 163.2 |
| 30-34 | 397.1 | 93.1 | 461.9 | 74.2 | 391.1 | 102.5 |
| 35-39 | 355.0 | 61.3 | 430.6 | 42.3 | 344.6 | 54.2 |
| 40-44 | 238.9 | 23.8 | 202.9 | 14.9 | 208.3 | 15.2 |
| 45-49 | 23.5 | 2.6 | 47.6 | 1.6 | 42.1 | 1.1 |

Source: Cook (1954:36).

As Lang and Göhlen (1985) have pointed out, Eaton and Mayer utilized completed fertility rates for family size which is a median and not a mean figure. Since median and arithmetic mean rarely ever coincide, later data which utilize a mean statistical projection may overestimate shifts in completed family size. Moreover, Lang and Göhlen recalculated Eaton and Mayer's data and produced a new median value of 9.4 and an arithmetic mean value of 8.97. These data apply to married women only and inclusion of non-married women drops the figure to 8.85 for all women over 45. Because Peters assumed a growth rate of 4.12 is probably rather inflated, the difference in the calculations between the population which he expected and the actual number enumerated should be smaller. Yet another problem are the actual population enumerations (the data) which were conducted by the Hutterites themselves. Not only do self enumerations often underestimate populations in artifactual ways, they are prone to manipulation where the size of a population is a regional political issue (as it is for Hutterites in the Prairies) or is a criteria for various forms of rural assistance (social, medical, agricultural, educational, etc.). Finally, samples drawn from even a sizeable number of colonies (see Peter 1987, for example) can be highly misleading because, as we shall soon see, the growth rates of colonies systematically vary as they go through their cycle of growth and periodic fission.

The extremely high population growth rates manifested by the Hutterites are best explained by a number of strongly held religious convictions which militate for pregnancy and birth, while concomitantly linking persons differentially to social structure. First, in order to participate fully in Hutterite society as an adult, one must be baptized and thereby accept moral accountability for one's actions. Second, one of the primary demonstrations of moral accountability is marriage and parenthood. Hutterites often say that a man without a wife is "like an untended garden." The metaphor is illustrative, indicating both a lack of order, and diffuse and wasted fertility for a man without a wife implies that a woman is without a husband as well. The brethren also accept the biblical admonition to "be fruitful and multiply" as God's chosen people. Third, birth control is regarded as wholly immoral and it is often said that persons who practice birth control will be visited by the souls of all their murdered children at their final judgment (Lee and Brattrud 1967:519).[2] Should pregnancy threaten the life of either or both a mother and child (as for example, with pregnancy-induced diabetes) the burden of guilt is borne by the physician should the colony preacher decide to allow surgical intervention. Although it has long been suggested that the preponderance of males rather than females among cohorts of aged Hutterites may be due to increased risks inherent in maternity when more than three pregnancies are experienced (Evans 1973:39, Guttmacher 1941), this "parity" hypothesis has been seriously questioned. Simply on statistical grounds, there appears to be no relationship between parity and mortality. (See Parkinson 1981; Stephenson 1985). Fourth, there are numerous customs which tacitly support high birth rates by elevating the prestige of women who have just given birth. A new mother becomes the focus of attention for several months after the birth of her child; she is visited by distant family and friends, is given special help either by her mother or by another older woman (this is perhaps the only time a young woman is in a position to dominate an older woman), has special food and kitchen privileges, eats at home, and is reintroduced to colony routine by planning and supervising a colony meal. Finally, in a culture where birth constitutes the key symbol and the most central concept of cosmology, it is not in the least surprising that high birth rates should accrue.

Children born out of wedlock are extremely rare – Hartzog (1971:9) found six out of 2,200 births among the *Schmiedeleut*, all of which were acknowledged by the brethren. The only culturally-appropriate control on the number of births seems to be delayed marriage on the part of women. Between 1918 and 1956 the mean age at first marriage increased from 20.8 to 22.0 for women and from 21.8 to 23.6 for men (Peter 1966). Many authors attribute the rise in age at marriage to the development of what the Hutterites term "girl power" in the colonies. While the Hutterites recognize the existence of cliques of unmarried young women in their midst, and such cliques are regarded as mildly disruptive, most Hutterites do not give the reason for their existence that researchers do – indeed they often give none. Peter (1966) and Hostetler (1974) both indicate that women who live in well-run and long-established colonies are often loathe to marry and, due to the patrilocal postmarital residence rule, move to newer and less comfortable colonies. This explanation is problematical because there are no data to indicate that women from established colonies marry at a significantly older age than those from new colonies. Furthermore, many new colonies, particularly those built by well established colonies (by admission of the women themselves), are better designed with more creature comforts (indoor plumbing, better heating, better kitchen facilities, better laundry facilities, etc.) than are old colonies. Finally, "girl power" does not explain the even greater shift in age at marriage for males, which is almost twice that of females. Since weddings are by mutual agreement, the causes for such a shift must be sought among both men and women.

**Fission and Colony Social Organization:**
**The Number of Managerial Status/Role Sets**

There are a limited number of occupational statuses with attendant roles in which persons must accept and demonstrate managerial decision-making capabilities within a large-scale mixed-farming operation on the North American prairies. Commercial enterprises have become highly mechanized to maximize the productivity of single individuals. Indeed, to yield a profit on virtually any prairie farm, the control of an enormous number of animals and/or amount of acreage by one person appears to be necessary. The Hutterites also have a fascination for clean, highly-mechanized production techniques which corresponds to their values and social organization which stress simplicity, dominion over "nature," and rigidly prescribed statuses and role relationships which often lead them to compare the colonies themselves to well run machines. I have occasionally heard the colonies compared to clocks or engines, and often to beehives by Hutterians.

The number of major occupational statuses is constrained by the nature of prairie land and the market as circumscribed by

North American dietary preferences and is limited to one managerial status for each species and sex of animal exploited (hogs, chickens, steers, cows). Pork, chicken, beef, eggs and milk constitute the animal foods most commonly eaten in North America and all can be produced on the prairies. Cereal grains such as wheat, oats and barley, and grains which can be rendered for oil, (rape or "canola" seed, sunflower) or into protein additives (soya beans) are also commercially viable crops. Most Hutterite colonies are too far north to produce maize in per-acre yields which are profitable. Grain (and soya) harvests are seasonal and involve the coordination of all the managers and young men of the colony under the supervision of one person — the "field boss." Some portion of the yield from these enterprises is held back for colony consumption, seed, and breeding; the remainder (and greatest bulk) is sold. A set of five managerial statuses may be said to exist which are viable adaptations to land and market conditions obtaining on the North American prairie and these are: "hogman," "chickenman," "cattleman," "dairyman," and "field-boss." Three of these (hogs, chickens, and dairy) are often what the brethren call "one-man-operations" in that only one person is needed to perform the day-to-day operation of the facility, which is completely mechanized. The cattleman normally tends the herds through his "helpers" who labor but do not make administrative decisions. The "field-boss" is responsible for the harvest, planting, and overall operation of all the commercial farm enterprises by distributing labor among them and overseeing transfers between operations. For example, because of inclement weather the "field boss" may shift a number of "helpers" from the cattle operation and re-allot them to the construction of a new facility, or to the harvest. He may also shift grain from storage to feed, etc. In a sense, all of these positions are "one-man-operations" inasmuch as one person is ultimately held accountable for their functioning on a daily basis, which is why I have termed them "managerial" statuses.

In order to keep highly mechanized forms of production in operation, a number of support facilities are required and each of these must in turn be managed. Thus, there is a blacksmith, electrician, mechanic and, to guide new construction and repairs to the physical plant itself, a carpenter. A set of four support statuses may then be said to exist, three of which have risen in stock as the colonies have become increasingly mechanized, and all of which rise and fall in relative importance, dependent upon the construction plans and needs of the colony as it grows.

There are also a set of two statuses with responsibility quotients of a managerial nature which satisfy the internal needs of a colony and these are German school teacher (*Lehrer*) and gardener. Hutterite custom calls for a dual form of leadership to oversee and coordinate all of these endeavours. One of the leaders (the *Wirt*) coordinates the commercial enterprises, while the other (the *Praediger*), insures that all transactions are performed in accordance with the tenets of Hutterite religious beliefs, and supervises the entire colony (especially the schools) in that context. Therefore, there is an effective maximum of 13 major occupational statuses in sets of {5} {4} {2} {2}, in most colonies where autonomous decisions can be made on behalf of the rest of the colony. The {13} also include statuses which are critical for internal colony needs involving leadership, socialization of the young, and the management of female and male labor pools (the latter being a function of the gardener and "field" manager). Klassen (1964) lists 18 occupations allowed by Hutterian doctrine. However, few *Dariusleut* or *Schmiedeleut* colonies appear to attain this maximum because occupations such as shoemaker, beekeeper, goosekeeper, and duckkeeper have been consigned to very young men, the aged, occasionally to women, or have been abandoned in some colonies. The participation of women is further limited by the commercial viability of the enterprises and shoemaking is proscribed for them. These occupations are often the responsibility of men performing other more important occupational roles and are part-time endeavors for them. Among the *Lehrerleut* these marginal occupations are more frequently the full-time tasks of men and an attempt to maintain them has been more actively pursued. *Lehrerleut* colonies are also usually larger than *Dariusleut* or *Schmiedeleut* colonies (refer to Table 5.2).

The {13} major occupational statuses must be filled by baptized and (usually) married men. Since most men retire at around the age of 60, and are baptized and married sometime in their mid-20s, there are approximately 35 years of managerial potential for a man. However, since the population doubles in at least half this time in a social organization where the number of managerial statuses must remain constant, the colonies cannot grow by simple replacement of managers. Therefore, although the population profile of the Hutterites is extremely stable, a "simple growth" nexus does not accommodate the rate of increment described.

**Table 5.2**
Mean Size of Hutterite Colonies in North America through Time

| Year | Total | S-*Leut* | D-*Leut* | L-*Leut* |
|------|-------|----------|----------|----------|
| 1880[a] | 111 | | | |
| 1922[b] | 101 | | | |
| 1931[c] | 105 | | | |
| 1947[d] | 113 | 111 | 97 | 142 |
| 1950[e] | 96 | 97 | 85 | 117 |
| 1964[f] | 94 | 97 | 83 | 103 |
| 1969[g] | 94 | 96 | 80 | 105 |
| 1972[h] | 95 | 97.2 | 85 | 103 |

Data Sources: [a]United States Census; [b]Clarke (1924); [c]Horsch (1931); [d]Ziegelschmidt (1947); [e]Eaton (1955), Eaton and Mayer (1955); [f]Hostetler (1965); [g]Friedmann (1970); [h]Ryan (1970), and Evans (1973).
After Evans (1973:69).

The solution for the Hutterites has been periodic binary fission wherein the population splits down through the population pyramid into two halves, one of which moves to a new site: these are respectively called "mother" and "daughter" colonies [*Mutter-Kolonie* and *Tochter-Kolonie*] (see Tables 5.3 & 5.4). Fission is primarily a 20th century growth phenomenon in the colonies which was adopted after the brethren moved from the Ukraine to North America. The *Hutterischen* term for this process is *schwärmen* [often glossed as "hiving," but more literally translated as "swarming"] which is an explicit analogy with bees which appear throughout the Hutterite *codeces* as a communal creature worthy of emulation. All Hutterite colonies contain an apiary as well because the brethren regard honey as the only

**Table 5.3**
Distribution by Age Cohort in a *Schmiedeleut* Colony
from Founding through Division

| Cohort | Colony Population | | | |
|---|---|---|---|---|
| | 1954 | 1969 | "Mother" | "Daughter" |
| 75-+ | 0 | 0 | 0 | 0 |
| 70-74 | 1 | 2 | 0 | 2 |
| 65-69 | 0 | 2 | 1 | 1 |
| 60-64 | 0 | 1 | 0 | 1 |
| 55-59 | 3 | 0 | 0 | 0 |
| 50-54 | 2 | 1 | 1 | 1 |
| 45-49 | 1 | 7 | 2 | 5 |
| 40-44 | 0 | 8 | 5 | 3 |
| 35-39 | 1 | 8 | 4 | 4 |
| 30-34 | 7 | 6 | 1 | 5 |
| 25-29 | 8 | 7 | 6 | 1 |
| 20-24 | 6 | 11 | 2 | 9 |
| 15-19 | 8 | 20 | 11 | 9 |
| 10-14 | 4 | 31 | 17 | 14 |
| 5-9 | 8 | 35 | 18 | 17 |
| -4 | 19 | 26 | 15 | 11 |
| Totals | 68 | 165 | 83 | 82 |
| % male | 50.0 | 53.3 | 49.4 | 57.3 |
| % female | 45.4 | 55.7 | 60.2 | 51.2 |

Data Source: Hostetler (1974:188).

**Table 5.4**
Fission Times by Decade and *Leut*

| Decade | *Lehrerleut* | | | *Dariusleut* | | | t Both *Leut* | | |
|---|---|---|---|---|---|---|---|---|---|
| | m | x | o | m | x | o | m | x | o |
| 1920 | 6 | 5.3 | 3.0 | 7 | 6.2 | 3.1 | 6 | 5.9 | 2.8 |
| 1930 | 14 | 12.6 | 5.1 | 12 | 10.3 | 5.5 | 12 | 11.4 | 5.2 |
| 1940 | 16 | 15.9 | 4.6 | 12 | 15.1 | 7.8 | 15 | 15.5 | 6.2 |
| 1950 | 15 | 15.2 | 5.9 | 17 | 16.9 | 7.7 | 16 | 17.0 | 7.7 |
| 1960 | 13 | 13.5 | 2.9 | 13 | 14.3 | 6.9 | 13 | 13.9 | 5.4 |
| 1970 | 19 | 19.0 | 4.2 | 15 | 14.0 | 1.4 | 16 | 16.5 | 3.9 |

Values expressed in years; $m$ = median, $x$ = mean, $o$ = standard deviation.

After Evans (1973:69).

proper sweetening agent for coffee, tea, bread, etc. Honey [*Honig*] is also a metaphor for the love [*lieben*] which results from living in harmony. The first time I asked one of my informants about the fission process he showed me the apiary of his colony and explained that just as there could not be two queens to a hive without strife among bees so could there not be two leaders in a colony or two managers of a farm enterprise without dissension as well.When speaking English, Hutterians refer to *schwärmen* as "splitting," "branching," or "budding." The person most responsible for this manner of expansion appears to have been Michael Hofer, who imbedded the concept of communal life within the concept of rebirth when he revitalized the brethren in Russia. The Hutterites' expansion accommodates unprecedented demographic vitality, not by altering the number of statuses relative to sheer numbers, but instead by altering the ratio of people of a relatively fixed number of statuses. The metaphor of the beehive [*Bienenschwarm*] is certainly apt.

Because a typical colony grows at an average of approximately 4% per annum, in order to fill its complement of managerial statuses with men over the age of 25 (assuming that all positions are to be filled by separate and single individuals) such a colony would consist of about 100 persons (see Table 5.2). If growth is relatively constant, when the population of the colony reaches 130 there will be two men potentially able to fulfil each managerial task. In fact, the entire colony at this time contains within it a "shadow" status hierarchy of assistants involved in each enterprise. At this point in the growth of most colonies an assistant preacher is nominated and the search for new land begins.

### The Fission Process and the "Will of God"

After an assistant preacher is selected by means of drawing lots among nominees, he serves for several years learning to fulfil the duties of his position prior to being ordained by the preachers of his *Leut*. The ordination (*Handauflegung*) of a new preacher usually occurs sometime between the selection of land for the new colony and the onset of construction.

The search for a site for the daughter colony by the leaders of a mature colony often involves the use of land agents, who keep track of local growth patterns and approach colonies which they think may wish to purchase land. Good land is not always easy to find in Alberta because pressure is often placed on prospective sellers by their communities not to sell to Hutterites. In the past this problem was compounded by the Communal Property Act which governed the amount and location of new land to be purchased by Hutterites. When land becomes available to a Hutterite colony it is quickly bought, but this is more than just a function of decision making under pressure wrought by previous government restrictions and current local prejudice. Although Hutterite leaders often state that they looked for a long time before obtaining land, they rarely look at more than four sites, or for longer than a year-and-a-half (Evans, 1973:101). In fact, it is not uncommon for a colony to buy the first piece of land it is shown, even where land restrictions and local prejudice are not mitigating circumstances (e.g., Saskatchewan). Evans (1973:104) states that the Hutterites often buy the first piece of land they look at because they regard God as having led them to that site through the unlikely medium of the land agent or retiring farmer selling his land. Indeed, the "hand of God" is thought to be present throughout the fission process. First, God's will becomes manifest in the choice of a new preacher, then in the selection of land, and finally in the division of the colony population and assets. The entire "daughter" colony is usually constructed without the benefit of prior knowledge indicating to which colony any particular person will be assigned, and cooperation throughout construction is thought to be engendered thereby. Among the *Dariusleut* it is possible for one group to "volunteer" to leave a colony where dissension among kin lines has developed. However, this practice appears to be the exception, not the rule. Among the other two *leute* the possibility of "volunteering" to leave is absent and is thought to be too disruptive to the construction of a new colony to be allowed. Among the *Lehrerleut* and *Schmiedeleut* a colony must receive permission from the other colonies of the *Leut* before creating a "daughter" colony. Among the *Dariusleut*, consent need not be granted although notice is nearly always given and advice and funds are often sought from other colonies.

The day prior to a move every person packs their few belongings and waits for the decision to be made informing them in which colony they will next reside. Cattle, sheep, items of small equipment (saws, drills, etc.) are all divided by use of lots. The older preacher of the colony places his name, and that of the assistant preacher, on a blackboard and sorts the colony members on the basis of stated preferences by heads of families and the aged, and by sex, age, and occupation, until a balanced distribution is achieved. The men of the colony are then informed of the make-up of each group. After church and the evening meal the two preachers draw lots to ascertain which group is to remain and which is to depart. The following day, the group selected leaves for the new colony with the assistance of other Hutterite colonies who loan them the means of transportation to move everything to the new site. Those who remain unpack their belongings and move back into the old colony, occupying larger quarters or moving where necessary. Although there is a strong attachment between people and the places they occupy, the Hutterites try to regard colonies as essentially the people who inhabit them and not their buildings, streams, and fields. The "mother" colony is therefore regarded as essentially a new colony, just as is the "daughter" colony. The unpacking by persons left behind to reoccupy the "mother" colony epitomizes the "rebirth" of the "mother" colony as well as the "birth" of the "daughter" colony.[3] The structural similarity between the earlier persecution-migration complex and the contemporary fission process is obvious: the latter is a ritualized version of the former, in which the element of chance (God's will) is still the deciding factor for where one shall live.

## Economy and Fission

The purchase of land upon which to build a new colony and set it into operation is costly. The minimum amount of land necessary to begin a new colony varies greatly by region and by the size of the population starting up the "daughter" colony. A wealthy colony in South-central Alberta might actually own over 10,000 acres, all of it bought when the colony was established in 1918. Of this perhaps 9,850 acres might be arable but at least 20% utilized for natural pasture too. The area surrounding Calgary in County Wheatland is characterized by heavy soils and production is spectacular. In 1971-72 one colony in this area had 1,227 acres in wheat, sold 74,380 bushels, stored 4,000 bushels and retained one ton for seed. A more modest colony within ten miles of the one just described owned nearly 7,000 acres, kept 1,300 acres in wheat and produced roughly 50,000 bushels. The smallest colony in the area owned nearly 10,000 acres but could only farm about 3,000 — the rest was unusable except as range. This small colony also leased land — a common practice for new daughter colonies given sharp rises in the price of good agricultural land. In southern Saskatchewan a colony with the same amount of land as the wealthy colony in Alberta (+/- 10,000 acres) would not be wealthy in terms of land at all. Soils are light, crops more specialized and yields lower, but land is also cheaper in Saskatchewan. In short, there is no rule of thumb concerning minimal amounts of land needed for new colonies. In my primary fieldwork area about 3,000 acres (owned or partly leased) would be needed but this would not be adequate for a typical northern Alberta, or southern Saskatchewan colony. The dollars needed to buy or lease land (which varies in value by region) is a more useful criterion for description and analysis. Between $200,000 and $280,000 was required to buy land depending on its quality and amount. The costs of purchasing new equipment, and financing the construction of new buildings are jointly borne by both mother and daughter colony either by remaining linked as the same corporation until all major debts have been absorbed, or occasionally by a terminal grant from the mother colony to the daughter sometimes amounting to more than $50,000. See Table 5.5 for the averaged financial statement of eight Hutterite colonies.

After a colony has begun operation it must invest heavily in production for maximum cash return in order to retire its debts to banks and other Hutterite colonies. At this point in time a colony tends to overplant its fields, raise animals in substandard environments, and take greater risks to maximize the margin of profit obtained from its commercial enterprises. After retiring its debts a colony begins to spend on more land, labor-saving devices, reduces cropping to standard 50/50 rotations, and develops water resources, fences, and buildings (see Bennett 1967:183-189). Finally, in its last five-ten years prior to division, a colony saves the money necessary to help sponsor a new daughter colony.

**Table 5.5**
Statement of 1971 Assets and Capital Equity on a Cash Basis

| ASSETS Current Assets | Mean of Eight Colonies |
|---|---|
| Cash | $ 61,238 |
| Investments | 133,516 |
| Loans Receivable | 64,671 |
| Total Current Assets | 259,425 |
| Fixed* | |
| Land Improvement and Equipment | 849,537 |
| Total, all assets | 1,108,962 |
| LIABILITIES | |
| Current | |
| Bank Indebtedness | 159,528 |
| Loans Payable | 26,775 |
| Total | 186,303 |
| Mortgage Payable | 55,452 |
| Capital | 867,207 |
| Total Liabilities | 1,108,962 |

*Book Value

Source: Alberta Government Report (1972).

The asceticism of Hutterian religious beliefs and their large-scale labor force allows for sufficient capital to be collected to create a daughter colony. Surplus capital is in turn depleted by the process of expansion and keeps the colonies from ignoring the concept of collective wealth and personal austerity. The average interval between divisions is between 15-16 years, all of which is best understood in terms of the process of fission and involves a shift from overemployment and high-risk farming to chronic underemployment and stabilized farming (see Figure 5.5 and Table 5.6).

When a colony reaches its plateau of affluence, the pressures placed upon the leaders, by ascendant young assistants and women, to spend more money and create new projects which they can use and be responsible for, increase dramatically. The doctrine of collective consumption and personal austerity which serves the colonies well in their developmental phase is not as effective against the short term projects planned by assistants when colonies become affluent. Men occupying prime managerial positions may also begin to try to expand their operations in order that younger brothers and/or sons can have meaningful (e.g., responsible) employment. Projects such as the construction of sidewalks, the planting of lawns, flowerbeds, sprinkler systems, and the extensive repairing of old buildings (such as "summer" kitchens, food storage facilities, and kindergartens) which have swept through the colonies in later years all appear to be examples of spending at the plateau of affluence. Clark (1974a, 1974b) found that wealthy colonies among the *Schmiedeleut* tended to divide more quickly than poorer colonies. Clark also constructed an index of inequality, based on father-son job succession rates (which were highest in poor colonies) which revealed that competition among underemployed young men increased as the interval between divisions grew longer.

The large unpaid labor force of the Hutterite colonies is a major factor in their successful economic adaptation to large-scale prairie agriculture. Generally speaking Hutterites do not occupy the very best agricultural lands in Alberta as a function of local prejudice, past government interference, availability, and their propensity for construing first encounters with available land as manifestations of "God's will." However, during the course of growth between property divisions, Hutterite colonies have the necessary labor to develop even rather marginal lands to their productive maximum. The sophisticated use of irrigation, fertilizer,

**Table 5.6**
Per Acre Income and Expense Comparison (1971)

| Receipts | Colony Avg./Acre | F.B.A. Avg./Acre |
|---|---|---|
| Grain Sales and Wheat Board Payments | $ 8.36 | $ 4.62 |
| Livestock sales | 14.89 | 14.94 |
| Livestock product sales | 4.95 | 11.92 |
| Interest and Dividends | 1.09 | 0.00 |
| Other Farm receipts | 1.58* | 0.73 |
| Total Receipts | 30.87 | 32.21 |
| Expenses | | |
| Equipment | 2.97 | 2.67 |
| Building repairs | 0.52 | 0.56 |
| Crops | 1.73 | 1.72 |
| Livestock | 8.06 | 11.64 |
| Overhead | 1.67 | 1.65 |
| Labor | 0.0+ | 2.14# |
| Tools and Hardware | 0.35 | 0.02 |
| Cash rent | 0.38 | 0.52 |
| Miscellaneous | 1.12 | 0.25 |
| Depreciation (Capital Cost Allowance) | 4.72 | 3.62 |
| Total Expenses | 21.52 | 24.79 |
| Profit (Receipts less Expenses) | 9.35 | 7.42 |
| Difference | +1.93 | |

*Reflects sales of garden surplus.
+Reflects ideology of *gütergemeinschaft*.
#Does not reflect minimum wage, but per acre cost over one year.

Data Source: Alberta Government Report on Communal Property (1972:23)

machinery and extensive planting of "test-rows," coupled to a supply of manpower which need only be fed and is not paid a wage, gives the Hutterites a competitive edge on most farmers in Alberta. Table 5.6 is a per-acre comparison of those farms registered in the Alberta Farm Business Analysis program (F.B.A.) and all Hutterite colonies in Alberta during 1971. The F.B.A. farms are in approximately the top 1/3 of all farms in the province on an income basis. The F.B.A. farms and Hutterite colonies each had incomes of just over $30.00 per acre ($31.21

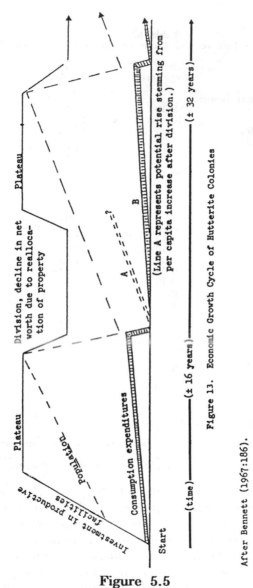

**Figure 5.5**
Economic Growth Cycle of Hutterite Colonies
After Bennett (1967:186).

and $30.87 respectively) whereas the mean for all Alberta farmers was $17.00 per acre. The expenses of F.B.A. farmers and Hutterite colonies were similar although the F.B.A. group was about twice as involved with livestock as were the Brethren and half as involved with grain sales. The most salient difference between the two groups with respect to actual profits is a function of labor costs which were $2.14 per acre for the F.B.A. farmers and nothing for the Hutterites. The net result is that Hutterite colonies show a mean profit of $1.93 more per acre than do F.B.A. farmers.

To summarize, the relationship of the Hutterite economy to the overall growth of a colony and eventual division is complex and involves the adaptive interplay of their ideology with external market conditions and the availability of land. Belief in collective ownership (*Gütergemeinschaft*) provides the Hutterites with sufficient surplus capital to insure its very depletion when a daughter colony is constructed to accommodate surplus population growth. The development of a daughter colony relieves the social pressures which mount due to the underemployment of young men who need to assume occupational statuses with at least a modicum of responsibility accorded them in order to realize through concrete behavior the moral accountability adopted at their baptisms. The choice of land is limited by local prejudice and cultural beliefs which often lead the Hutterites to select more marginal land than is necessary. The development of even the most marginal farm land is in turn facilitated by the existence of an unpaid labor force, but which (due to its diminished and overemployed state) also involves high risk agriculture in order to retire debts. The underemployment situation also augurs for the adoption of highly-mechanized techniques to relieve colony members of excessive work loads. Mechanization limits the effective number of managers involved in commercial activities but leads to increases in the level of responsibility attached to the roles of mechanic, electrician, blacksmith, and carpenter. In the later phases of growth, the machine shops also become more fully developed and utilize a warehouse approach parts and repairs. After a colony reaches a population of approximately 100 persons, underemployment, coupled with the necessity of saving for the purchase of land for a daughter colony, begin to produce strains on face-to-face relations which are particularly uncomfortable and unwanted in this pacifist, communal society. At this stage, short term projects to "improve" a colony's physical plant may provide a temporary outlet for the social pressures inherent in the underemployment situation. Ultimately relief comes when a daughter colony is constructed after a period of usually between 15 and 16 years (see Figure 13). With the construction of the daughter colony, the carpenter, blacksmith, and electrician – statuses often held by younger men – assume a level of prominence in colony affairs previously unaccorded those statuses. The interval between divisions is therefore nearly equivalent to the rate of growth which doubles at approximately 16 years as well. In the ideal fission experience, doubling time for the population would be the same as the interval between actual divisions of the population.

**Leut Variation and Fission**

The mean size of Hutterite colonies manifests general concordance but nevertheless does vary typically by *Leut*. The *Lehrerleut* maintain the largest populations in their colonies and the *Dariusleut* the smallest, while the *Schmiedeleut* occupy an intermediate position between the other two (see Table 5.5). *Lehrerleut* mothers are significantly less fertile than are their *Schmiedeleut* counterparts perhaps due in part to genetic factors (according to Hartzog 1971:30-35). The *Lehrer* population grows by doubling in about 21 years at 3% per annum, whereas the *Schmiedeleut* population doubles after 16 years at 4% per annum. The mean number of live births per family are 8.75 and 10.23 respectively. The mean age at marriage for the two *leute* has risen significantly since 1810 but the increase has been sharper for the *Lehrerleut* than the *Schmiedeleut* (4.1 vs 2.1 respectively). Nonetheless the difference does not account for the total decrease in fertility for mothers born after 1900 (Hartzog 1971).

The *Lehrerleut* tend to occupy more marginal land than either of the other two *leute* and tend to have only one man per occupational status while attempting to fill nearly all 18 traditional occupations. The *Dariusleut* are at least as fecund as the *Schmiedeleut* people but they maintain smaller populations in their colonies in part because traditional occupational categories are often the part-time responsibilities of men primarily engaged in other tasks (and also because traditional occupations have either lapsed or have been adopted by women).[4] Additionally, *Dariusleut* colonies are smaller because their expansion is not controlled by the *Leut* as a whole and is perhaps facilitated by land-based economic solvency as well. The *Dariusleut* colonies in my fieldwork area were not quite as conservative with respect to financial lending institutions as were the *Lehrerleut*.

Table 5.7 contains information on 12 colonies (6 *Darius*, 6 *Lehrer*) which have divided between 1964 and 1972. *Lehrerleut* colonies in this sample are slightly larger than are the *Dariusleut* colonies, take longer to undergo fission, and yet produce colonies which more closely approximate one another in size after division has taken place. Among the *Dariusleut* colonies the mean difference between mother-daughter colony pairs in terms of final populations is twice that of the *Lehrerleut* colonies despite the fact that they are smaller to begin with. This difference probably stems from the *Dariusleut* procedure which allows one group to volunteer to leave should factions develop. The existence of a strong minority faction promotes greater population differences in mother-daughter colony pairs among the *Dariusleut*.

The practice of volunteering to create a new colony among the *Dariusleut* is more than merely a reflection of arbitrary differences in *Leut* rules. *Dariusleut* people interviewed on the subject of fission often allowed that they found the prospect of moving into a frontier situation to be exciting, rewarding, and a fulfilment of God's admonition "to be fruitful and multiply." One old *Dariusleut* man summarized this attitude in a convenient metaphor of struggle by stating that "building a new colony puts you into the front lines of the true Christian faith." *Lehrerleut* people with whom I have spoken have never expressed this attitude but their explanations are nonetheless circumscribed by ideas about fertility. *Lehrerleut* people often stated that building a new colony should be done "carefully," or with "orderliness" and occasionally intimated considerable fear of failure concerning

Table 7.   Comparison of Fission in Six *Dariusleut* (D) and Six *Lehrerleut* (L) Colonies 1964-1972[5]

| *Leut* | 1. 1964 Pop. | 2. Date Div. | 3. Interval | 4. Pop. @ Div. | 5. 50% of 4. | 6. 1972 Proj.* | 7. Actual Population (Mother) | 8. Actual Population (Daughter) | 9. Mo-Da Difference |
|---|---|---|---|---|---|---|---|---|---|
| *Dariusleut* | 90 | 1970 | 15 yrs. | 109 | 55 | 60 | 60 | 60 | 0 |
| *Dariusleut* | 119 | 1966 | 13 yrs. | 129 | 65 | 82 | 70 | 78 | 8 |
| *Dariusleut* | 98 | 1970 | 21 yrs. | 122 | 61 | 66 | 70 | 46 | 22 |
| *Dariusleut* | 120 | 1967 | 15 yrs. | 125 | 63 | 76 | 70 | 55 | 15 |
| *Dariusleut* | 115 | 1968 | 15 yrs. | 133 | 66 | 77 | 87 | 65 | 22 |
| *Dariusleut* | 97 | 1968 | 13 yrs. | 112 | 56 | 65 | 69 | 70 | 1 |
| *Lehrerleut* | 124 | 1969 | 16 yrs. | 151 | 76 | 86 | 78 | 77 | 1 |
| *Lehrerleut* | 142 | 1964 | 12 yrs. | 142 | 71 | 93 | 90 | 99 | 9 |
| *Lehrerleut* | 122 | 1969 | 18 yrs. | 148 | 74 | 83 | 73 | 88 | 15 |
| *Lehrerleut* | 131 | 1966 | 18 yrs. | 142 | 71 | 90 | 90 | 91 | 1 |
| *Lehrerleut* | 128 | 1970 | 22 yrs. | 161 | 80 | 86 | 80 | 80 | 0 |
| *Lehrerleut* | 120 | 1968 | 20 yrs. | 130 | 65 | 76 | 70 | 78 | 8 |

*Computed @ 4% compound rate.

D = Summary of $\bar{x}$ computations:   3. 15.33;   4. 121.67;   6. 71.00;   7. 71.00;   8. 62.33;   9. 11.33

L = Summary of $\bar{x}$ computations:   3. 17.67;   4. 145.67;   6. 85.67;   7. 85.67;   8. 85.50;   9. 5.67

**Table 5.7**
Comparison of Fission in Six *Dariusleut* (D)
and Six *Lehrerleut* Colonies 1964-1972[5]

the expansion process. Both groups give rationalizations of a religious nature when describing their respective patterns of expansion. The *Dariusleut* seem to regard expansion as a form of elutriation which ends or avoids friction and consider it concomitantly to be a fulfilment of God's will to be pursued with zeal. The *Lehrerleut* regard expansion with more obvious ambivalence and consider failure in the expansion process to be a breach of the same sacred trust to "be fruitful and multiply." In any case, none of the three *Leut* appear to fail more often than the others. Although there are many factors which impinge upon the interval between divisions in the fission process, in all cases the interval varies in accordance with differences in the doubling time of specific colonies and characteristically by *leut* affiliation.

## Marriage Patterns

Each of the three endogamous *Leute* can be further subdivided into land holding kinship groups which expand via the vehicle of periodic binary fission. These kinship groups are neither clans nor segmentary lineages in the usual sense because they are not unilineal and exogamous, so I have termed them patrifiliated kindreds − or patrikindreds for brevity. All Hutterite colonies in Canada derive from the populations of those colonies originally established in 1918 after migration from the United States. There were four *Lehrerleut*, six *Schmiedeleut*, and seven *Dariusleut* colonies established at that time. Since postmarital residence is customarily patrilocal, the male members of each patrikindred are descendants of the males of founding colonies.

Marriage is far from random within the colonies of the three *Leute* because, although a person may marry anyone outside the first cousin incest prohibition in the reckoning of kinship, the majority of marriages occur within extended-patrikindreds. Although the majority of marriages are to persons outside the colony of residence, the number of marriages which occur within the colony is significant as well. Bleibtreu (1964) found that among the *Lehrerleut* two-thirds of all marriages were patrikindred-endogamous (he termed them "clans") and that marriage was more likely to occur between persons of the same colony, between relatives, and between persons of two siblingships where a previous marriage had already taken place. Hartzog (1971:18) found that 42% of *Lehrerleut* marriages were between members of the same colony and that only at distances greater than 200 miles were marriages outside the colony but within the patrikindred more common than those to different patrikindreds.[6] *Lehrerleut* men are an average of 1.8 years older than their wives.

The degree to which these patterns hold for the entirety of the other two *Leute* is unknown but specific colonies among the *Dariusleut* with which I have worked manifest similar patterns. Logically, the basic *Leut* difference is that the percent of marriages within colonies drops slightly with a decrease in average colony size.

Founding colonies are in close geographic proximity to one another and discuss issues among themselves before passing on their evaluations of any particular problem to their respective daughter colonies, which in turn pass information to their daughters, etc. Thus, the position of a colony in the collective kinship structure is largely a product of its age and relationship to its mother colony — a recent daughter gets information from a founding mother colony sooner than the daughter of a daughter. Since most major innovations (technological adaptations, changes in house styles due to new building materials, etc.) occur during the construction of new colonies and the "jump" to a new site, and because founding colonies tend to produce slightly less technologically conservative daughters which in turn produce slightly less conservative colonies than themselves, information tends to proceed from a conservative base line through to more modern colonies along a gradient. Information thus transmitted gains a kind of inertia due to its repetition and remains untransmuted yet condensed. Serl (1964:98-99) also points out that as preachers move from colony to colony when important matters are under discussion, the stated purpose is to gain a wide range of opinions. However, the effect is to present single colony leaders with an ever-increasing complement of elders favoring a certain viewpoint — inevitably a conservative one.

Thus, leadership, policy, and social control originate from founding colonies, and are transmitted through a communication network constructed along kinship lines running from the oldest to the newest colonies.

## The Fission Cycle: Baptism, Marriage, and Growth

As indicated throughout the preceding pages, baptism is an event of cardinal importance to a Hutterite. Through baptism today's Hutterite identifies with the martyred ancestors, the apostles, the suffering of Christ, and gains membership in the *Corpus Christi* or reconstituted and reborn savior as His successor (the *Nachfolge*). Christ and the past are reborn in the Hutterites and they are reborn through him. The decision to seek baptism is the most important one of Hutterite's life and must be carefully considered. When a person feels that "the spirit has been born within" them, he or she seeks out the *Praediger* and discusses baptism with him and then with the *Aufsehern*. The candidates for baptism are then privately discussed among the elders and if any have serious and irrevocable objections to particular candidates they may be denied baptism. It is generally the preacher's role to act as an advocate for the candidate under such circumstances and consensus is usually the result – only occasionally is baptism denied a candidate upon first petition, and I know of no cases when the second petition was denied; the interval between baptisms is probably sufficient (two-six years to avoid a second refusal.

After baptism a person becomes morally accountable for his or her actions and thoughts. Therefore, if there is no available social venue where one can make decisions to actually be held accountable for, then quite likely baptism will be delayed. Should baptism be delayed, then marriage will consequently be delayed as well. Therefore, the probability increases that actual population growth will diminish as a colony matures. It is apparent that baptism constitutes a model of rebirth which is collectively recapitulated in colony fission whereby a "daughter" is born to a "mother." Baptism is therefore at the crux of decisions made by persons within a sacred belief system which has led to rapid population growth. This in turn denies later members access to responsibilities as a by-product of growth initially engendered by granting those same responsibilities to others earlier (e.g., marriage). Exactly how baptism serves to augment and diminish growth at various stages of the fission process is illustrated in Tables 5.8, 5.9, 5.10, and Figure 5.6, where three fission cycles of a *Dariusleut* colony are represented.

As the colony grows in size the mean age at baptism rises just over two years on the average and the frequency of baptisms increases. The mean interval between baptism and marriage does not vary significantly so the increase in baptismal age is not appreciably effected by a decrease in courting time. This state of affairs stems partly from the proscription of marriage during the days surrounding Christmas and between

**Table 5.8**
Fission: Cycle 1

| | | | | | | | | |
|---|---|---|---|---|---|---|---|---|
| n. people in colony | 61 | 94 | 105 | 125 | 135 | 139 | D* | 71 |
| n. people baptized | 5 | 7 | 5 | 9 | 6 | 4 | - | 5 |
| n. of baptismal cohort | 5 | 7 | 7 | 10 | 11 | 12 | - | 5 |
| % cohort baptized | 100 | 100 | 71.4 | 90 | 54.5 | 33.3 | - | 100 |
| % colony baptized | 8.2 | 7.4 | 4.7 | 7.2 | 4.4 | 2.8 | - | 7 |
| x age at baptism | 19.1 | 20.2 | 20.4 | 20.2 | 20.9 | 20.9 | - | 19.7 |
| x age at marriage | 22 | 22.5 | 21.4 | 22.5 | 22.7 | 23.1 | - | 21.9 |
| x baptism-marriage interval | 2.9 | 2.3 | 1.4 | 2.3 | 1.8 | 2.2 | - | 2.2 |
| interval between baptisms (in yrs.) | - | 6 | 3 | 5 | 4 | 2 | - | 2 |
| growth rate**(%) | | 7.1 | 3.7 | 3.5 | 2.0 | 1.5 | - | -48.9# |

fission interval = 20 yrs. x growth @ 3.9% per year.

*Division of colony.
**Computed for x year of interval between baptisms.
#Division expressed as a negative growth rate.
x Mean

**Table 5.9**
Fission: Cycle 2

| | | | | | | | | |
|---|---|---|---|---|---|---|---|---|
| n. people in colony | 71 | 82 | 97 | 118 | 123 | 126 | D | 82 |
| n. people baptized | 5 | 5 | 4 | 7 | 1* | 4 | - | - |
| n. of baptismal cohort | 5 | 5 | 7 | 8 | 1* | 10 | - | - |
| % cohort baptized | 100 | 100 | 57.1 | 87.5 | 100* | 40 | - | - |
| % colony baptized | 7 | 6.1 | 4.1 | 5.9 | .8* | 3.2 | - | - |
| x age at baptism | 19.7 | 18.3 | 19.9 | 20.8 | 21.8* | 22.2 | - | - |
| x age at marriage | 21.9 | 20.4 | 22 | 22.7 | 23.9* | 25 | - | - |
| x baptism-marriage interval | 2.2 | 2.1 | 2.1 | 1.9 | .5* | 2.8 | - | - |
| interval between baptisms (in yrs.) | 2 | 3 | 5 | 6 | 1* | 2 | - | - |
| growth rate (%) | | 7.2 | 3.4 | 3.3 | 4.1 | 1.2 | - | -34.9 |

fission interval = 19 yrs., x growth @ 3% per year.

*The baptism of one person here is anomalous and was precipitated by an older widow marrying out who was joined by a younger sister in a double sibling-sibling marriage.

Easter and Pentecost. Marriages at spring planting and during harvest are exceedingly rare as well. The largest number of marriages occur in November and early December (around 40%, Mange 1963:34). If a person does not marry within the preferred months following baptism (mid-summer, or late fall) the likelihood that he or she will wait an additional year is great. The increase in the age at baptism is mainly precipitated by males who cannot advance to managerial positions. Since a large number of women marry men of their own colony — particularly in larger colonies — they too stave off baptism. Those women who choose to marry-out (more than half) are lost to the overall population of the colony as occasionally are a few frustrated men who tend to leave colonies at the peak of their growth curves because of the lack of opportunity for advancement at that phase of the fission cycle. Here, I think, is the reason why there is an older average age at marriage for men than for women. Women who

**Table 5.10**
Fission: Cycle 3

| n. people in colony | 82 | 100 | 115 | 125 | 135 | 142* | D* | 63* |
|---|---|---|---|---|---|---|---|---|
| n. people baptized | - | 4 | 4 | 7 | 4 | 11* | | |
| n. of baptismal cohort | - | 4 | 5 | 8 | 10 | 11* | | |
| % of cohort baptized | - | 100 | 80 | 87.5 | 40 | 100* | | |
| % of colony baptized | - | 4 | 3.5 | 5.6 | 3 | 7.7* | | |
| x age at baptism | - | 18.9 | 19.1 | 20.9 | 21.5 | 22.3* | | |
| x age at marriage | - | 21.1 | 21 | 23.1 | 24.7 | - | | |
| x baptism-marriage interval | - | 2.1 | 1.9 | 2.2 | 3.2 | - | | |
| interval between baptisms (in yrs.) | - | 3 | 2 | 3 | 3 | 5* | | |
| growth rate (%) | | 6.5 | 6.9 | 2.8 | 2.5 | 1* | -55.6 | |

fission interval = 15 yrs., x growth @ 3.6% per year

*Mother and daughter colonies baptized together after dividing just after Christmas.

move out to marry men in other colonies leave behind a set of bachelors whose only immediate prospects are for a delay in their search for a responsible position, and whose difficulties in attracting a wife are compounded by the desertion of many remaining marriageable women from their colony. Perforce, they must wait until their colony divides and they can attract a wife from another colony in the late stages of its growth. It is easy to see that changes in farm technology which yield a concentration of responsibility and power in only a few "one-man operations" could be at the root of slower colony growth, increased factionalism, later age at marriage, lower population growth, and increased defection. As a colony grows, the number of persons baptized falls from as high as 7% to 3% of the total colony. This is less than half of the potential for individual age cohorts based on the youngest person baptized in the previous baptismal cohort. The net result of the concatenation of all of these factors is that growth is inhibited after the mean size of

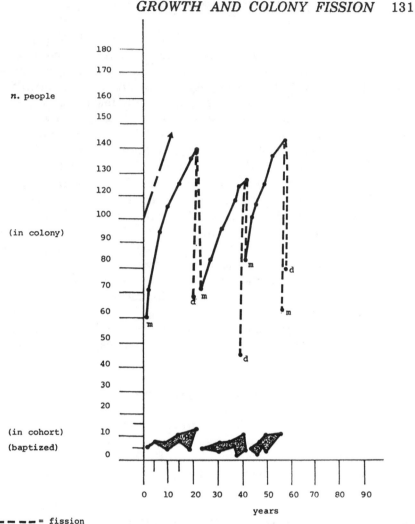

= fission

shaded area = difference between **n.**baptized and **n.**of baptismal cohort

= growth @ 4% per year

m = mother colony, d = daughter colony

**Figure 5.6**
The Fission Cycle of a *Dariusleut* Colony

the colony is reached over its fission cycle and is engendered prior to this. The fulcrum of this transition from a positive to a negative feedback situation is baptism and the consequences of adopting *gelassenheit*. In baptism one adopts an attitude of Christian resignation; "gives up" the desire for material rewards and ambition in a sacred ceremony and is thereby accorded responsibility over and for those material things which comprise the general welfare of the colony. Where there is no context within which to demonstrate sufficient responsibility to gain acceptance of one's petition to the elders for baptism, no petition is made. Indeed, in a large colony in a state of underemployment, cliques tend to develop and their behavior is sometimes anything but responsible. The Hutterites are fond of saying that "the Devil finds work for idle hands," and in colonies at the peak of growth in the fission cycle the phrase finds ready application to the activities of youths living in a protracted state of childhood. This is because it is during these "casual" years that young adults usually investigate the "outside world" anyway; often by leaving the colony for short periods if they are young men. As the age of these defectors increases, the likelihood of permanent, or long-term defection also increases. Disaffected youths may also visit towns where they sometimes buy small transistor radios, and miniature tape recorders. While driving in rural Alberta and listening to my car radio, I was once stunned to hear a phone-in request from a young Hutterite girl for a popular country-and-western tune which she wished to dedicate to "Mary, my brother George, Elias, Rachel, Katie, and all the other boys and girls down at "Rosebush." "Rosebush" was indeed a Hutterite colony, and the accent was as obviously Hutterian as were the names. Teen-age Hutterites establish cliques differentiated by sex and these constitute effective conformity enforcing peer groups. Even if such teen-age cliques break a colony rule and go see a movie in town, or listen to a radio, they will normally all break the rule together. This makes their activities difficult to hide, and in large colonies the evidence of their conformist approach to breaking the rules is everywhere because after the age of 15 they are out of school but do not yet have responsible jobs. Older non-baptized Hutterites are more likely to be solitary and at greater risk of leaving the colony for longer periods partly due to the loss of peer pressure itself.

Following colony division, the age at baptism drops dramatically and the percent of both the potential cohort and the colony which is baptized increases to full proportions within the colony population structure: everyone who can be baptized undergoes the rite. In a new daughter colony hard working young men are given every chance to prove themselves and are actively encouraged to seek baptism via the approbation of their acts. Consequently marriages abound in new colonies. In the positive feedback phase of growth, marriages between colony members are also augmented by the infusion of brides from outside the colony and a profusion of small children soon sweeps through the colony.

"Girl power," and differences in age at marriage between men and women, are largely artifacts of the growth process itself because the adoption of new technology largely takes place during the construction of a new daughter colony. However, Boulding's assertion that all growth is "structural" is simply too simplistic to be easily supported or denied by the evidence presented in this chapter. The actual number of managerial statuses does not increase with the exception of the election of an assistant preacher who constitutes a second nucleus for the social mitosis of fission itself. Instead, the number of colonies increases as a product of changes in the numbers of persons who vie for a limited number of statuses with attendant role requirements where responsibility may be demonstrated. The relative importance of different statuses changes as the colony grows and the relationships among the membership of colonies change as well. Whether this constitutes Boulding's definition of "structural change" is dubious and minimal at best. If the plane of analysis was the growth of the number of colonies rather than of individual persons then Boulding's statement would be supportable to a greater extent. Of course, the number of colonies is ultimately derivative from population increases but it is the relationships between and among colonies which may ultimately result in regulatory committees (a structural element) struck from the assemblies of all preachers of their respective *Leute*. Although the Hutterites use terms like "mother colony" and "daughter colony," it is difficult to assign colonies the labels of status and role as they are used in conventional social science parlance. I will return to this issue in the conclusion because it bears on communal evolution. Finally, if retirements were considered to be statuses (however, retired men actually remain members of the *Aufsehern*) then this too might support Boulding's assertions.

Fission is a process which includes the entire history of a colony between its divisions and is not just the final division itself. The fission cycle is quintessentially change: yet it is repetitive, periodic, and at present relatively stable. Periodic oscillation, like homeostasis, is not the lack of change – it is a special kind of change. *Beigiessungstäufe* and the belief system which adheres to it (*gelassenheit, Nachfolge, Corpus Christi*, and calendrical marriage proscriptions) and the social and demographic concomitants of it, render baptism the centerpiece of the fission cycle in a dialectic between the ideational and material domains epitomized by sacred beliefs and raw demographic increase.

We have moved thus far from the historical features and universal symbols of birth in the demography and "salvation" of Hutterians in the Middle Ages to their fusion in the baptismal cycle of fission practices today. How these are entwined within the lives of individual Hutterians involved in the performance of ritual today is the subject matter of the next two chapters. It should be evident that for Hutterian people the nature of this connection to the past goes back through the Middle Ages to apostolic times and ultimately, in their minds, to Jesus as the personification of God.

## NOTES

1 Numerous equations have been promulgated for the ogive curve, ultimately they are only descriptive, however, and not explanatory. Courtis (1937) suggests that even flat description via mathematics has the advantage of revealing cases where the equation does not fit. The "law" of gravity led to the discovery of the outer planets in just such a way (Boulding, 1956:67fn.). I have used Boulding's summary here because his discussion is based on the assumption of constant growth rates or compound rates expressed in exponentials. More recent efforts at general theory construction such as Thom's (1975) theory of catastrophe are devoted to discontinuous phenomena. Since Hutterite demography has long evinced a

very stable pattern of population expansion (ff. Ch. V), I have used Boulding as a foil for my argument (see Zeeman 1976 for a review of catastrophe theory).

2 It should be noted that Boldt and Roberts (1980:116fn) have also recalculated Eaton and Mayer's statistic and arrived at a higher earlier growth rate and larger decline, which they attribute to the use of birth control and not to later age at marriage. They do not, however, provide any direct data to support this suggestion. Whatever decline in growth rates has occurred is likely to be a product of both later marriage and some use of birth control as well as increases in non-married rates and deflection to other charismatic religious groups (See Peter 1982).

3 Hostetler (1974:189-190) gives a nearly identical account of a typical "moving day" in a *Lehrerleut* colony. My description derives from information collected in *Dariusleut* colonies.

4 If the overall growth rate for all Hutterites is still about 4%, and the *Lehrerleut* grow at 3% and the *Schmeideleut* at 4%, then logically the *Dariusleut* must grow at a rate in excess of 4% for the average to be sustained. However, the data on total growth rates are too old to accurately estimate from. Nonetheless, the fact that *Dariusleut* colonies divide more quickly and at smaller peak sizes is suggestive and might accrue from overall birth rates in excess of 4%. Birth rates and absolute growth are not to be confused with growth rates and percentiles of individual colonies charted later in this chapter. In the latter case growth includes occasional outmigrations of men and outmarrying women and are therefore lower than absolute population growth for an entire *leut*, or for all Hutterites.

5 Some of these data were first published by Evans (1973:76) and have been augmented with my own data.

6 Hartzog is critical of Bleibtreu's hypothesis that marriage practices are designed to insure close relationships among males of the landholding kin group from generation to generation on the basis of this "nearest neighbor" criterion of marriage. However, she ignores the fact that marriage within the colony itself would be sufficient to support Bleibtreu's contention even without the figure of one-third extra-colony, patrikindred-endogamous marriages. She also ignores the rule of patrilocality and stated reasons of Hutterites themselves for preferring such marriages over others, which also supports Bleibtreu's hypothesis (as indeed does the contention that patrikindreds exist at all).

7 To preserve community anonymity the graph is a composite drawn from 3 separate colonies. That is, division 1 is from colony A; division 2 is from colony B; division 3 is from Colony C. All three colonies were *Dariusleut* and all three show the same trends over three divisions or more.

# CHAPTER VI

## HUTTERIAN *ETHOS* AND *EIDOS*

"The basic problem with empiricism is not whether we trust the
evidence of our senses but whether we accept their transmutation into
the constructs of the mind."
                                R. Murphy 1971:206


Ritual has often been defined as a communication event by
anthropologists who note that ritual behavior is stereotyped or
repetitive and includes the presence of symbols which occur in
predictable sequences and in association with certain phases of
repetitious behavior (see Leach 1954:14, Turner 1967, Goffman
1956). Perhaps the greatest difficulty in defining ritual with
precision has stemmed from the fact that although it is a central
feature of religion, ritual cannot easily be separated from the
wholly secular practices represented by certain kinds of repetitive
physical labor without reference to its communication function and
the meaning of a particular ritual's resident symbols (see Wallace
1966:234). All this complaint descants is that although ritual is
generally defined in terms of its communication function, this has
been done neither explicitly on the basis of solely observational
criteria, nor strictly via an abstract comparison with the functions
of other non-ritual behaviors. In this chapter I have been content
simply to conclude that what the Hutterian People regard as a
"special event," or "ceremony" is in fact, a ritual. No amount of
definitional impedimenta which are imposed from without by
rather dualistic theorists are likely to alter the units of analysis
much if we simply begin with local meaning, and ask how it is
then communicated by special (ritual) activity. Furthermore, if
there is information communicated in ritual which is significant
in a pragmatic sense, but which the participants might not be
aware of, then how are we ever to pry this underlying

significance loose, if we do not at least begin with the more prosaic meaning which is ours for the asking? We cannot begin by assuming that all things are unknown in order to conclude that they are also "uncognized." This is the stuff of communication research, and so I have appealed to information theory to get started on the business of teasing meaning out of various ritual contexts in Hutterite religious practice. Eventually, however, the ethnographic description will wend its way back to the concepts it has been launched by to catalyze them. This is in the interest of generating an ethnographic understanding which is eventually freed from the umbilicus to its parent theory. The metaphor is intentional of course – the birth of our understanding has its analog in both individual and collective indigenous representations of Hutterite world view; in other words, "consciousness."

The terms I have drawn from communications theory have rather specific meanings which are quite distinct from what is generally implied by them in common parlance, so I must define them prior to moving further into the description and analysis of Hutterian ritual. First, the amount of information which a signal or sign conveys is a function of the frequency of its occurrence within a series of these comprising a message. Information is a statistical measure of the degree of non-randomness in a series – in effect it is the negative of entropy. Second, this measure of information applied to a sequence of signals yields the relative redundancy of a code. Redundancy, coupled with its constituent information, is a formal statement of what scientists conventionally call "pattern" which is perhaps the most time-honored and shopworn metaphor of analytical thought. Third, the quantity of information conveyed by a symbol is inversely proportional to the probability of its occurrence.

The greater the redundancy of a code from which messages are drawn, and the more these are repeated, the less information it and they possess. However, the more redundant the code or message is, the more likely the message is to be understood should some sort of interference (noise) occur between the source of the signals and the receiver. Therefore, although redundancy diminishes the quantity of information transmitted, it also increases the probability of successful reception. Emergency beacons, doorbells, S-O-S signals, sirens, "mayday," etc. are all messages which obtain from joining the preceding propositions (see Bateson 1967, 1968, Cherry 1952, 1957, Rapoport 1953, Shannon and Weaver 1949).

The perspective whereby ritual may be regarded as noninstrumental, yet still a communication event, is commonplace in anthropology as well as in general ethology. However, within this very conventional wisdom there are a number of competing statements regarding the efficacy and content of ritual, the disposition of information in it, and the respective theoretical hegemony of either the "etic" or "emic" approaches to ensuing analysis. In any case, the methodological interpenetration of beliefs and acts is usually foresworn by proponents of one or another of the competing interpretations of ritual as a communications event. This seems to stem from the proclivity of many investigators to treat information as an analytical category, but to confuse ritual as both an analytical category and a particular culture-specific context.

For example, according to Anthony F.C. Wallace 1966:233):

> Ritual may, perhaps, most succinctly be classified as communication without information: that is to say, *each* ritual is a particular sequence of signals which, once announced, allows no uncertainty, no choice, and hence, in the statistical sense of information theory, conveys no information from sender to receiver. It is, *ideally* a system of perfect order and any deviation from this order is a mistake [my italics].

Wallace's statement is grounded in a deep-seated assumption of many writers who seem to regard ritual as a form of socially-formalized neurosis. The roots of this conceptualization are to be found in Freud, who regarded ritual as a compromise act which neutralized anxiety by controlling opposed values repeatedly through time.[1] It is my contention that this view has effectively strangled the investigation of whatever empirical import ritual may have other than as a kind of representational display of social structure and those changes which are recurrent within it (see van Genep 1960:1-15, Turner 1969, Young 1965, Gluckman 1965:250-303).

In an evolutionary sense, ritual is the final arbiter of

adaptation and subtly changes as more and more information is collapsed and stored within it. Over time an increased storage of information in the form of increasingly stylized pieces of behavior renders them into arbitrary symbols differentiated from their evolutionary or historical roots. This process goes on all of the time in the evolution of communication systems. For example, in languages, the increased use of a term generally seems to yield its phonetic abbreviation. The more a word is repeated, the more it is shortened and concomitantly the more abstract its meaning tends to become as well. This phenomenon is commonly known as Zipf's (1965) law after its first proponent. To gain an immediate appreciation for this feature of languages simply open any dictionary to the words "it," "the," "for," "a," etc. and compare them with any polysyllabic word. Abstract color nomenclature (basic color terms) also appears to have evolved this way from metonymic origins (Stephenson 1973, Conklin 1974).[2] Ritual may be regarded as the vortex of abstraction in which repetition simply means that the communicants may increasingly assume a form of common "consciousness" or "shared awareness." An emphasis on ritual performances of increasing exactness is essentially the process whereby ritual simultaneously evolves while it imbeds increasing amounts of information within the members of a culture, via the avenue of their "consciousness." Ritual is not merely an expression of pent-up but dangerous and conflicting emotions, it is, far more broadly, a compression of both collective historical and personal experience: it is where they meet. The pursuit of ever more perfect performances (contrary to Wallace's remarks) is more the working of evolutionary change than it is a resistance to it. In ritual *plus ça change, plus ça reste la même* finds its natural inverse; for the more we try to match a performance against its unattainable ideal, the more it evolves and so the more information it comes to contain.

Within the body of ethnography proper, Wallace seems to have ignored a distinction between the ideal and actual behaviors of people at rituals and all of the variation that occurs around the always unrealized ideal. Furthermore, by concentrating on the performance of an ideal within an externally imposed typological definition of ritual, Wallace has obscured those differences which exist between and among the several rituals to be found within a single culture. One typical approach in anthropology has been to approach single rituals and explicate them in terms of an overarching definition of ritual and to ignore the more widespread appearance of symbols and their general distribution within a whole system of rituals (see Firth 1973 for example). If ritual is a general analytical category, then a single ritual viewed over time can certainly constitute the locus for an examination of trends specific to itself. However, meaning and its communication via abstract symbols in ritual are not completely analyzable within the confines of a single contextually specific ritual alone. A description of all of the rituals of a society, the relative frequency of their occurrences, the distribution of symbols within them, the demography of participation in them, and their individual and collective relationship to the ordinary mundane activities that they correspond to and have in part arisen from, is necessary to an interpretation of culture through the analysis of ritual. This may also allow us to move beyond simply saying that an action is either a ritual or not, and toward a conceptual notion of ritualization as the central process of both culture creation and social reproduction.

## The Daily and Weekly Matrix of the Trinity

Among the Hutterites, the most frequent ritual observances are the daily church services which are held before dinner in the late afternoon. These services culminate at week's end with a Saturday evening service and two services held on Sunday which are longer than daily services and often convey a single theme across all three days in the sermons which are read. The rhythm of daily life is highly repetitive but there are day-to-day differences which are integrated along a weekly dimension. Each age group and sex have slightly different time schedules which hinge upon both the nature of their specific tasks and the relationships which obtain among groups.

The day begins for the cook at an extremely early hour — around 4:00 A.M. during the summer growing season. The dairy workers follow the cook to work within an hour. Still an hour later, a large, centrally-located bell is rung (6:00 A.M.) to awaken the colony.[3] The breakfast bell for adults is sounded at approximately 6:30 A.M. Throughout the day, the bell is tolled to mark changes in work activities and to call people to meals (with the exception of the evening meal and church). After the adults have eaten their breakfasts, the room is cleared by the women on kitchen duty and the German school children then eat while the kindergarten children are also being fed at school. Following these groups, infants will be fed in the family apartments by their mothers. After breakfast, some of the girls clean the children's dining facility. The daily chores at this level are invariant but some jobs vary from one day to the next: women launder on Monday but, as with eating, always along a continuum of age in which the oldest women wash first and the youngest last. Younger women (in particular) also work in the colony garden later in the week. Some job assignments (baking and milking) are changed on a weekly basis, and the constituency of certain crews (kitchen duty) changes as well. The transition of jobs from one person to the next, one crew to the next, occurs on Saturday after a general cleanup of the venue for that job on Friday. Saturday afternoons are weekly bath days and most barbering occurs then as well.

The menu of a colony changes with the season and some items are tried for awhile and then dropped. Occasional surprises are cooked too. I was once served "chowmein" on the birthday of an elderly preacher (it was his favorite meal) who had learned to cook it while in prison as a conscientious objector during World War II. But for the most part, food does not vary greatly. Generally speaking, if one eats borscht on one Tuesday, one will eat it the following Tuesday too. Fowl – duck whenever possible – is served on Sunday and re-served cold on Sunday night.

Saturday night and Sunday church services are long and people wear their best clean clothes to them. The three major services involve three changes of dresses for women: Saturday afternoon calls for one dress, Sunday morning for a second, and Sunday afternoon for a third. These end-of the-week services last for several hours and involve the reading of prescribed sermons which are usually integrated around a common theme – indeed sometimes all three are really parts of the same sermon. Weekday services tend to employ shorter sermons chosen for their instructional nature and are more discretionary on the part of the preacher. They deal obliquely with current events, current discipline problems, etc., but they too, are drawn from the *codeces* and are not written by the current preacher.

The marking of this stream of events is complex but basically it involves the separation of the men from women, age grades from one another, Hutterites from the world, and the sacred from the secular. Men and women sit on different sides of the dining hall and church, the old eat and wash prior to the young, and the age grades all eat in different locales with some degree of overlap. Hutterites say prayers upon both rising and retiring and both before and after eating. The last activity of one group of persons is the first part of that same activity for another group. The interface between these transitions in the matrix of activity is marked by prayer. These prayers are invariant, recited collectively, and even repeated by the smallest of children to invoke the Trinity of God the Father, God the Son, and God the Holy Spirit.

The intrusiveness of the world is controlled and compartmentalized by holding *Grosschul* prior to as well as following the English school every day. Hutterite children generally attend the English school to the legal minimum of age 15. If a Hutterite child becomes 15 in the middle of a school year he or she will leave school then. Likewise, if the child turns five years of age during even the last week of school it will attend.[4]

The quotidian passage of time is marked by prayer and the invocation of the Trinity while weeks are marked by a Trinity of services at week's end. During the year there are also three major rituals, each lasting for a duration of three days. The calendrical ritual year begins with Advent and a discussion of the coming of Christ as prophesied throughout the Old Testament.

**The Trinity of High Rituals**

1. *Weihenachten* [Christmas or "consecration eve" in literal high German.] I have often heard a literal use of the word *Wehenachten* as a pun meaning "night of birth, or labour." *Wehen* means labor and many Hutterites intentionally mean they celebrate Christ's real birth, and not our form of "consecrated" (*Weihe*) Christmas, but using *Wehenachten* rather than *Weihenachten*. I prefer to use their pun on the word normally employed by the outside world to represent the Hutterian sense of Christmas — that of the nativity where spirit becomes flesh. This also anticipates a basic manner of symbolic representation among the Hutterian people. By using a pun, or by inverting practices of "the world," the Hutterian symbolic universe becomes simultaneously highly abstract and very literal: a finely honed subtle fusion of the spiritual with the corporeal where a bare minimum communicates so very much (*see fn. 6).

*Wehenachten* is then the celebration of the birth of Jesus Christ, the son of the Trinity where one day is devoted to the Father, one to the Son, and one to the Holy Spirit of the Trinity. Work is proscribed. *Wehenachten* texts are chosen from *Luke* 2:1-20, *Isaiah* 11:1-7, *Micah* 5:1-3, *Isaiah* 9:6-7, *Isaiah* 49:1-4.

2. *Oster* [Easter]. Sunday, Monday, and Tuesday are segmented in terms of sermon topics as follows: on Sunday, the sermons stress the unity of the Trinity and the purpose of the celebration of the Lord's Supper [*Abendmahl*] (literally: evening meal; the Hutterites avoid prefatory use of *das Helige* [holy] which implies actual transubstantiation). *Abendmahl* is held on Monday and involves two long services. On Tuesday *Auferstehungs Tag* [Resurrection Day] (literally: rising-up-from-the-dead day) is celebrated. Work is proscribed. The texts used in the sermons are: *Exodus* 12:1-51, *I Corinthians* 10:1-24, (*Oster Tag*); *I Corinthians* 11:213-32 (*Abendmahl*); *Matthew* 28:1-15; *John* 20:1-18 (*Auferstehungs Tag*).

3. *Pfingsten* [Pentecost, Whitsuntide] begins nine days after Ascension Day [*Christihimmelfahrt*] (literally: Christ's-flight-to-heaven) and the sermons deal with communal life and the origin of the Hutterites as the rebirth of Christianity via the "pouring

out of the Holy Spirit." Occasionally, although rarely, baptisms are held at *Pfingsten*. The basic texts for the sermons are: *Acts* 2:1-47 and hundreds of other shorter passages (Anderson 1972, Vol. 2:400-409). Work is proscribed.

Generally, baptisms are held on *Palm Sonntag* [Palm Sunday] but are not exactly calendrical because there are not always candidates. Baptism is an event which synthesizes the Trinity of High Ritual days for the candidate by involving him in the *Nachfolge* and *Corpus Christi* for the first time. Although actual baptism is outside the Trinity of High Rituals, it is via the baptism that the candidate is incorporated into them. On *Palm Sonntag*, the concept of *gelassenheit* is preached following Christ's example of humility as exemplified by riding a donkey into the city of Jerusalem. *Karfreitag* [Good Friday] and *\*Gründonnerstag* [Maundy Thursday − literally green Thunderday] emphasize suffering, self-sacrifice, and the voluntary death of sacrifice by Christ on the eve of his betrayal. Finally, at *Oster* on *Abendmahl* the candidates join the rest of the *Nachfolge* of the *Corpus Christi* by eating the meal of remembrance with the rest of the baptized members of the colony. So, the individual Hutterite is ushered into potential salvation through the metaphor of Christ riding along with the candidate into the new Jerusalem on humility via a voluntary death of self-sacrifice.

## The Trinity Elaborated

The Hutterites do not view the Trinity as solely or distinctively a culmination of the coming of Christ into the world but rather interpret the Old Testament festivals as earlier manifestations of the same Trinity at work. In the Pentecostal sermon the relationships are made explicit as follows:

1. The Feast of Tabernacles, or Christmas, was celebrated by Israel when all the harvest had been gathered from the threshing-floor and the wine-press. In view of this we must ponder the great love of God, how he has bodily communicated the heart to us, and has given and sent to us his beloved Son, Jesus Christ, the heavenly fruit.

2. On Easter Day they slaughtered the lamb and celebrated the Passover memorial, remembering their deliverance from the bonds of Egypt. That was the meaning of Christ, the true Easter lamb, slain for our sins.

And thus the Easter festival is being held for thanksgiving, remembrance, and recalling the suffering and death of Christ.

3. On the Feast of Pentecost, Israel received the Ten Commandments at Mount Sinai: This was a prelude to the mission and the outpouring of the Holy spirit (translation, Anderson 1972, Vol. 1:49).

*Wehenachten* is the heir to the Feast of Tabernacles, *Oster* to Passover, and *Pfingsten* to the Feast of Weeks which comprises the moral rules by which humanity can live together harmoniously.

The Trinity was also present at the origin of life itself in that the major division of order made from chaos by God was characterized by the presence of the "Spirit" moving on the face of the waters whose first manifestation was light (Spirit) who then separated the water from heaven and distributed it. The waters (Father) then became the domain of life which went on to propagate itself eternally (Christ). Finally, after the preceding events had transpired, God said, "Let *us* make man in *our* image after *our likeness*." Note that God the subject has one likeness but takes the first person plural.

The Trinity is then the source of all life and also of a new eternal life for the baptized who become children of God – like Christ [*Christlichen*].

> For whatsoever is born of God overcometh the world; and this is the victory that overcometh the world, even our faith.
> Who is he that overcometh the world, but he that believeth that Jesus is the son of God?
> This is he that came by water and blood, even Jesus Christ; not by water only, but by water and blood. And it is the Spirit that beareth witness, because the Spirit is Truth.

> For there are three that bear record in heaven, the Father, the Word, and the Holy Ghost: and these are one.
> And there are three that bear witness on earth, the Spirit, and the water, and the blood; and these three agree in one. – *I John* 5:4-8.

The *Pfingsten* sermon emphasizes the unity of the Trinity as the perfect coordination of mind with action via the body which results in a perfect outcome or result. In a sense the Trinity is a state of perfect being stemming from total communication: the Trinity is conceived of as perfect and eternal life.

In the sermon three parts are given attributes which correspond to the unity of mind (thought), body (being), and activity (behavior), as follows:

1. First, God the Father, who has the power and might to order and command. [Mind, Thought.]

2. The Son, who derives power and might from the Father, and who executes His work. [Body, Being.]

3. The Holy Spirit, who is the power which comes from him who orders, and from him who carries out the commandment, and is he who executes the will of god everywhere. [Activity, Behavior.]

God as a Trinity exists in a perfect state of being because, as the sermon continues: "the intimate love of their communion is so great that everything exists as one thing, is of one mind, of one will, of one plan, of one beginning, means, and end" [my translation].

There are a number of metaphorical expressions utilized to illustrate the Trinity by the Hutterites and the earliest (1565), the best known, and most often repeated comes from Peter Riedemann (1950:37):

> For even as fire, heat and light are three names and yet one substance, one nature and essence, even so are God, the Father, Son and Holy Spirit three names and yet but one being. And even as fire, heat and light do not separate or depart one from the other (for where one is, there are all three, and where one is lacking, none is present) even so the Father, Son and Holy spirit. . . . For just as little as one

can take heat and light from fire and yet leave fire, even so and still less can one take the Son and Holy Spirit from the Father.

The Hutterite conception of the Trinity is that of a perfect state of being after which the human individual must struggle while plagued by doubts and selfish desires. This state of perfect being is also expressed as the unity of life in the Garden of Eden prior to humanity's fall from a state of "grace" which is an undifferentiated oneness with God. The fall from grace was a product of the human propensity for behaving selfishly and knowingly as if there were only one life and no possibility of eternal life or eternal damnation. There is no way to overcome the vagaries which human imperfection brings to living, however, without struggling against these faults, while still accepting them as a given which one comprehends can never be fully overcome, even the possibility of eternal life is denied. *Beigiessungstäufe* is the first step towards the ultimate salvation. The second step is the adoption of *gelassenheit* as evidenced by a subsequent marriage which must be the harmonious dwelling together of disparate entities; one with authority and power (father), the other an agent of reproduction and dispersion (mother) of progeny (sons and daughters). The harmonious marriage is expressed as something which effectively combats time. The *Pfingsten* sermon states, and individual Hutterites often note, that 20-30 years in a good marriage "seems only 6 or 7 years." Marriage is the primary example of a state of harmony which defeats time after the pattern of the Trinity itself but the Hutterites give other examples as well. Bees and sheep are communal animals which are said to be useful in the Bible but solitary animals like wolves are pictured as destructive because they attack sheep and goats which are protected by the good shepherd – the most common metaphor for Christ. Harmonious living is understood as productive and fertile: "and where this unity prevails, there lives the Holy spirit. There the fruits of the love of God will bloom and grow" (translation, Anderson 1972, Vol. 1:62).

Knowingly sacrificing one's life as Christ did in a voluntary death is thought to be the antithesis of the sin of knowledge, or knowingly acting in a selfish way. Christ's act, from a human

Hutterite perspective, was only possible because he comprehended that it actually meant a unity with all life such as existed prior to Adam's "fall" from grace. As such, the crucifixion is understood to be an affirmation of life, not death. The Hutterites attempt to reconstruct the life of the apostles as a group who witnessed Christ's resurrection into an eternal life, and who lived and ate with him and had "all things common" as represented in the concept of the *Corpus Christi*:

> For as the body is one, and hath many members, and all the members of that one body, being many, are one body; so also is Christ.
> For by one Spirit are we all baptized into one body . . . (*I Corinthians* 12:12-13).

The harmony of the reborn body of Christ is a statement of Christ's corporeal existence and perfection which is also a state to which humanity should aspire. The unity of mind with body in the act of self-sacrifice is Christ's state of being, otherwise his voluntary death on the cross could not have been possible. Christ

> . . . is the image of the invisible God, the firstborn of every creature:
> . . . And he is the head of the body, the church: who is the beginning, the firstborn from the dead;
> . . . And, having made peace through the blood of his cross by him to reconcile all things unto himself; by him, I say, whether they be things in earth, or things in heaven.
> And you, that were sometime alienated and enemies in your mind by wicked words, yet now hath he reconciled.
> In the body of his flesh through death, to present you holy and unblameable and irreproveable in his sight . . . (*Colossians* 1:14 . . . / . . . 22).

The self-sacrifice of the individual Hutterite, of Christ, and the collective resurrection of Christ the individual through reborn individuals after his pattern, and the harmony of marriage, are all one Trinity-like isomorphism: a reconciliation of intent with acts, of mind with body through action. This, in turn, must characterize a meaningful life. The body of Christ is reborn in the baptized members who have been informed of eternal life by him, and who struggle against doubt to believe in an eternal life that is only possible through self-sacrifice as expressed in collective living. The disavowal of material wealth to the extent that martyrdom should be preferable to apostasy is a covenant with Hutterite history, as well as with God.

## Ethos and Eidos

The concept of the Trinity, the metaphors which explicate it, and its structural relationship to birth and the idea of rebirth are all logically related, and in this way they represent Hutterian *eidos*. *Eidos* was first used by Bateson (1958) as a foil for the concept *ethos*. The *eidos* of a culture is the way ideas are schematically linked together by the anthropologist as a reconstruction of the cognitive domain of the people he or she has worked among. *Eidos* is the ethno-"logic" of the ethnologist and is his or her construction of the abstract structure of indigenous explanation; the logical vertebrae upon which the structures of ethnobotany, kinship nomenclature, etc., hang. In contrast to *eidos*, *ethos* may be regarded as "the system of emotional attitudes which governs what value a community shall set upon the various satisfactions and dissatisfactions which the contexts of life may offer" (Bateson 1958:220).

Geertz (1973) utilizes *ethos* in much the same manner as Bateson, but prefers "world-view" to *eidos*, although he seems to mean the same thing by it. Consider the following passage:

> In recent anthropological discussion, the moral (and aesthetic) aspects of a given culture, the evaluative elements, have commonly been summed up in the term 'ethos,' while the cognitive existential aspects have been designated by the term 'world view.' A people's ethos is the tone, character, and quality of their life, its moral and aesthetic style and mood; it is the underlying attitude toward themselves and their world that life reflects. Their world view is their picture of the way things in sheer actuality are, their concept of nature, of self, of society. It contains their most comprehensive ideas of order (Geertz 1973:127).[5]

It appears that the attempt to bridge the discontinuity between *ethos* and *eidos* (or "world view") in ritual is the apotheosis of religious expression. The accommodation of logic with emotion is understood as a rephrasing of the statement that religion is an existential resolution of doubt via faith. Doubt is a contingency of knowledge (logic) which is overcome in an emotional defeat of death and linear time. This analytical view of religious expression is quite general, but it ignores the fact that in ritual people unconsciously seek to abolish the very distinctions by which as analysts we consciously seek to construe it. Existential belief is antithetical to "systemic" knowledge and logic. For the Hutterians, just as for the Javanese whom Geertz describes, faith is logical, and the explanatory precepts of the analyst are obliterated by this, although the goals of an ethnographer should not be. Among the Hutterites the existential taproot of religion is simple naked belief unfestooned with a rich symbolism of icons, fanciful architecture, sculpture, etc. They attempt to abolish theology as merely another sterile branch of vain cleverness. The Hutterites no longer interpret the Bible, or write their own sermons – that has been done adequately in the past – today the Bible is read and the sermons are copied. The eternal truth is replicated not embellished.

According to Geertz (1973), meaning can be "stored" in sacred symbols like the cross, crescent moon, feathered serpent, etc. These symbols seem to "sum up" for the believers their knowledge of the world and the quality of the life which the world encompasses.

> Sacred symbols thus relate an ontology and a cosmology to an aesthetics and a morality: Their peculiar power comes from their presumed ability to identify fact with value at the most fundamental level, to give to what is otherwise merely actual, a comprehensive normative import. The number of such synthesizing symbols is limited in any culture, and though in theory we might think that a people could construct a whole autonomous value system independent of any metaphysical referent, an ethics without ontology, we do not in fact seem to have found such a people. The tendency to synthesize world view and ethos at some level, if not logically necessary, is at least empirically coercive: if it is not philosophically justified, it is at least pragmatically universal (Geertz 1973:127).

Basically, while I agree with Geertz, I think we must go further in this matter. The nature of an "intentional" or "utopian" society such as the Hutterites may stretch the boundaries of his discussion somewhat, mainly because they were a people founded on principles of faith which separated them from the religious practices of "the world" and the conventions of its "metaphysical referents." Geertz hedges here – he never actually says 'symbols' although by "metaphysical referent" he appears to mean not simply the metaphysical *significata* (gods, demons, etc.) themselves but also their points of reference in the domain of physical objects – their *designata* – which he regards as symbols.

The history of the Hutterites has taken their religious ideology on a very fast five century trip across the same rough territory which other religions have often traversed through the relative quiet of millenia. Because the persecution of the Hutterites has been extreme, so has been their retreat from "the world." The Hutterites have also adopted personal austerity and collective moderation in material wealth as dictates of their beliefs. I have already suggested that the evolution of ritual is characterized by a positive feedback loop in which the process of abstraction leads to increasing amounts of information being imbedded as givens within the "collective unconscious" of members of a culture. Correspondingly, the more resonant a symbol may be in the unconscious of persons of a culture, the more redundant, abbreviated, and abstracted it should tend to be (Stephenson 1978).

The Hutterites appear to bear this observation out completely by representing so much with so little that, to the naive observer, there would appear to be no symbols at all. It is just these obvious absences which are so filled with significance – which are symbolic. There are no feathered serpents in their ritual, there is no crucifix, indeed, there is no church building. The brethren regard arbitrary material symbolization in most instances as constituting graven images. At the end of the same rather long passage from *John* which I quoted earlier in this chapter he admonishes: "Little children, keep yourselves from idols. Amen" *I John*:5-21. Metaphorical extrapolation was feared by early *Täufer* writers who kept very close to the scriptures in their sermons and did little interpretational writing. For example, Meno Simons stated that "I dare not go higher or lower, be more stringent or lenient, than the scriptures and the Holy Spirit teach me" (Hershberger 1957:172). It was felt that the truth, as revealed by the Holy Spirit and spoken by the prophets, took its fullest form in the person of Jesus Christ. Therefore, the

Hutterites did not earlier do more than comment upon the Scriptures of the Bible, which they consider to be the revealed word of God which contains a basic plan for living. The "word" is also a metaphor for Christ. If the preachers of the past were loathe to do more than comment upon scripture, those of the present exemplify the same tradition even more intensely by refusing all commentary – there are no sermons being written today.

There is a principle here that is worth examining in detail because it is the key to beginning to understand the manner in which Hutterian *ethos* and *eidos* are synthesized. Among the Hutterian people, things can resonate meaning precisely because they are absent. These absences are recognizable in the stream of both contemporary events and history because, like the pun for Christmas, they contrast with items which are present in either a nonsacred Hutterite milieu, or a non-Hutterite milieu, or both concomitantly.

Let us take, for example, the bell which calls the brethren to rise, to work, and to meals. In the stream of events that make up the Hutterites' day the bell serves to coordinate the work activities of the commune. However, the one time when the bell is not rung is that time when people are most aware of the bell's deepest significance: the bell is not rung in order to call people to church before the evening meal. People are attentive to the silence, to the not-ringing of the bell. In effect, I am suggesting that the brethren really hear the silence and that this is not some clever ethnographic trope. Perhaps the following quote from my field notes will lend this statement a more concrete note of credibility.

> I asked [him] if he ever was late for church in the evening and he said 'almost never.' I continued, 'but how do you know when to go to church if you are out some distance from the center of the colony? – where there is no clock . . . and remember you don't wear a watch! He answered that he 'could just tell' and mentioned that 'it gets kind of quiet.' I then asked if he ever felt hungry and if that 'sort of told' him that it was getting late in the afternoon and so must be time for church. He said yes, but 'you must feed the soul before the body, Peter!'

The most frequent signal which the bell makes is its sounding at

regular intervals. But there is an interruption in the regularity
of the pattern during the late afternoon when hunger pangs begin
to set in, and people are tired; when the cows come in from the
pasture and the light begins to fade slightly. It is in this context
that the silence of the bell becomes sacredly significant, for it is
a different quality of silence than the one which represents the
background against which the peals of the bell are normally
heard. This pre-church silence is a higher order silence altogether,
for rather than constituting the background against which the bell
is heard, the bell constitutes the background pattern against
which the silence is heard. The quiet hush that envelopes the
Hutterite colony at the "spiritual" silence of the bell ushers them
into the realm of the eternal "word" and they quietly assemble
as the "body of Christ." However, they do not gather in a
church, but rather in a school house converted for use as the
place of gathering. If a colony is just being built and the school
is not yet usable, they will meet elsewhere – in a dining room,
or the cellar of a longhouse under construction. The exact place
of worship is irrelevant as the fact that they customarily meet
in the school occupied for most of the day by the worldly
intrusion of the English teacher demonstrates. What is most
significant about the place is that it is *not* a "worldly" building
decorated with icons and stained glass. The building must be
chaste and undecorated by any religious paraphernalia – even the
sermon book must be carried to the meeting by the preacher.
The ritual of the worship service occurs in sacred time and is
apart from the mundane goings-on of the day. The service is also
set apart from the "blasphemous" worship of the outside world.
The churches of the worldly represent "the temples of the un-
Godly" to the Hutterites. Just as the people of the world ring
bells to call persons to church, so the Hutterites, who are not "in
the world" but have been chosen "out of the world," refuse to
ring bells to call the truly faithful to church. The historical origin
of this practice probably goes back to the persecution of the
Hutterites during which they were forced to meet in persons'
houses, caves, forests, and dungeons. Once Jacob Hutter even
celebrated *Oster* in the open fields. A refugee people in a
perennial state of migration do not build beacons to attract

attention to themselves (Stephenson 1978:438-439).

The absence of iconic symbols is also related to the separation of the world of the flesh from that of the spirit – as the quote from my informant demonstrated. The antimaterialistic orientation of the brethren and the emphasis on unity through the works of the Holy Spirit are also epitomized by the pattern configuration of absences constituting symbols. The hog barns of the brethren are often luxurious in comparison to their own houses which, although they are sparsely furnished by most North American standards, are far more individualized and cluttered than the schoolhouse generally used for the church services. Within the belief system of the Hutterites this all makes perfectly good sense because the Spirit is a force and not a thing. Things are of temporally-defined dimensions whereas the Spirit is eternal and therefore cannot be symbolized by a temporary physical entity – Geertz's "metaphysical referent," or symbol – without it constituting idolatry.

The absence of signs can have great import as messages in a digital communication system. If I don't send in my income tax form I shall elicit a specific response from the government of Canada. Likewise, if I fail to send my best friend a Christmas card, I insult him. When the bell does not ring in association with an impending meal it is "time to feed the soul" as the Hutterites say. Among the brethren the most sacred symbol is the conscious absence of material designations of meaning altogether. This simple observation means that Hutterian symbolic behaviour is *de facto* a form of symbolic consciousness, or awareness which can evaluate all things as "symbolic."

Where things do serve the antimaterialist ideology of the Hutterians they do so because they are thrown up by recent history and are simply recognized as evidence of the omnipresent Holy Spirit. This means that everything can be a sign of the presence of the Holy Spirit's work – abandoned wagons and the like – and that precisely nothing at all can serve to symbolize the Holy Spirit itself. Sometimes this antimaterialist bent of the Brethren takes on the most ironic proportions imaginable. For example, I once held an old Hutterite bible – let me emphasize that by old I mean hundreds of years old, having survived the ravages of the very earliest persecutions. This bible would be considered a museum piece by people who think about such things but to the Hutterians it is ultimately, simply a bible, and so a few of the torn pages have been taped together and it has names written down the margins with a few notes scribbled here and there. It also has a bookmark. The bookmark is a newspaper clipping about the oldest bible in Canada which contains some quibbling about whether it is one in Quebec, or another one in Manitoba. The bible I held in my hands was much older than those described in the newspaper clipping. While the Hutterians recognize the fact that it is an old book and it has historical significance to them because it has survived all manner of disasters just like they have, it is still, when all is said and done, a bible, and it is the words on the scotch-taped pages that have true meaning. The bookmark itself stands as a continuing reminder of the great and foolish store that the worldly place upon things rather than "the word"; it is a fresh reminder with every reading. The old bible is rendered most significant by the "found" object which is its bookmark, just as a rotting wagon on the landscape gains significance because it stands as a historical marker too. They are signs directing one's attention towards the underlying spiritual meaning which lies invisibly within everything. Such a symbolic landscape is rich with significance though barren of the kinds of symbols which line museum cases.

The most pervasive conceptual Hutterite metaphor is birth and its attendant symbols which are also extremely sparse. The most important Pentecostal aspect of the Trinity – that which is everywhere to be reckoned with "like the wind" – is the invisible "spirit." The Spirit is both literally and figuratively an atmosphere. Water is a sign comprised of the most ubiquitous substance itself which is only used at baptism to indicate public recognition of the coming of the Spirit within individuals. The major exception to the rule of symbolic absence among the brethren is not to be found in clothing – for uniform dress means the absence of personal ownership; nor is it to be found in the ownership of forbidden items like cowboy boots – for these are fads; nor in the small items of personal wealth – for those are idiosyncratic. The one important exception to the rule of absence is the actual use of red to stand for the blood of the innocent which protects humanity from those omnipresent evil demons which personify the devil.

## The Evil Eye and the Forces of Good (Angels of God) and Evil (Demons of the Devil)

> The mystery of the seven stars which thou sawest in my right hand, and the seven golden candlesticks. The seven stars are the angels of the seven churches: and the seven candlesticks which thou sawest are the seven churches.
> from *The Revelation of St. John the Divine* (1:20)

The Hutterites conceive the only perfection to be the Trinity and they strive to approximate as best they can the harmony which the Trinity represents to them. For the brethren this striving is both individually and collectively demonstrated. The Trinity is also regarded as an historical manifestation as well as a synchronic (timeless) entity. The Hutterites think of the history of the world as divided into three epochs, or "hours." The first of these was the destruction of the world and its rebirth via the waters of the flood through "Noah the believer," the second hour extends from "the law" (Moses) until the coming of Christ, and "the final (third) hour is approaching" when the Holy Spirit will do its work and the final judgment will be made at which only the reborn children of God shall be saved.

The harmony of the Trinity is thought to be nowhere more apparent than in Christ's sacrifice which is the focus of human existence — both historical and personal. The Hutterites realize that their striving after this harmony can never be fully accomplished because of the imperfection of mankind which is born into a state of original sin. This struggle after perfection is a travail which contains within it the core of an existential dilemma. The state of perfection which must be pursued can never be obtained because of original sin, yet the original sin is itself the belief that one has attained some sort of perfection. The paradox is that one must both strive for perfection but concomitantly recognize the impossibility of its attainment. The brethren regard this struggle as constantly occurring within human beings and its temporal pervasiveness assumes logical consistence in their use of the number seven. The perfect world was created by God in seven days only to be spoiled by man's desire for more. The Hutterites break up the week into a period of seven days as well and, like the Lord, they rest on the Sabbath to celebrate his perfection set amidst their own imperfection.

For the Hutterian People the Trinity is encapsulated within Saturday evening and the Sabbath day which culminates the sequence of seven. The unit of seven manifest in the origin of the world and the contemporary week may also be seen in the Old Testament as the pattern of existence of the Hebrews. Peter Walpot (1957 edition:25-26), an early Hutterite *Vorsteher*, wrote:

> Six years could Israel gather in their fruits, each man for himself, but the seventh year was a year of release, and it was proclaimed that the land should hold a solemn Sabbath unto the Lord, and they might not gather in, but what it bore in the seventh year was common them, to the father of the household and his servant and to the cattle and beast of the land. And he who had been bought was released in this seventh year with all manner of gifts and presents. In the same way whatsoever had lent his neighbor and brother ought, might not ask it back in the year of release, but had to let it go . . . . Which year of release is the acceptable year of the Lord, as the prophet himself doth interpret it, when those who their whole lives have been subject to the bondage and power of the devil are redeemed. Therefore we should have all goods which God hath given us in this time in common, through Christian love, and enjoy them with our neighbors, brothers and household, and not make the same our own. For it is now a much more glorious and festive proclamation of the year of release, yea, of the year of grace, than in the Old Testament.
>
> Men will observe a great Sabbath, yea, they will have one Sabbath after another and will lead the most peaceful life on earth where they have laid aside these two words – 'Mine' and 'Thine' which do *not* belong to the nature of things. . . . For he that seeketh much lacketh much, and he that desireth much needeth much. Now that is the greatest poverty and the most unpeaceful life on earth – which Christ desireth not in His house, among those who have entered upon the true Sabbath, Pentecost, and Easter Day.

The Hutterites conceive of there being seven major evil spirits (represented by demons) which engage with seven major good spirits (represented by angels) which are in a constant state of conflict within human beings. There are also minor spirits (guardian angels for instance) but these are idiosyncratic spirits related to specific people: perhaps as saintly ancestral ghosts, or Cherubim.

The continuing struggle is between the domain of "the flesh" and that of the "spirit"; it is the struggle of the Christian with the world, of the prince of light with the prince of darkness. The struggle can only be won by persons who have recognized the workings of the Holy Spirit (which is omnipresent) within themselves, and who comprehend that they have a free will and that choices are theirs to make every day of every week of every year throughout their lives. The battle with the seven evil spirits must always be carried out in order that the faithful may live in harmony with one another. The demons who do the devil's work are counterposed by angels who perform God's work. The evil spirits play upon the natural inclinations of humankind which can be subordinated by certain qualities which the Hutterites believe are engendered by living communally.

The qualities of the good spirits are drawn from *Isaiah* 11:2:

> And the spirit of the Lord shall rest upon him, the spirit of wisdom and understanding, the spirit of counsel and might, the spirit of knowledge and of the fear of the Lord . . . .

which continues:

> And righteousness shall be the girdle of his loins, and faithfulness the girdle of his reins.
>     The wolf also shall dwell with the lamb, and the leopard shall lie down with the kid; and the calf and the young lion and the fatling together; and a little child shall lead them (11:5-6).

The reborn child of God, whether he be Christ, an apostle, a *Täufer* martyr, or a modern Hutterite, obliterates polar opposites by faith. To the six qualities listed in *Isaiah* the Hutterites have added "art," but not representational art, rather the abstract notion of art as a synthesis of diverse intents manifest in "the art of living together": a description of harmonious arrangement as a process. These good spirits are felt to drive out evil and to usher in Christ just as in *Mark* 16:9 Christ the reborn is first seen by Mary Magdalene: "Now when Jesus was risen early the first day of the week he appeared first to Mary Magdalene, out of whom he had cast seven devils."

The qualities of the seven evil spirits are: arrogance, greed, envy, anger, gluttony, impurity, and laziness. These seven evil spirits are named as demons in the Bible throughout which the horrible, chaotic result of giving in to them is detailed. Anderson (1972) has listed these references and so I shall not repeat all of them here. Instead, I have counterposed each of the demons together with its principal quality, against the angels together with those qualities which belief in the messages they bring from God brings about. Each of these is juxtaposed by the name of a person who exemplifies the virtuous resolution of the struggle between the two domains via faith in God as demonstrated in a story from the Bible.

1. *Beelzebub* (arrogance) is thwarted by wisdom as characterized by the guardian angel of humility which assisted Joseph the husband of Mary. Joseph found Mary to be with child before they were married and sought to avoid the marriage altogether but was visited by an angel in a dream who told him that the child was of the Holy Spirit, that it was to be named Jesus and suggested that he should have faith and marry the woman. Joseph, being a humble man, did all of these things "And knew her not till she had brought forth her firstborn son: and he called his name Jesus" (*Matthew* 1:25).

2. *Mammon* (greed) is thwarted by understanding characterized by the guardian angel of composure which assisted Moses by helping him to leave the wealth and riches of court life and subsequently lead his people from Egypt (*Exodus* 23:20).

3. *Leviathan* (envy) is thwarted by counsel characterized by the guardian angel of love which assisted Abraham in his migrations into and out of Egypt (*Genesis* 11, 12) and also helped Joseph to escape from his brothers who envied him for his coat of many colors (*Genesis* 37).

4. *Abaddon* (anger) is thwarted by art as characterized by the guardian angel of patience which assisted Job to overcome the temptations of Satan (*Job* 2) and protected David from Saul (*Psalm* 34:7, and throughout *Chronicles* I, II, and III).

5. *Behemoth* (gluttony) is thwarted by knowledge as characterized by the guardian angel of moderation which assisted

Judith to refuse the meal ordered by Holophernes for her (*Judith* 12, 13 [*Apocrypha*]) and who also helped to protect Esther from defilement by Haman who wished to murder Mordecai and all other Jews (*Esther* 7).

6. *Asmodi* (impurity) is thwarted by might as characterized by the guardian angel of purity which assisted Joseph by keeping him safe from the approaches of a lewd woman married to the master of the house in which he was overseer (*Genesis* 39) and also protected Susanna from false witness given by the elders who lusted after her (*Daniel and Susanna* [*Apocrypha*]).

7. *Belial* (laziness) is thwarted by the fear of God as characterized by the guardian angel of vigilance in the parable of the five wise virgins who remembered to fill their lamps with oil and so could find their grooms (*Matthew* 25:1-13). The angel of vigilance also protected Tobias the son of Tobit on the road to Media (*Tobit* 5 [*Apocrypha*]).

The first names of contemporary Hutterites include the names of all of those persons assisted by angels as evidenced in the Bible. In fact these names constituted about half of the names in all of the colonies in which I worked, other common names (chiefly those of the apostles) came from the Bible as well. Very few non-biblical names are used and these are usually employed when the confusion of multiple Johns and Marys becomes too great. Nonetheless I have often recorded nuclear families where two sons are named "Paul," or two daughters have been called "Sarah." One Sarah would be named for her mother, another for a favorite aunt. This follows from Hutterian symbolic awareness – who the name stands for is significant, not the name itself. The havoc this nonetheless brings to both social relations and kinship reckoning is quite impressive – and often funny. Nicknames are often employed to avoid confusion and these too can become the source of humor. "Shorty" may be 6'2" tall, but is shorter than his wife, whose nickname is "Tina."

The struggle against the forces of evil in which the individual Hutterite engages is a never-ending, daily affair which has not changed since Biblical times. The struggle is basically between the "spirit" and the "flesh" which are in immutable opposition to one another.

> For the flesh lusteth against the Spirit, and the Spirit against the flesh: and these are contrary the one to the other: so that ye cannot do the things that ye would.
> But if ye be led of the Spirit, ye are not under the law.
> Now the works of the flesh are manifest, which are these; Adultery, fornication, uncleanness, lasciviousness, idolatry, witchcraft, hatred, variance, emulations, wrath, strife, seditions, heresies, envyings, murders, drunkenness, revellings, and such like: of the which I tell you before, as I have also told you in time past, that they which do such things shall not inherit the kingdom of God.
> But the fruit of the Spirit is love, joy, peace, longsuffering, gentleness, goodness, faith.
> Meekness, temperance: against such there is no law.
> And they that are Christ's have crucified the flesh with the affections and lusts.
> If we live in the Spirit, let us also walk in the Spirit.
> Let us not be desirous of vain glory, provoking one another, envying one another (*Galatians* 5:17-26).

The flesh is an impermanent and imperfect universe of life whereas the spirit is the infinite and perfect universe of heaven (*Himmel*) which is thought to be a place of perfect communal living. Hutterites generally wish to avoid the appearance of self-importance and so they do not praise God via *beauty* which is an impermanent state of the flesh. For example, Hutterites do not sing in melodious voices. The socially-approved manner of singing is not pleasing to the ear for such sounds are "aus Fleisches Lust" [from the lust of the flesh]. Songs must be sung from the heart to please God (the Trinity) which is the only perfection. Beautiful melodies are thought to make people pleased with themselves and accordingly do not please God for they are idolatrous (see Stephenson 1979:250-254).

The Hutterites comprehend the very nature of aesthetics as an issue to be side-stepped so theirs is a world where the culturally acceptable does not coincide with a set of graded aesthetic ideals. Beauty is comprehended and significant in its absence . . . its presence can be a threat. In some colonies persons with bad eyesight are given plain, black-plastic-frame glasses or wire-rims. While most people need these I was aware of two young women (both of them very "pretty" by North American standards) who wore these glasses although their eyesight was said to be quite within the range of normal. When appraised by a female friend that some young Hutterite women also wore fancy petticoats, I asked an older Hutterite man about this "worldly" practice. Ironically, his response was "It doesn't matter if they wear it underneath their dresses. . . . If we can't see it then it isn't important . . . it might as well not be there."

Similarly, English school teachers report that Hutterite school children do not respond to individual encouragement in their studies. Praising an individual child is dangerous to both the person making praise who mistakenly elevates a matter which should be of no consequence (a thing of the flesh) to an inappropriate level of importance (the domain of the "Spirit"). Concomitantly, the person who has been singled out for praise is tempted to feel him- or herself to be overly important.

Hutterians rarely praise one another but will often criticize each other. To the uninformed outsider this criticism can be too easily taken as dissension when it is no such thing at all. Hutterian people feel that the open criticism of individual faults fosters learning, betterment, humility, and brings unity. As with other important arenas of Hutterite life there are often-repeated proverbs which accompany the act of criticizing another colony member.

*Aus and Fehler, kannst du Nutzen ziehen, dusiehst den Fehler ein und kannst ihn leichter fliehen.*

[From the faults of others you can draw advantage . . . you recognize the fault and can avoid it more easily.]

*Ein Fehler den man erkennt, der ist schon halb gebeszert.*

[A fault recognized as such is already half amended.]

As previously stated, the one visible and abstract symbol which I found the Hutterites to use has specific Biblical roots and involves the color red. Infants have red ribbons tied around their wrists to protect them from *Pshrien* ["the evil eye"]. I have used the dialect term "Pshrien" — pronounced Pshry — rather than the modern German *Beschreien* because the active belief in evil eye seems to be theirs alone. The Hutterites believe that some people are more prone to have the "evil eye" than others but it is not defined in terms of individual people. Any person can be possessed of the "evil eye" which is a specific manifestation of the existence of evil (as witchcraft) in the world as indicated by St. Paul in the foregoing quote from *Galatians* 5. *Pshrien* does affect some persons more often than others; but anyone is a potential host for the devil personified. The result of *pshrien* is the severe and abrupt onset of a fever, which progresses quickly through thirst, weakness, and rolling eyes to a loss of consciousness which can ultimately and quickly lead to death.

This suffering can be inflicted by a person possessed of *pshrien* upon anyone but most typically it affects infant human beings or young farm animals. It is said that the only way to cure a person or animal who has been "afflicted" is to quickly wipe the eyes and face of the victim with a red cloth. Infants are felt to be especially vulnerable and so they are made to wear a red ribbon around their wrists. It is the flesh which is weak and temporary so in the symbolism of spirit, water, and blood it seems most apt that it should have a material referent — if only a colour.

The following are typical case histories of *Pshrien* episodes (from Stephenson, 1979:255-6).

Case #1. The fieldboss in a colony mentions to a visiting cattleman from another colony that his *group* has just acquired a young stallion. He describes it as "a pretty animal" to the visitor. Later in the day the visiting cattleman goes to see the animal alone . . . he quickly returns but mentions how much he would like to have such an animal at his own colony. About 30 minutes later the fieldboss goes into the barn to find the animal sweating profusely. It quickly sickens and dies. It is widely believed that the visitor killed the animal with *Pshrien*.

Case #2. A woman (A) goes to see a newborn calf (described by the informant as "a pretty animal") while the dairyman is out of the barn. She returns home and the calf dies within an hour. The dairyman, perplexed by these events, attempts to save the calf but fails. *Pshrien* was suspected by one of the old

women who later told the dairyman to ask (A) if she had gone
to see the calf and had admired and thereby "killed" it. (A) had
been widely believed to be possessed of *Pshrien* on other
occasions. The answer to the dairyman's question was "yes" on
both accounts and the woman was heavily criticized by other
colony members.

Case #3. Shortly after a new bullock arrived at a colony a
young cattleworker (an older helper) spoke very highly of its
beauty. Soon after this the bull became feverish and at attempt
was made to save it by rubbing its eyes with a red cloth. The
bull eventually recovered but *pshrien* is widely suspected.

Case #4. A preacher visiting a nearby colony was asked to
give the Sunday sermon there. He did so but the following
events, as described in his own words, ensued:

> At the very end of the service I suddenly felt hot, and I started to
> sweat . . . it just poured out of me. I also got thirsty. Well, you know
> I almost couldn't get out of the building I felt so bad. Right after I got
> outside my legs started to feel weak and then this woman that I knew
> as a boy . . . we grew up together . . . she came up to me. [Note: this
> action of accosting a preacher after a sermon is very unconventional .
> . . normally all would file quietly into the kitchen for dinner, except
> the preacher who eats alone in his quarters.] She said, 'Sam, it surely
> is good to see you and to hear you preach. I don't think I've ever
> heard such a fine sermon before . . . no, that was the best I've ever
> heard!' After that she must have noticed that I was pale and sweating
> because she slapped the side of her face and said, 'Oh Sam, I've
> "pshried" you!!' Well, they ran and got a piece of red cloth and got
> back to me just before I passed out and I rubbed it all over my face
> and wiped my eyes with it. And you know, all of a sudden I felt just
> fine! It just happened in a second, I was almost passed out, then I
> was fine – felt like nothing had even happened. Now you know me,
> Peter, I have to be shown a thing first before I'd believe it. Before
> that I wasn't too sure about *Pshrien*, I'd only heard what the people
> say ... but it happened to me! (Stephenson 1979:256).

[Everybody believes this is an example of *Pshrien*.]

These cases are typical of the *Pshrien* that I was told by
Hutterites or, in several cases, directly observed. In the great
majority of cases, young, or newly-acquired farm animals are
involved. The admirer of the animal is often a visitor who shares
the same status, or a highly related one as the manager of the
operation to which the affected animal belongs. The suggestion of

*Mammon* (envy) and *Leviathan* (greed) at work is strongly apparent, as well as *Beelzebub,* for praise is understood to be a function of arrogance. In most instances the admirer gossiped about the animal after having visited it while an attendant was away. New animals are quarantined and access to young farm animals is usually limited for reasons of infectious disease prevention, (perhaps also because of their susceptibility to *Pshrien*) so the colony rules were also being secretively broken by the admirer in most cases. The animals affected are inevitably described by informants as "pretty." Red cloth is almost always used in the attempt to save the animal. There is no negative sanction, except criticism and sometimes mild ostracism, used against the person thought to have cast evil eye upon something or someone. Each case is characterized by the admiration of another being as if it were a perfect entity, so *Pshrien* is in effect a form of idolatry, which is extremely dangerous and involves three demons. As such, it is the devil (Lucifer) personified and deified as a Trinity. *Pshrien* is the epitome of the struggle of the spirit with the flesh and is original sin recapitulated (Stephenson 1979).

**Red, Red Ribbons, and the Protection of the Innocent from Pshrien**

The Hutterites often told me that children could be killed by *Pshrien* but gave me no examples (that is, they refused to name anyone). Instead, they focused on a rather elaborate means utilized to avoid having children affected by *Pshrien.*

The color red represents the "blood of the innocent" and as such protects the helpless from evil and a final death. The blood of the lamb which protected the ancient Israelites from the "angel of death" at Passover, and the blood of Christ who suffered in humanity's stead are both referents for the red cloth used in *Pshrien* episodes. I have also heard mentioned an obscure reference to Moses protecting the Tabernacle with some scarlet cloth.

The red cloth is clearly an abstract symbol which refers to multiple *significata* which share a common theme. Blood shed for and by believers (the baptism of blood) serves to protect those afflicted by other persons possessed by a trinity of demons, e.g., the devil. When asked why red protects the afflicted I was told "because of Jesus, 'In whom we have redemption through his blood for the forgiveness of sins' — *Colossians*, Chapter one, 14th verse."

This is a rather different use of symbols from the classic use of icons, or relics, to protect their wearer. The Hutterites do not regard the cloth as empowered to protect — red is only a reminder to the afflicted, the perpetrator, and any witnesses of "the blood which was shed for you" — nothing more. The red cloth is only a temporary link with faith which also functions as a kind of warning beacon.

The red ribbon worn by children is somewhat more complex with respect to its symbolic referents. The ribbon is worn until a child does one of two things; either attempts to comb its hair, or strikes back when struck. After a child has done one of these things it is said to be "self-willed." Once a child is recognized as "self-willed" its prestige plummets to the very bottom of the Hutterite social hierarchy and as such it is no longer admired. Previous to this, however, it is very highly valued. Babies are much played with and are quite literally "shown off" at every possible opportunity. This certainly stems in part from the extreme fondness which Hutterites have for the children of "the children of God" as signs of hope. But more generally, it is probably just human nature to admire babies . . . if it wasn't there probably wouldn't be a human species (See Stephenson 1978:24fn., 27-30, also Dunn 1976, Jones 1972, Richards and Bernal 1972).

Hutterite babies are certainly no exception to the general findings of human ethology; they too are admired, praised and are the focus of much attention although these are regarded as highly inappropriate ways to behave towards other adults or even small children (See Ch. IV). To protect infants from *Pshrien*, until by playing with a comb (or striking back) they demonstrate those same qualities which inhere within its use, a red ribbon is tied about babies' wrists. The Biblical reference for the ribbon comes from the story of Jacob and the daughters of Laban in *Genesis*

29-32.

Briefly, Jacob was charged by his father Isaac to take a wife from among the daughters of Laban, his mother's brother. Eventually, Jacob agreed to serve Laban for seven years in return for which he would be given Rachel, Laban's "beautiful and well endowed" daughter whom he loved. However, after seven years had passed Laban tricked Jacob into marrying his oldest daughter, Leah, who was "tender-eyed" (but not beautiful). Laban explained away his trick by stating that it was not customary in his land for a younger daughter to marry prior to the eldest. Laban then forced Jacob to work for him an additional seven years to pay for Rachel, whom Laban eventually relinquished to him. Since God saw that Leah was "hated" and Rachel "loved" he rendered the latter barren and the former fertile. Jacob appears to have learned much about the nature of false beauty from these experiences for when it finally came time for him to depart from Laban with his wives, in order to provide for his large household they made a bargain in which Laban's arrogance, greed, and envy were overcome by Jacob's wisdom, composure and love of God. This struggle epitomizes *Pshrien*: a battle between Lucifer as represented by three minions and God by three of his messengers (angels). The bargain struck by Laban with Jacob stated that Jacob would take only those "spotted, speckled, and ringstaked" among Laban's flocks and cattle, while Laban would keep all of the perfectly-colored animals.

Jacob stripped away pieces of bark from the branches of green poplar, hazel and chestnut trees and mounted these over the troughs where the flocks watered so that when they conceived they would bear marked offspring. Jacob also placed similarly-striped stakes in front of the eyes of only the strongest cattle when they mated and when the feeble mated he did nothing. As a result of these actions Laban's cattle were feeble and his flocks diminished while Jacob's were respectively strong and flourished.

The ribbon around a Hutterite child's wrist is said to represent the bark strips torn from the branches used as stakes in front of which the flocks and cattle of Jacob conceived. The ribbon is said to be red to represent the sacrificial blood found throughout

*Leviticus.* The burnt offerings of *Leviticus* are made whenever a man sins out of ignorance. By combining these two stories we can see something of the meaning behind the red-ribbon symbolism and of the logic which links these matters together.

First, the red ribbon protects both the child and those adults who may admire it. The child can only sin out of ignorance for as yet it is unself-willed. It is passive with only a proclivity towards sin which has not yet been manifested. The adult Hutterite by admiring the infant cannot be admiring it for its perfection, because it has been marred like the speckled flocks. This is a situation wherein the adult is trapped by a conflict between, on the one hand, a deeply-rooted cultural valuation and a biological inheritance which attracts him or her to children, and on the other hand, a core belief which establishes that the admiration of beauty is a form of idolatrous devil worship. This conflict is resolved by the red ribbon because not only is the child flawed by the ribbon, all those who reproduce after having regarded it will produce children who are strong in their own recognition of their imperfection, not weak and enfeebled by being overly cognizant of their beauty. The red color is a reminder to all of "the redemption" via the voluntary death and rebirth of Christ and the child-life-saving quality of the blood of the Passover lamb. Children are "gifts of God," and sins with respect to admiring children are unconsciously committed out of ignorance (see Stephenson 1979:257-258; 260). It seems altogether fitting that since Hutterian symbolic consciousness resides in avoiding more conventional physical icons, that their one concrete symbol (red ribbon) represents a lack of awareness itself.

All of the major Hutterite rituals are calendrical, which is also to say that they are completely predictable and represent the redundant background against which the three noncalendrical (high information) rituals of baptism, marriage, and burial may be viewed. In these latter three rituals the status of a person changes. The articulation of these noncalendrical rituals which vary in frequency, with those obligatory calendrical rituals which do not, will be further elaborated in the next chapter. For now we have shown that symbolic consciousness among the Hutterites serves as a guide to how meaning is to be found in the world of things. Next we must look at actual behaviour in the context of those rituals where one changes status — that is, where meaning is created in the world of persons.

## NOTES

1  The transition from individual to societal levels of abstraction with respect to "neurosis" was not merely a function of the adoption of Freudian concepts by scientists interested in collective representations of individual sentiments (e.g. Roheim 1950, LaBarre 1954). Freud (1928:77) explicitly espoused this view himself: "What appears in a minority of human individuals as an untiring impulsion towards further perfection can easily be understood as a result of the instinctual repression upon which is based all that is most precious in human civilization." This is a later statement which summarizes the position which earlier (1913) dominated an entire work (*Totem and Taboo*) which was (not untellingly) subtitled" *Resemblances between the Psychic Lives of Savages and Neurotics*, and seems to have grown out of Freud and Breuer's earliest work on hysteria (cf. Freud and Breuer, collected 1966).
2  Take, for example, the English basic color term "blue". It is monoleximic and denotes a color without reference to another noun (it is not used in the manner of "blood colored," "earth colored," etc.). "Blue" is blue. The word appears to stem from the somewhat longer word "bloom" which probably originally referred to "blue" flowers. Bloom now simply means flower, or to flower, and cannot be utilized to encode color information, whereas "blue" (which is phonetically shorter) encodes little else. Both Stephenson (1973) and Conklin (1974), working independently, found that all English basic color terms derive from longer, metonymic sources. Durbin (1972) and Hays *et al.* (1972) also reported that the average number of phonemes of basic color terms in Berlin and Kay's samples (1969) decreased with the relative hypothesized antiquity of the terms.
3  These are summer hours. The colony schedule varies with the season and slightly from one colony to another and from *leut* to *leut*. The Hutterites do not go on "daylight-saving time" during the summer partly because they tend to regard time as invariantly progressive and linear. The changeover to daylight-saving time by the rest of "the world" is thought to be just one more example of the "worldly peoples'" silly penchant for playing with eternity in an essentially scornful and dangerous way. From the Hutterite perspective, if one wanted to change the amount of daylight available for work, one should simply rise earlier or open up shop earlier. To change the hours themselves is the act of a lazy people who have wrongly attempted to co-opt God's prerogative for controlling destiny — the time humans have to live and work within. The time difference between the colony and "the world" is a very obvious manifestation of the Hutterians' separation from "the world" — one which a researcher visiting the colonies during the summer is constantly aware of. One always meets the brethren on their terms within their time.
4  Attitudes towards education are changing in some of the more liberal colonies (notably the *Dariusleut* in Montana) where occasionally students have finished high school by correspondence. Some Hutterites have also taken college courses by mail and a very few have attended teachers colleges. Change in this section will probably come but, as Bennett

(1975b:126-127) has indicated, it will be slow. In many past instances the Hutterians' experiences with higher educational institutions have resulted in confusion, resentment and apostasy.

5  I have adopted *eidos* over "world view" because the latter connotes a visual and perceptual relativity with which I do not sympathize. "World acoustic" would presumably be as acceptable as "world view" and the fact that it is not, is in itself a demonstration of the bias inherent within the term "world view." I am less interested here in perceptual variation than in the logical connections among precepts which emerge from the ethnologist's (my own) articulation with a local epistemology.

6  Throughout this work unless otherwise noted (*) I have utilized the modern German rather than the old High German. In rendering Hutterite speech I have also utilized modern German because the dialect is unwritten, thereby rendering translation into High German equally as distorting as conversion into modern German. Modern German is simply of greater convenience to the reader and the writer. Finally, it should be noted that in Hutterite dialect most of these proverbs are given over to rhyme and alliteration. The metre is typical of many childens' sayings throughout the German speaking world.

# CHAPTER VII

## THE PROXIMITY OF BELIEF: SPACE AND THE SYMBOLISM OF ANTIMATERIALISM

"Spatial changes give a tone to a communication, accent it, and at times even override the spoken word. The flow and shift of distance between people as they interact with each other is part and parcel of the communication process."

Edward T. Hall (1959:160)

In the preceding chapter it could be seen that the relative absence of material things; of a church building, of qualities of beauty in music, and even of sounds, imbues Hutterian life with meaning. Hutterian asceticism requires an antimaterialist symbolism which has led to the use of absence itself — absence of symbols utilized in the concupiscent "world" — to communicate about Hutterian events and emotions. *Ethos* and *eidos* were useful concepts to apply to the emotional tone and the logical connections of Hutterian ideology but they are poorly suited to the analysis of ritual as actual behavior. In the following several paragraphs two terms are defined which stand in relationship to one another as *ethos* does to *eidos*, and which may be useful for the analysis of observable behavior.

### Analogic and Digital Communication

The two communication modes thought to be most basic to the relative abstraction of information are distinguished as digital and analogic. Digital communication occurs in a binary or base 2 code in which information is conveyed on an all-or-none basis (+/-), (1/0), (yes/no). The limitation of the code to 2 choices has the interesting feature of rendering all signals as simultaneously dual: 1 concomitantly transmits as "not 0," and 0 as "not 1." The nervous system apparently operates in this modality since chemical information at synaptic junctures results either in the facilitation or inhibition of firing by the neuron. I have made the case that Hutterian symbolism works in much this same way — only it is the "0" which often has great value in their system... which as a form of consciousness is the same as "not 1."

Analogic communication accrues from the manipulation of different magnitudes of information relative to originals that they are meant to approximate. Wind tunnels, slide rules, and "'Grandfather' clocks" that tell the phases of the moon and tides are all examples of analog computers.

Among most social animals other than human beings (and probably Cetaceans), open communication systems comprised entirely of gestures appear to predominate.[1] Unlike the digital communication of information in terms of probabilities of presence and absence, analog communication via the strictly behavioral channel of acts has no complete negative ("no") for the simple reason that behavior has no opposite other than the conscious recognition of death. Other than by voluntary death it is impossible to "not be" in the same sense that it is impossible to not communicate because the attempt to do so communicates the attempt, which is *de facto* communication.

Negative qualities — although not quantities — can be expressed in the analogic mode but only in a very cumbersome manner through ritualized (that is, exaggerated, foreshortened, etc.) behaviors which connote relationships. For example, the common canine behavioral sequence that enables one animal to communicate "don't" with respect to conspecific aggression involves a mock (ritualized) attack by the submitting individual to initiate the sequence, followed in turn by an identical mock response by the second animal, followed by the adoption of infantile posture and behavior (urination, whining, prone position) by the initiator, which finally triggers the parental response of licking it dry by the animal initially attacked (see Schenkel 1967). Given an inhibition in a species against attacking its own offspring, the effect of this sequence is to prevent aggression although ritualized combat has occurred. The analog of the ritual combat expresses a relationship (parent-child) and the content of the communication digitally expressed is roughly "I am child to you." It stretches the digital conception of negative somewhat to construe such an exchange as "don't" as Bateson (1968) has suggested we might.

Since behavior has no opposite, the analog modality has no intrinsic equivalent to the digital construction of "truth" in opposition to "falsehood." However, since true and false entail absolute probabilities, all 16 truth functions of calculus can be represented in binary code on a digital computer (see McCulloch and Pitts 1943). This means that information transmitted in the digital mode is often inherently falsifiable and on the basis of experience is often understood by the communicants to be so. Since behaviour "has no opposite" it can therefore be too easily construed as "unconscious" by analysts who reside outside the stream of local behaviour itself.

Human beings communicate simultaneously in both analogic and digital modes (speech and gesture) in a complementarity: most content is relayed digitally and relationships tend to be conveyed analogically. However, by becoming aware of this distinction, and by wresting conscious control of the analog modality from the fabric of acts, they too can be falsified. It is here that an awareness of behaviour dons the mantle of "consciousness" and departs the problematic interpretation ethologists make of dogfights.

The knowledge that one is falsifying behavior in an analogic mode occurs in many human contexts and is even revealed in the etymology of the words for such occasions. Theater, sport, and childhood behaviors are the primary arenas where the analogical and digital modalities become collated. Children "play" and "actors" or "players" appear in "plays" of one "act" or more. The neighborhood or club "show," and school "play" constitute the developmental interface of these. "Play" is often topically discussed as a buffered learning situation where the core beliefs of a culture are expressed and various social problems are rehearsed which adults in particular cultures must characteristically face. Play is also widely hypothesized to be an activity which draws in children by partially resolving basic psychic conflicts incurred by the withdrawal of some parental care associated with infancy. The resolution is never complete, but represents a temporary measure which may in turn be repeated again after more escalations in the discomfiture resulting from parental rejection, this further necessitates the adoption of additional "independent" behaviors. Independence is then supposedly softened by incorporation within a greater whole (the group or culture) via play (see Roberts and Sutton-Smith 1962, Roberts *et al.* 1959).

Athletic events seem to occupy the structural position between theatre and childhood game activities, they too are games involving "players" in which core beliefs are stressed in highly analogic and programatic ways. Theater can be a platform for the examination of moral dilemmas and in classical forms, existential motifs are pervasive and so their portrayal becomes rigorously stylized.[2]

Religious ritual seems similar to all of these, but to a greater degree it incorporates, through performance, both players and audience as an integrated whole. Religious ritual does more than just lend credibility to digital information, it is the ultimate collation of the two modalities in which the falsifiability of information is rendered moot by a virtual fusion of the two modes. This is at least partly a function of the complete incorporation of all participants: there are few critics of ritual and nobody ever keeps score. A search for the digital dimension of ritual must leap from the most inclusive aspect of performance (is it occurring or not [+/-]?) into the most idiosyncratic context of an individual mind. To accomplish this, the unconscious must be regarded as something other than a convenient personal burial ground for the unpleasant memories of childhood which is, unfortunately, the popular construction of the concept in much of social science today including the depiction of "play" I just alluded to above. The unconscious renders the brain efficient, for without it we would drown in details: consciousness presumes an unconscious storehouse of information. If rituals are understood as repetitive, and probabilistic, then they can also be said to be highly redundant codifications of information. The information content of ritual is therefore low, but it is also insured against noise (misinterpretation, or easy reinterpretation). Finally, as Bateson (1972) has cogently argued, redundancy apparently imbeds information in the unconscious. The most repeated bits of information are the most expected and thus constitute the background against which new information is examined. However, the highly probable background remains unexamined and from this the epistemological error of accepting cultural assumptions as eternal truths can obtain (see Bateson 1967). But the point is not that ritual constitutes itself in religion as an epistemological error. The point is, instead, that by insuring itself against one kind of "error" (noise), ritual may predispose another form of error: rigidity.

Since *ethos* is a term for the emotional tone of life in a culture, it corresponds to analogic communication processes which are largely about relationships and which involve gesture. *Eidos*, however, corresponds to digital communication processes because both of these concepts are basically a function of logic. In Hutterian society, the expression of changes in relationships found in ritual has been highly restricted: there are no dances, melody in music is distorted by antiaesthetic principles, and there are no material icons to represent the people as a whole. Given this state of affairs, it is not surprising that the spatial organization of people at church services takes on meaning when these are compared with the spatial orientations of people in secular settings. A comparison of (and among) services predicated upon an initial set of meanings, derived by comparing the spatial orientations of persons in church to persons outside church, should also be revealing. However, prior to analyzing the proxemics of Hutterian rituals, the purposeful distortions of the music which accompanies them will be taken up. "Accompanies" implies a sense of background which is too pale: Hutterian singing surrounds their ritual in a loud and dissonant vocal protest. It is — like the absences of icons that have been discussed — a nimbus of special ritual awareness which envelopes religious practice in a Hutterite colony.

## The Analogs of Hutterian Hymnody

Since there is really no iconographic symbolism in the church services of the Hutterites, we must ask — and seek to answer —

how things are communicated in them without it. If the sermon was simply read, then communication would be largely digital, and the essential analog ingredients of ritual communication would be absent. Much of the digital information of the service rests in the sermon but the sermon does not comprise the dominant aspect of services; it is only part of a compound whole. The order of events in a church service are as follows: 1) meditation, 2) hymn, 3) preface, 4) prayer, 5) text, 6) admonition to hear, 7) sermon, 8) blessing of the sermon, 9) hymn continuation, and 10) dismissal. Weekday services are slightly abbreviated forms of the same sequence. The order is inviolate, and although the hymn, preface prayer, text, and sermon vary by specific day; the meditation (silence), admonition to hear, blessing, and dismissal are invariants.

The longest amount of time during the services generally is spent in hymn singing. Music is a highly analog form of communication which seems to arrest time by encapsulating a different time within its own construction. In Hutterite hymn singing, the chant-like antiaesthetic, studied cacophony of voices is an analog expression of human imperfection. Furthermore, Hutterite hymns are sung in a redundant, canticle-like format wherein the preacher first sings out a line and the rest of the people repeat it — beginning their phrase just prior to the end of the preacher's. This line-by-line redundancy "analogizes" the hymn effectively and is consistent with the words of many of the songs which were written by martyrs as communiques to their brethren. The Hutterites identify with their martyrs through songs via a repetition of the martyr's testimonies of faith — hymns written in 16th century prisons. The phrase-by-phrase rendering of hymns should be understood as having more than a simple didactic significance. These songs were often composed by groups of prisoners singing back and forth to one another, or by one person singing out a line which other prisoners in other cells then repeated. In today's service the preacher's phrase comes to the congregation as a voice from the past which is recapitulated in the present (Stephenson 1978:440).

Acrostic is often found in the hymns as well so the first letter (or word) of each line (or stanza), when read down the page of lyrics, contains a message distilled from the meaning of the combined verses. The meaning of the acrostic is sometimes the name or names of the *Sendboten* who first sang the hymn. More often, the acrostic comprises a message which summarizes the contents of the hymn itself. Typical of such acrostic is a song written by a small group of Hutterites imprisoned at *Aach* (*Aix-la-Chapelle*) probably in 1558. The acrostic for this hymn reads: *HANS HEINRICH Mathias TILMAN HANS WERNER SAMBT UNSERN LIBEN SCHWESTERN Taten Euch Zu Wissen Wie Es Uns Geht In Dem Horen (Hern)*. [Little Hans, Heinrich, Mathias Tilman, Hans Werner and our dear sisters (read wives) inform you how we fare in the Lord.] The lower case letters mean that the entire first words of verses form the acrostic (capitals indicate an acrostic of first letters of words) (Martens 1969:48-50). The Preacher-Congregation-canticle format is unified in the acrostic and serves to make the singers more aware of it than if the hymn was simply sung outright. The *Ausbund* (hymnbook) is rarely referred to by the Preacher and no other person even brings a hymnbook to church. The hymns are sung from memory reinforced by the fact that all of them have been laboriously copied at the German school during prebaptismal religious instruction. The Songs of Solomon, Psalms, and the voice of King David are all models for the Hutterian hymnody which is a revealed living history connecting the singer with a past filled by martyrdom and faith. These are songs of conviction – not tunes or airs for entertainment. The first time I heard Hutterite singing I was shocked by how loud and dissonant it was and it never failed to make the hair on the back of my neck stand up.

*The Proxemic Background of Hutterian Rituals*

Hutterite colonies are generally located a distance of a mile or more from hard-surfaced highways and are denoted by a small sign. The colonies are usually further isolated from view by being located in the bottom of a small river-cut gorge – what, on the prairies, people call a "coulee." The access road into a Hutterite colony leads first to the farm buildings, where machinery and animals are housed. Most commercial dealings – deliveries of fuel and the like — are carried on in the immediate context of the farm enterprises themselves. The longhouses, school, and communal kitchen/dining facility, are located in greater privacy at a short distance from the colony's business operations, often behind a blind of "cottonwood" poplar trees. In this way, the inner life of the colony is spatially removed from "the world." This settlement pattern is very widespread and exceptions to it are the result of road building by provinces and states after the initial construction of colonies.

A typical Hutterite colony is laid out in a four-square, city-of-Jerusalem manner, directly on the axes of the compass. Although the exact location of buildings varies, the usual pattern is for there to be four longhouses with a kitchen and dining-hall building located in their midst. The kindergarten and English school are usually located outside of this central cluster. The way in which people are organized within this architectural plan is presented abstractly in Figure 7.1.

In the sleeping arrangements of adolescents in the attics of the longhouses, and also in the sleeping arrangements for napping children at kindergarten, males are located in the western aspect of the axis ($x'$) and females in the east ($x$). The pattern also pervades the seating arrangement at meals and even the locations of washrooms at the school. During school hours children may sit in this orientation as well but they are sometimes mixed according to criteria established by the English school teacher (age, rate of progress, discipline, etc.). The exception to this arrangement is the axis of orientation of church which inverts the normative pattern. At church, men sit in the eastern aspect ($x$), women in the west ($x'$), and all face south. I was told once that the reason "the people" sit facing south was "because when Noah's three sons went forth to replenish the earth they went south, east, and west but not north" (see *Genesis* 10). Other than this one statement there was never any rationalization of this inverted pattern offered. When asked directly about the pattern, people initially seemed to be quite unaware of it and when it was demonstrated to them, stated that, "it just seems right that way." I would suggest that the spatial inversion of the Hutterite church from the more quotidian

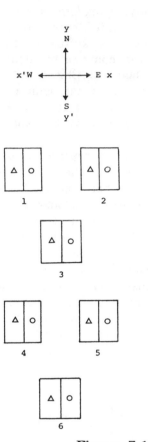

**Figure 7.1**
Spatial Orientation of Persons on the Axes
of the Compass in a Typical Hutterite
Colony

Key:
1, 2, 4, and 5 are longhouses
3 is the dining hall and kitchen
6 is the kindergarten
7 is the English school and church building
l is the lavatories at school

orientation of persons is a direct (and unconscious) expression of the Spirit/Flesh, World/Colony, Kingdom of Darkness/Kingdom of Light, Heaven/Hell, God/Devil, Life/Death, Mind/Body dichotomies with which Hutterite ideology is suffused. The Hutterites are called to church by silence and convene in silence in the presence of the Spirit as the reborn body of Christ. A closer examination of the exact seating order at most church services further supports and elaborates this representation of Hutterite cognitive distinctions; especially with respect to the spirit, the body, and rebirth.

Figure 7.3 is a diagrammatic representation of the seating order at everyday church services. The exceptions to this format are at certain key rituals where status changes: baptisms, marriages, and funeral. The order includes a two-fold scaling of age in which the youngest persons sit to the front of the room and to the outside as well. Two correlative statements may then be made concerning age relationships:

(1) oldest:youngest::back:front ($y$ axis, south-north)
(2) younger:older::outside:inside ($x$ axis, east-west)

By marking increased age (oldest, older) with [+] and relatively less age (youngest, younger) with [-] we may abstractly represent these relationships along the $x$ and $y$ axes as follows:

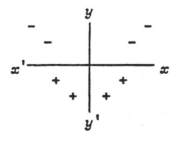

Figure 7.2

Phrased in this manner it can be seen that the proxemics of age converges with that of sex. If two lines are drawn between the oldest male (1) and the youngest (20) and between the oldest female (a) and youngest (w), an approaching convergence of the

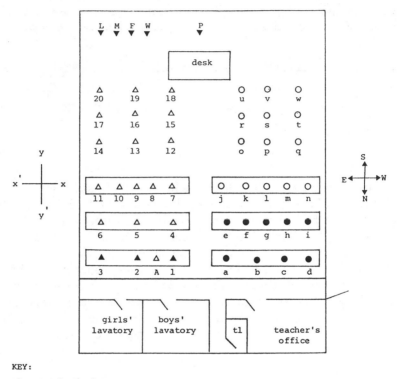

KEY:

tl = teacher's lavatory
□ = unbaptized
■ = baptized
P = Praediger
W = Wirt
F = Fieldboss
M = Aufsehern member
L = Lehrer
1. . .20 = males, oldest to youngest (excluding Aufsehern)
a. . .w = females, oldest to youngest
2,3,i,g and f are baptized but unmarried
A = Anthropologist

**Figure 7.3**
Proxemics of a Hutterite Church

two sexes becomes visible. The origin of these two lines is at the youngest children and they converge increasingly through baptized and baptized-married persons as shown below:

```
_____△_____0_____unbaptized_____

_____▲_____●_____baptized_____

_____▲=●_____baptized & married
```

**Figure 7.4**

The *Praediger* [Preacher], who is "minister of the word" [*Diener am Wort*] faces the congregation and children. Children are said to be "gifts of God" and the baptized are often referred to as "God's children." Age increases with corresponding increases in the distance between the preacher and persons seated in front of him. The *Aufsehern* [elders] sit to the preacher's right. There are a number of things which this order expresses. First, the $y$ axis (age) may be regarded as time while the $x$ axis segments the sexes. Thus the primary social vertebrae of colony life are rendered at once discrete and dynamic by this seating arrangement.

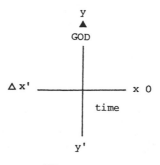

**Figure 7.5**

As representatives of the reborn body of Christ, the baptized members of the colony spatially encapsulate the children, whose salvation is assured by the suffering of Christ, as shown below:

```
__Aufsehern, Praediger, males, baptized.............................:[+]___
__children, boys and girls, unbaptized.............................:[-]___
__men and women, baptized........................................:[+]___
```

## Figure 7.6

As a Hutterian becomes progressively aware of the Holy
Spirit, the freedom to choose between good and evil, and human
fallibility, the distance between oneself and the preacher as the
voice of God, increases. Distance from the preacher along the $y$
axis is then a measure of responsibility accrued by any individual
in the congregation. This is inverted along the $x$ axis where
members of the *Aufsehern*, who are responsible for not just their
actions but also for the actions of the commune as a whole, sit
increasingly closer to the preacher as they accrue responsibilities
and age.

A person moves progressively to the right (males) or left
(females) and back in the seating arrangement as he or she
proceeds through life according to the rate at which others die
and are born. A man may, if elected through the manifest "will
of God," proceed to the front where he sits at the right of the
preacher. The structure of the service quite exactly represents
the life of the colony, of the individual Hutterite, and also the
life of the reborn body of Christ, in spatial terms. Christ was,
as the apostles' creed tells us, "born of the Virgin Mary" [the
flesh]... etc., and "ascended into heaven where he sitteth on the
right hand of God the Father..." Thus church also represents
the sacred order of things and approximates the structure of
heaven – a place about which the Hutterites speculate little but
nonetheless regard as a place of perfectly harmonious communal
living.

After church the brethren file out and walk directly to the
dining hall. The order in which persons leave the church and re-
enter the dominion of the flesh, and the spatial ordering which
obtains in the dining hall, both corresponds to and contrasts with
the preceding remarks on the structure of Hutterite church

services (see Figure 7.7). the first person to leave church is the oldest man who does not sit with the *Aufsehern* – he is also the closest to the door (among men) as well. My own position was usually to his left – thus encapsulating me within the adults but excluding me from the *Aufsehern*. All males, except the preacher and elders, then file out in descending order of age. The males are followed in turn by all the females who depart similarly. These both are followed by the elders and finally the preacher. *En route* to the dining hall there are two patterns which this order of departure renders evident. First, there is a digital sequence:   [baptized ▲ +/- △ unbaptized]...[baptized ● +/- 0 unbaptized]...[baptized ▲ +]. Thus there is an interdigitation of baptized [+] with unbaptized [-] in a [+/-/+/-/+] schema in which the central *persona* is that of the baptized woman. A second meta-message unfolds when the sex of the persons in the sequence is the superordinating criterion of pattern formulation, rather than simple baptismal status. Within the single-file processional order of departure from church, males (1,2...5,6) encompass females (...3,4...). A collimation, or alignment, of these messages reveals an expression of the reproductive nature of womankind. If the convergence of the sexes is apparent in the proxemic analysis of the church service which occurs in the domain of the spirit [-]; and the working structure of the colony is apparent in the dining hall which directly supports the body (the domain of the flesh [+]); then the mediational status [+/-] of the procession itself should be understood to express a synthetic principle which is fundamental to both domains. The principle which links the eternal living domain of Christ to the existence of the Hutterites is simply birth, for Christ was "born of the flesh" as well. In the Trinitarian conceptualization discussed in Chapter III, God "the Father" (paternity) synthesized the worlds of "the spirit" and "the flesh." Submerged in this idiom of "God the progenitor" who is a spiritual entity, is the material notion of procreation and woman as genetrix. Males invested with the Spirit may administer and rule colonies in the image of a male God of Father and Son, but the colonies they run are "mother colonies" which produce "daughter colonies." Men and women are born of womankind; they are reborn of Christ

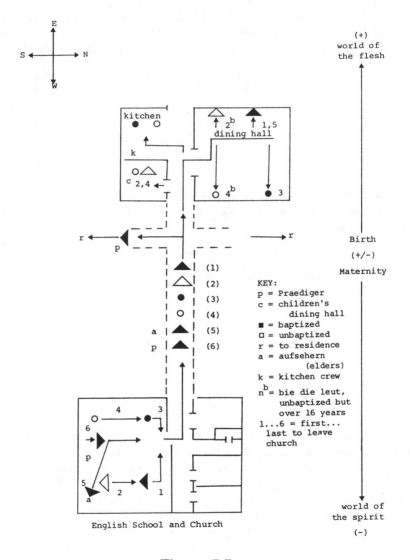

**Figure 7.7**
Proxemics of Church/Dining Hall Inversion

who was also born of womankind. Within the procession itself, which now moves through time on the $x$ axis, women can be seen as producers of both unbaptized (young) males and females.

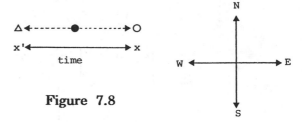

**Figure 7.8**

Only mature, baptized (reborn) men move on to assume responsibility for sustaining the body of Christ (the church) through time.

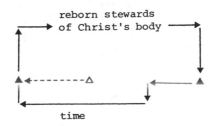

**Figure 7.9**

Women, however, oscillate between a newborn status and a reborn (baptized) status which allows them to reproduce men and other women to reproduce other men *ad infinitum.* The reproductive oscillatory structural pattern exhibited by women may be understood to combat time via fertility, while the reborn pattern of men combats time by their taking responsibility for collective fertility, through time, via the communally realized metaphor of the reborn body of Christ. If rebirth in Christ is eternal life, likewise are women responsible for an eternity of human lives because they are fertile.

As the procession enters the dining hall, the oldest men (1) proceed to the tables at the end of the northern and western

axis (*y*,*x'*) where they are joined later by the *Aufsehern* [5].
Those boys of age 16 and over sit at the southern end of the
eastern axis (*y'*,*x'*). Children under 16 eat apart from adults and
those adolescents who are eating *Bie die Leut* [with the people].
Young children eat in a set order in some colonies and not in
others. I have also found there to be significant variation with
respect to the younger children within single colonies depending
on who is supervising the children's mealtime. Women follow men
into the dining hall in a similar order, the only exception being
the kitchen staff which serves the meal and cleans up
afterwards. One man usually assists the women and sees to it
that there is always bread on the tables... this task is thought
to exemplify humility, much like Christ's serving the last supper.

The most senior man at dinner usually says the prayer
preceding and following the meal itself. The preacher does not
eat in the dining hall and neither does the steward [*Wirt*]; they
eat alone in their apartments. This may be due partly to the
administrative exigencies of their posts – for they must often be
absent from dinners due to their absence from the colony itself.
In the case of the *Wirt* this is more often the case than with
respect to the *Praediger* (unless, of course, they are the same
man). With respect to the latter individual, however, it is also
appropriate to keep the domain of the "spirit" as proclaimed by
the "*Diener am Wort*" separate from that of the flesh. Practical
consideration aside, I suspect that this is the real reason for the
Preacher's separate dining arrangements, if for no other reason
than the fact that they are actually absent far less often than
are various farm enterprise managers.

### Baptism and the Lord's Supper, [*Biegiessungstaufe und Abendmahl*]

> For John truly baptized with water; but ye shall be baptized with the
> Holy Ghost not many days hence.
> (*Acts* I:5)

It is necessary to discuss these two rituals in direct association
with one another because the latter confirms the former. The
proxemics of the baptism are simple: the candidates, after having

taken instruction, are baptized by a sprinkling on of water during which they assume positions directly in front of the rows of children of their respective sexes. The candidates are: "Buried with him [Christ] in baptism wherein also ye are risen with him through the faith of the operation of God, who hath raised him from the dead" (*Colossians* 2:12). In the scriptural texts which the baptismal sermon takes as basic to the rite itself, the candidates are told:

> . . . ye must be born again. The wind bloweth where it listeth, and thou hearest the sound thereof, but canst not tell whence it cometh, and whither it goeth; so is every one that is born of the Spirit (*St. John* 3:7-8).

> that whosoever dwelleth in him should not perish but have eternal life (*St. John* 3:15).

> Know ye not, that so many of us as were baptized into Jesus Christ were baptized into his death? Therefore we are buried with him by baptism into death: that like as Christ was raised up from the dead by the glory of the Father, even so we also should walk in newness of life.
> For if we have been planted together in the likeness of his death, we shall be also in the likeness of his resurrection:
> Knowing this, that our old man is crucified with him, that the body of sin might be destroyed, that henceforth we should not serve sin.
> For he that is dead is freed from sin.
> Now if we be dead with Christ, we believe that we shall also live with him. (*Romans* 6:1-8).

The vows of baptism follow.

Questions asked of the applicants before the prayer:

1. Do you now acknowledge the doctrines, which have hitherto been taught to you, as being the truth and right foundation to salvation?

2. Do you also believe in and agree with the twelve articles of our Christian faith which comprise: 'We believe in God the Almighty . . .'

[Each repeats the Apostles' Creed.]

3. Do you also desire the prayer of intercession of the pious that God may forgive and remit the sins committed by you in ignorance?

4. Do you desire to consecrate, give and sacrifice yourself to the Lord God in the covenant of Christian baptism?

Here follows the prayer.

(After this prayer, while kneeling, follow these six questions:)

1. Do you now sufficiently understand the word of God and acknowledge it as the only path to life eternal?

2. Do you also truly and heartily repent of the sins which you have in ignorance committed against God and do you desire henceforth to fear God, nevermore to sin against God, and rather to suffer death than ever again to sin willfully against God?

3. Do you also believe that your sins have been forgiven and remitted through Christ and the prayer of intercession of His people?

4. Is it also your desire to accept brotherly punishment and admonition and also to apply the same to others when it is needful?

5. Do you desire thus to consecrate, give and sacrifice yourself with soul and body and all your possessions to the Lord in heaven, and to be obedient unto Christ and His church?

6. Do you desire thus to establish a covenant with God and all his people and to be baptized upon your confessed belief?

Note: All of these questions must be answered with a "yes." The minister, laying on his hands and sprinkling with water, speaks the following words:

On thy confessed belief I baptize three [sic][3] in the name of the Father, the Son, and the Holy Ghost. God Almighty in heaven who has given you grace and mercy through the death of Christ and the prayer of His Saints, may clothe you with fortitude from on high and inscribe your name into the book of eternal life, to preserve these in piety and faith until death. This is my wish to thee through Jesus Christ. Amen (Trans. Hofer 1955:26, Hostetler 1974:337-338).

Following the Palm Sunday baptisms by one week is *Oster* [Easter] where at *Abendmahl* [the Lord's Supper] the candidates are incorporated into the body of Christ by partaking of bread and wine together with all of the baptized members of the colony.

At *Abendmahl* the baptized partake of a special rich bread and of wine. The wine is generally bought especially for the occasion because wine made of grapes is called for. The minister first breaks the bread in half and hands one piece to his right where it begins its journey down the age hierarchy beginning with the members of the *Aufsehern* and ending with the youngest (and most-recently) baptized male. The other half of the bread is likewise passed from the *Praediger* to the oldest woman at the rear of the church where it begins its journey down the age hierarchy of baptized women. The Hutterites do not regard the bread as constituting the actual transubstantiation of the body of Christ. Indeed, children are later fed on the same special bread at mealtime. Rather, they regard the process of sharing bread as a "knitting together in love" of disparate persons into one body — the body of Christ reborn. In 1565 Peter Riedemann (1950 ed.:86) wrote that in the notion of transubstantiation the act of Christ instructing his apostles "had been twisted by the deceiver and made into idolatry." According to Riedemann (1950:86), Christ taught the apostles that "... they are members of his body, and as the bread is made a loaf by the bringing together of many grains, even so we, many minds and purposes are led by faith into one, and have become one plant, one living organism and body of Christ..." Through direct knowledge of salvation through Christ and freedom of choice for eternal life, humanity (according to Riedemann) can be spared a final death.

After the *Praediger* circulates the bread he pours wine into a number of cups and distributes these to the eldest baptized member of each row of men and women who each drink from the cups in a pattern which proceeds from inside to outside on the x axis.

Riedemann (1950 ed.:87) continues in his discussion of the knowledge of God and free choice and uses wine didactically:

> Through this knowledge, however, man is led to God, is grafted into and becometh a fellow-member of his nature and character, whereby we are also all led into the one mind and will of Christ. For this reason he giveth them wine, since many grapes have become one drink, and saith, 'This is the new covenant in my blood, as though he meaneth to say, that is ratified or made strong and confirmed by my blood...'

and concludes: "Thus, the meal or the partaking of the bread and wine of the Lord, is a sign of the community of his body, in that each and every member thereby declareth himself to be of the one mind, heart and spirit of Christ." In the Hutterian celebration of the Lord's Supper the "body of Christ" is not eaten. It is the baptized brethren who reconstitute the body of Christ, not the bread and wine, and they are nourished and fused into one body at *Abendmahl*. It is the reborn Christ who is fed at the Lord's Supper — the brethren are fed in the dining hall. The Lord's supper is celebrated in order:

> That there should be no schism in the body; but that the members should have the same care one for another.
> And whether one member suffer, all the members suffer with it; or one member be honoured, all the members rejoice with it.
> Now ye are the body of Christ, and members in particular (I *Corinthians* 12:25-27).

### *Zusammenstellen* ["Public Engagement"] and *Zusammengeben* ["Marriage"], (Literally, "Putting Together," and "Joining Together, or Giving Together" in Marriage)

At wedding ceremonies the couple (or sometimes, couples) are situated next to one another at the very front of the congregation. The ceremony itself is in two parts and takes place during the course of regular church services. The final wedding [*Zusammengeben*] takes place on a Sunday in most instances while the public engagement ceremony [*Zusammenstellen*] generally takes place several days prior to the former. Both of these are usually preceded by parties [*Hulba*, or "shivaree"] first at the colony of the bride and later at the colony of the groom (provided the newlyweds come from separate colonies), where courting, visiting, secular singing, and large quantities of food and drink prevail. Immediately following the final exchange of vows, there is a wedding meal attended by all the members of the host colony and their visitors.

At the *Zusammenstellen* and *Zusammengeben* ceremonies, the bride and groom are situated at the front of the church, side by side, in front of the youngest children. At the wedding dinner, the bride and groom sit at a central table next to one another, flanked by the *Praediger* and their parents. The vows follow:

The Engagement Vow [*Zusammenstellen*]:

> *Introduction*:
> As the brethren have talked to you individually they have understood that before God each one of you will accept the other as a gift of God in

good faith. Neither a resolution nor your final approval have yet been heard.

*Question to the brother:*
1. Thus I ask you my brother first, do you desire to accept this sister without complaints and with good will? Say yes, so that she hears this.
*Answer:* Yes.
2. Do you desire to go before her in such a way that she finds in you a mirror and an example of honesty and will be led to the Lord through you, so that you may live together as Christians, one being of benefit to the other?
*Answer:* Yes.
3. Marriage has its share of grief and not every day is filled with happiness, but brings suffering, too, as the women are the weaker ones. Thus I ask you, do you desire to have her for good, in health and in sickness, in love and in sorrow, never to leave her, until the Lord separates you through death? If this is not difficult for you, you may affirm it.
*Answer:* Yes.

*Questions to the sister:*
My sister, you have heard the good intentions of the brother, which will be of comfort to you.
1. Thus I ask you, will you also accept him with good will and without complaints?
*Answer:* Yes.
2. Since God has ordained that the husband is and should be the head of the wife, I ask you: Do you wish to obey him in all right and godly things as it is the duty of a wife, so that you can serve each other in godliness?
*Answer:* Yes.
3. Whether the husband can always enjoy better health than the wife is in God's hands. Will you therefore serve him also in health and sickness, in happiness and in sorrow, and never leave him? If this is not difficult for you, you may answer with yes.

*Summary:*
Because of your declaration of intentions we want to publicly state before the congregation that with the counsel of your parents you want to come together. You also ask the Lord that His will be done to the glory of His name. For this the congregation will gather once more. Now you may be seated, or you can leave. Amen.

## The Marriage Vow [*Zusammengeben*]:

*Questions to the brother:*
1. I ask you brother first whether you still wish to accept this sister that was introduced in good faith as a gift of the Lord?
*Answer:* Yes.
2. Are you willing to be a good example for her in honesty and godliness, so that she may be brought closer to the Lord through you?
*Answer:* Yes.
3. Are you willing, brother, to take the introduced sister for good in love and sorrow, in health and sickness, never to leave her until death will part you?

*Answer*: Yes.

4. I ask you, brother, if it should happen that one or the other from the congregation should suffer shipwreck of his faith (which we would not hope for you and which God forbid) will you then be satisfied with yourself and not desire that your wife follow you from the right to the wrong and leave behind the community and the church? And would you on behalf of your woman not cause us any trouble with the authorities; If so, you may answer with yes.
*Answer*: Yes.

*Questions to the sister*:

1. My sister, you have heard this brother in his good intentions, which will be of comfort to you. Therefore I ask you, too, do you desire to accept him in good will without complaints?
*Answer*: Yes.

2. Because it is ordained by God that the husband is the head of the wife, I ask you, do you desire to be obedient in all good things, as a good wife ought to be, so that one can help the other toward godliness?
*Answer*: Yes.

3. Whether the husband can always enjoy better health than the wife is in God's hands. Will you therefore serve him also in health and in sickness, in happiness and in sorrow, never leave him, until death will part you?
*Answer*: Yes.

*To both*: In closing, I ask you once more, brother and sister, before His church, which is a witness of this honest assembly: Will you in all that pertains to your marriage bond be faithful to each other and to your faith and never leave one another, until death will separate you? For what God has joined together, let no man put asunder. If so, both parties may answer with yes and join hands.
*Answer*: Yes.

*Whereupon the blessing is given*: We herewith bear witness that you marry each other as godfearing partners according to the order of God and the example of the forefathers and with the knowledge and counsel of the elders of the whole congregation. May the God of Abraham, Isaac and Jacob bless and keep you, may He lead you Himself together and bless you. May all godfearing husbands and wives live together peacefully and serve God all their lives. This we wish you once again from God through Jesus Christ. Amen (Tschetter 1913; trans. Reist 1965, See also Hostetler 1974:339-341).

At baptism men and women are located at the front of the room just as they are at weddings. The fundamental difference is simply that at weddings the couple are located right next to one another directly in front of the preacher. The convergence which is approached as one moves back through baptized and married persons in the proxemic arrangement of church services is attained at the wedding and carried into the wedding meal by the newlyweds at marriages. At a wedding the newly-married couple(s) leave after the children and directly in front of the

*Praediger*. Weddings amplify the messages which I have drawn from the preceding structural analysis of the procession between church and the dining hall. The complementary relationship between God the progenitor and woman the genetrix is discussed as a mysterious yet interdependent parallelism in scripture as follows:

> Submitting yourselves one to another in the fear of God.
> Wives submit yourselves unto your own husbands, as unto the Lord.
> For the husband is the head of the wife, even as Christ is the head of the Church: and he is the saviour of the body.
> Therefore as the church is subject unto Christ, so let the wives be to their husbands in everything.
> Husbands, love your wives, even as Christ also loved the church, and gave himself for it;
> That he might sanctify and cleanse it with the washing of water by the word,
> That he might present it to himself a glorious church, not having spot, or wrinkle, or any such thing; but that it should be holy and without blemish.
> So ought men to love their wives as their own bodies. He that loveth his wife loveth himself.
> For no man ever yet hated his own flesh; but nourisheth and cherisheth it, even as the Lord the church:
> *For we are members of his body, of his flesh, and of his bones.*
> *For this cause shall a man leave his father and mother, and shall be joined unto his wife, and they two shall be one flesh.*
> *This is a great mystery: but I speak concerning Christ and the church.*
> Nevertheless let every one of you in particular so love his wife even as himself; and the wife see that she reverence her husband [my italics] (*Ephesians* 5:21-33).

## *Bestattung* ["Funeral"]

> And as it is appointed unto men once to die, but after this the judgement:
> So Christ was once offered to bear the sins of many; and unto them that look for him shall he appear the second time without sin unto salvation (*Hebrews* 9:27- 28).

Just as Christ is said to have risen again from the dead after three days, likewise are Hutterian funerals supposed to be conducted three days after a death, if possible. A wake is normally held for two days prior to the actual burial itself [*Beerdigung*], during which the family and friends mourn in the very same room previously occupied by the deceased. The body is attended through both the day and night during which short testimonials are given. Food and drink are served at fairly brief intervals throughout the wake.

On the third day following death the funeral service takes place. At funerals the *Praediger* (if the person is older there are also usually several visiting preachers) sits facing the open casket which lies longitudinally in the *y* axis of the church. All of the men and women sit to their usual sides, generally facing the casket.

The funeral sermon theme stresses the brief duration of human life and the reward of eternal life to those who believe in Christ. (See especially *Genesis* 3:19, *Psalm* 33; *Ecclesiasticus* (or *The Wisdom of Jesus Son of Sirach*) [*Apocrypha*]:17; *The Wisdom of Solomon* [*Apocrypha*]: 1-5; *Baruch* [*Apocrypha*]: 2:16-18, 4:21-24.)

Both at wakes and at funerals, mourning follows a pattern similar to the distributional pattern of bread and wine at *Abendmahl*: testimonials, sobs, shaking, shuddering and tears all tend to begin with the eldest and proceed through to the youngest person present. Following the service, the persons present file out of the church in the standard format: men first and women second; oldest to youngest. The exceptions to the standard procession format are the exclusion of very young children from the funeral service itself, and the pallbearers who carry the body from the building last, followed only by the preacher(s). Thus, the deceased departs from church for the last time in that position normally held by the very youngest of children (who are absent) with a final rebirth into eternal communal life.

The casket is transported to the colony cemetery where it is quickly and quietly buried with a brief prayer. Hutterite graveyards are sparse: some earlier graves are marked with wooden crosses but more recent ones often have very simple tombstones. The cemetery is often located on top of a rise (if one exists) with a panoramic view of the prairies above and the colony in the "coulee" below. The cemetery is not tended on a regular basis by anyone, it is left to run wild with sturdy prairie grasses and transient tumbleweeds. The graves remain undecorated save for occasional bunches of wild roses, daisies, and Indian paintbrush left by children.

## Summary

The calendrical rituals of Hutterian culture are performed as a replication of Christ's life: his birth (*Wehenachten*); his suffering and sacrifice (*Oster*); and his rebirth to eternal life (*Pfingsten*). These rituals also reconstitute the harmony of the Trinity and represent it. The distribution of individuals in these rituals is the same as at weekly and daily services, although attendance is more complete as one ascends from daily through weekly to annual celebrations. The church service is a proxemic inversion of the distribution of people in nonsacred contexts such as meals, sleeping arrangements, and school.

Those rituals where individuals are "reborn" (*Beigiessungstaufe*), marry (*Zusammengeben*), and are buried (*Bestattung*), are not calendrical and vary in frequency. As such, they include digital information about changes in the potential actual size of the colony when shifts occur through newly-adopted responsibility for work, marriage, and death. This information about the colony (the condition of "the body of Christ") is expressed analogically by changes in the spatial organization of persons participating in the rituals. The candidates at *Beigiessungstaufe* assume the position of children and are accordingly reborn; the betrothed at *Zusammengeben* assume the position of the children which their marriage anticipates; and the corpse at *Bestattung* leaves life as he leaves the church – like a child reborn to eternal life.

The three noncalendrical rituals celebrate birth (marriage), rebirth (baptism) and death (burial as a final rebirth) and are consistent with Christ's life and the calendrical rituals which recreate it. Thus, *Wehenachten* [Christmas, but literally "esteeming birth," or "labour"] corresponds to the less-sacred *Zusammengeben* [marriage, literally "giving together"] which precedes birth. Marriage is proscribed during the month surrounding *Wehenachten*, which celebrates the immaculate (virginal) birth of a perfect man (Christ) and not the sexually-initiated birth of an imperfect human being. Likewise, baptism [*Beigiessungstaufe*] precedes the Easter [*Oster*] celebration of "The Lord's Supper' [*Abendmahl*] at which the new member of the decision-making layer of the colony hierarchy is incorporated into it when "the body of Christ" is fed. *Beigiessungstaufe* then articulates with *Oster*: if it is not a year in which baptism has occurred then the body is reaffirmed at Abendmahl. If change in colony organization is to ensue as a result of baptisms having taken place, then the new structure is confirmed when the body is fed. The same hierarchical pattern of colony organization is sometimes revealed at funerals when grief is expressed. The metaphor of the body allows the rigid hierarchy to be expressed as a whole, and the metaphors of wine (many grapes mingling as one) and bread (many grains combining as one) used in the ritual meal also further identify the individual as a contingency of the group. The *Bestattung* [funeral] is equilibrated with *Pfingsten* [Pentecost] which for Hutterites is the primary celebration of *gütergemeinschaft*. Just as the Hutterites suppose that Christ rose from the dead approximately three days after being entombed, so then is a man buried three days after he has died, and if he merits eternal life in a *himmel* [Heaven] of perfect communal organization, then God will grant it.

The noncalendrical rituals are analogs of existential crises in the lives of individuals (birth, marriage, death) which correspond to the putative life of the heroic Christ who is thought of as continuing to live on as an individual in the collective *personae* of the group itself, expressed as an individual being which eats and – in the feminine gender – reproduces itself. Digital information concerning the intent of persons to seek meaningful work, to marry and to reproduce is contained within noncalendrical ritual, and as such these rituals contain more information (the probability of their occurrence shifts) than calendrical rituals which give them import by constituting a background against which they occur.

At the outset of this work I discussed Rappaport's (1971) cybernetic model of ritual. Among the *Tsembaga*, the episodic ritual cycle of periods of war and peace was dependent upon: conscious decisions (the slaughtering of pigs, the uprooting of the *Rumbin*, the planting of the *Rumbin*); the trustworthy nature of digital information about relationships (alliances) communicated within the analog mode of ritual; and the long-term cycle, being beyond the awareness of participants in it. In the Epilogue which follows an attempt to answer similar questions concerning the colony fission process and the rituals of the Hutterites will be undertaken. Are the brethren aware of the relationship between baptism and the cycle of colony fission? How did the fission process develop and how did baptism become the centerpiece which integrates the process? Is there a plausible way to model communal evolution? How do systems which replicate themselves, form out of constituent parts whose replication actually constitutes growth, which if uncontrolled, augurs for systemic disintegration rather than replication? What part do self-referencing symbols play in the institution of control in evolving hierarchies? These are all questions raised by the arrival of the Hutterian People as a culture which 500 years ago did not exist but which today flourishes across the prairies of Canada and the great plains of the United States.

## NOTES

1   Bateson (1966) has suggested that among Cetaceans, information about relationships has been funnelled into a vocal medium instead of appearing in a visual one. This is an inversion of the human system which is constrained by the characteristics of light in a terrestrial habitat whereas among sea mammals the nature of the constraints is very different.
2   For a review of classical drama and its development in may different cultures see Kroeber (1944:409-443).
3   I am sure that this example of a printed *parapraxis* is the flotsam of translation and was probably meant to be "thee" or possibly "thee thrice."

# CHAPTER VIII

## METANOIA:
## EVOLUTION'S EPILOGUE

To drift is to be in hell, to steer is
to be in heaven – G.B. Shaw

### Preface to an Incomplete Conclusion

Evolutionary theory has long resided in the camp of deterministic philosophy whereas theories of decision making tend to accept human beings as conscious, rational *personae* making free choices. As such, the two perspectives seem condemned from the outset to be immiscible. And indeed, attempts to link the two have been fraught with conceptual difficulties (see Bee 1974:138-140, 223-234). To get away from this conceptual logjam, I have adopted a pragmatic stance towards decisions and the evolution which emerges from them in which there are no "prime movers"; hope replaces predictability; and any attempt by myself or the other persons described here to completely control all the variables of their lives would be regarded as oppressive and vainglorious (if not completely insane). I have opted instead for an ethnographic version of Godel's (1931) theorem which, in essence, states that all systems capable of internal self-reference via symbols are necessarily incomplete. This is because internal consistency and self-reference allow statements to be made which are both axiomatically provable which simultaneously proclaim themselves to be unprovable. This also means there are problems which can be posed specifically which cannot be solved. Therefore, descriptions (including ethnographic descriptions of cultural evolution and decision making) are necessarily incomplete and are

202 *THE HUTTERIAN PEOPLE*

ongoing. For example, there is no algorithm for predicting exactly when a computer will stop, a baby will be born, a person will die, or a Hutterite colony will divide, although the computations could be defined with precision and currently all of these things are happening (see Middleton 1969:103).

In this work, numbers and formulae are used to convey the structural nature of colony fission (see Chapter V) but they should be understood as heuristic, descriptive categories of thought. Here, numbers are the shadows which events cast, they are not the events themselves, nor should they play a part in the mystification of social life. The numbers are derived from dates of birth, marriage, and baptism as set down by Hutterite preachers in notebooks at various colonies. These records should also be regarded as the shadows of events whose loci are not really notebooks at all – birthdates are not actual births. It seems odd, perhaps, to point this out, but it is by way of warning off extreme materialists who still haunt this world with the "thought" that their materialism itself is not an ideology.

A perspective which would wed evolutionary and decision-making factors should not offer a complete conclusion but rather, should seek to render complex events somehow more comprehensible. It is an understanding of the course of Hutterite society over the past 465 years that I am after, not a total explanation of it via some pet theory. To explain a thing completely would only explain it away – abolishing it forever from inquiry and consigning it to the dustbin of what is universally assumed. Of this possibility, Wittgenstein (1951:188), once remarked: "...even if *all possible* scientific questions be answered, the problems of life have still not been touched at all. Of course there is then no question left, and just this is the answer."

There are a few concepts which might prove useful for the interpretation of Hutterian history if we are to reformulate it as an example of cultural evolution. These are advanced in a tentative fashion, keeping in mind that they are all subject to testing by the very data I would hope they elucidate. The introduction of these ideas is aimed at a better understanding of the Hutterians themselves when eventually they re-emerge from their history to join with the evolutionary interpretation itself. The digression may seem long, and at times the reader may gasp for air during such an abstract excursion, but ironically the argument is complex, despite the subject – which is the evolution of simplicity itself. Nonetheless, the argument is that complexity is exactly the evolutionary path leading to simplicity – not the reverse.

## Hierarchies and the Evolution of Decisions

One of the characteristics of an open-ended hierarchy is the relativity of what are usually recognized as wholes and parts. In open-ended hierarchies there are no absolute wholes or parts, for each new level in the hierarchy makes wholes of former parts and vice versa. Based on some similar observations, Koestler coined the word "holon" to replace our static conceptualization of parts and wholes as absolutes (see Koestler, 1967:48). A particular system is a special kind of ongoing process in which, at any point, change in one variable yields change in at least one other variable. The formal definition of system here, can be Hall and Fagan's (1956:18) often quoted one: "a set of objects together with relationships between the objects and between their attributes." The "objects" are *holons*, attributes their properties, and relationships tie them together. Since this is all in a hierarchy, *holons* can be understood as systems themselves.

The idea that the outcome of systematic interaction in open systems is not a by-product of initial conditions but is determined instead by the nature of the process of interaction itself, that is, by "system parameters," was first enunciated by von Bertalanffy (1962:7) and termed "equifinality." Basically, equifinality means that identical outcomes may spring from what may be regarded as different origins. However, there is a descriptive paradox here: it must be recalled here that the origins are not, by definition, origins at all for it is the ongoing process of system interaction which is regarded as in some sense "causal."

Several things should be increasingly apparent to the reader at this point. First, the origin/system parameter problem, and the evolution/decision problem, are both confusions which might have a common basis. Second, these are basically problems compounded by our inability to readily conceive a means for passage between *holons* at different hierarchical levels in either descriptive or structural milieus. We must find a way to link different levels of abstraction to one another over time, without being reductionistic. Within the context of the present discussion, this might allow: 1) decisions to evolve, and 2) evolutionary outcomes to be the product of decisions, without generating those undue misgivings which arise from internal contradictions inherent in the free will/determinism intellectual *cul-de-sac*.

## The Evolution of Self-simplifying Systems

There are several different trains of thought regarding evolution and the conceptualization of hierarchy which must be stitched together here.

First, it has become increasingly clear over the past fifteen years that a conventional Darwinian theory of evolution which operates solely on the principle of chance variation (mutation, random drift) and random search in reproductive populations is inadequate to explain: 1) the level of complexity of life given the time in which it is thought to have evolved; and 2) great variation in the speed at which observed evolutionary episodes occur. Finally, we are also saddled with the imposing problem of why, as life has evolved to greater levels of complexity, more and more species have become extinct (the general evolution of culture to a state of complexity also rests on increased numbers of specific extinctions). Somehow a graph which represents increased complexity of function and greater internal system control ...

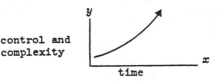

control and
complexity
time

**Figure 8.1**

seems fundamentally inconsistent with the omnipresent ogive curve describing extinctions and all growth ...

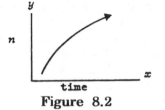

**Figure 8.2**

The following several paragraphs digress rather far afield from the Hutterians. Yet, I think the reward for this expansion might be a far greater understanding of cultural evolution in both a general sense and in this specific instance. To flesh out points one and two summarized above, plunges us into the problem of the "improbability" of evolution itself. First, the requisite search space for random search to "find" a functional organization is far too vast to inhabit the world with those life forms which exist. Mathematically, for example, a single functional enzyme (comprised of 200 amino acids) necessitates on the order of $20^{100}$ trials, which as Pattee (1971:38) has pointed out is not within any reasonable probability range for the age or size of the universe itself. Related to this is the problem of adaptation, which is sufficiently local and discrete in terms of fitness peaks that, in topological terms, no evolutionary pathway can be found to move from one fitness peak to another without passing through lethal valleys. In other words, natural selection (random search) is adequate to explain single adaptations (peaks) but the number of dimensions of the fitness landscape certainly exceeds one for any kind of complex life form (see Levins 1973).

As a number of authors have pointed out, these two problems grow exponentially with the growth of complexity itself. Complexity, understood in terms of information, is a function of the number of units (degrees or dimensions) of freedom which the evolving system enjoys with respect to its environment. Yet, the more complex and insular systems are, the less likely they are, as well (see Moorhead and Kaplan 1967).

Living hierarchies include "programs," or "elementary

information processes" which control a system through time. These can be referred to as the hierarchy of final causes, or simply, "the mind." Since these controls reorient an organism *or any other hierarchical system* within a field of variation producing factors in its exchanges with the environment, they are in an abstract sense, decisions. They are either/or choices based on information exchanged in feedback loops with the environment. Therefore, they are another systemic process which includes the environment by summarizing the organism's relationship with it. These controls are of the same nature as those controls which operate in the development of an organism — in fact they emerge from its development. Structural development never really ceases, it just slows as the information controls themselves develop — expanding their influence from a retrospective of the organisms's ontogeny to a stabilizing control over its more equilibrium oriented present (See Figure 8.3). Nonliving aggregates where all operations are reversible can be termed "heaps." However, in functionally adapted living units, simple aggregates form into collectives. Where these collectives can disband themselves, their constituent *holons* can be termed "loosely coupled" and they are not under "control" (Simon 1973:23). Colonies of bacteria, the migrating pseudopodium of a slime mold, the disbanding of a fire brigade, and the dissolution of a commune are all examples of reversibility in collectives. Grobstein (1971:33) has termed collectives of this nature "facultative."

Contrasting with facultative collectives are "obligate" collectives in which component sets (*holons*) sustain very different properties in isolation from the collective states they may comprise. In other words, the whole is greater than the sum of its parts to the degree that the parts in effect are no longer discrete parts. While obligate collectives are not reversible, they must still be able to reproduce themselves, so such hierarchical structures are "controlled." Evolution can be understood as a transition from an inorganic heap, through facultative, to obligate collectives, which must be recursive in order to avoid the improbability associated with the evolution of complexity. In brief, evolution (or growth) must rely on a principle of self-simplication. When a system reaches a controlled obligate state where system parameters

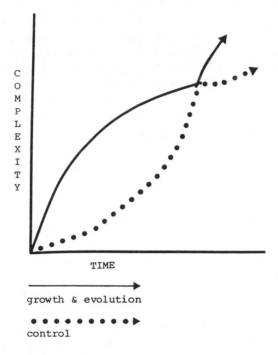

**Figure 8.3**

govern rather than original conditions, then there exists a situation which represents both an increase in complexity, and in a sense, a decrease in it too. For, as an inexorable slowing of the process of growth occurs, and the apogee of the ogive curve is approached, control — which is a function of complexity — is incurred. If this control event is reproduced, then we may speak of evolution as having occurred. In a stable homeostatic state, the system can be regarded as an individual *holon* itself — once again prone to repeat the same transition from facultative to obligate states.

The organism understood as a *holon*, is then a relative

construct, because groups of organisms in a facultative collective can become an obligate collective which may then become one of another facultative collective and so on. Such a theory may better allow us to understand the evolution of colonial hydrozoans of the order Siphonophora. The genus *Physalia* (the Portuguese man-of-war) is the best known of these. Basically, in Siphonophora, once independent organisms now perform the functions of organs and ultimately the colony takes on the reproductive task. Colonies of colonies also develop: *Nanomia* colonies can combine into *Forskalia tholoides* and as such, may live longer than single *Nanomia* (see Wilson 1975:383-387). Since random search (natural selection) operates on differential reproduction, it is evident that it operates on the unit which reproduces itself. Since the unit of reproduction is relative, it has its own internal evolutions. Finally, we are left with a picture of an evolution within evolution in which that which formerly "evolved' now "grows" and reproduces at another level in the hierarchy, eventually to "evolve" again. This process has been briefly sketched in biochemistry and biophysics by Pattee (1971, 1973a, 1973b) and is called the evolution of self-simplifying systems. Such a view implies much for the ongoing debate over "individual" (Trivers 1971) *versus* "group" (Wynne-Edwards 1962) selection models of evolution because the unit which reproduces itself is a *holon*: it is both an individual and a group. I think it also implies much for how a communal culture like the Hutterites has evolved.

One of the major problems in achieving some sort of broad applicability of evolutionary concepts within hierarchy theory seems to me to be the development of an understanding of how control emerges in such hierarchies as something of a complementary evolution of information. Control seems to evolve by first lagging behind the initial stages of structural development, then catches up in the facultative dimension and, finally, exerts itself when an obligate stage is achieved. This increase in complex information, in what may variously be called "the mind," or "superstructure," which occurs in inverse proportion to the ogive curve of structural evolution or growth, is an evolution of information.

The obligate and facultative stages used in the foregoing description of collectives is remarkably similar to Ruth Benedict's use of the terms "high" and "low" *synergy* and Abraham Maslow's later elaboration of the same terms to describe the variable level of nonaggressive cohesion in cultures. According to Benedict[1]:

> . . . societies *where non-aggression is conspicuous have social orders in which the individual by the same act and at the same time serves his own advantage and that of the group* . . . . Non-aggression occurs (in these societies) not because people are unselfish and put social obligations above personal desires, but when social arrangements make these two identical.

> I shall speak of cultures with low synergy where the social structure provides for acts which are mutually opposed and counteractive, and cultures with high synergy where it provides for acts which are mutually reinforcing . . . *I spoke of societies with high social synergy where their institutions insure mutual advantage from their undertakings, and societies with low social synergy where the advantage of one individual becomes a victory over another, and the majority who are not victorious must shift as they can* [my italics].

Maslow and Gross (1964) are perhaps no less cynical with respect to human nature than Benedict but expand her ideas to the point where morality is nonetheless expressed in highly synergistic cultures.[2]

> Those societies have high synergy in which the social institutions are set up so as to transcend the polarity between selfishness and unselfishness, between self-interest and altruism in which the person who is simply being selfish necessarily reaps rewards for himself. *The society with high synergy is one in which virtue pays* [my italics].

Let us return for awhile to the control of hierarchies through the form of information regulation which writers like McCulloch and Pitts (1953), Bateson (1972) and Laszlo (1963) refer to as "mind" and which artificial intelligence systems, theorists refer to as "superstructure."

To better understand the nature of control hierarchies the concept of "constraint" must be clearly stated. In common parlance, constraint implies a limitation of freedom which is externally imposed – but I mean more than this by it. Constraint is not merely a deterministic increase in the probability that an event will continue to occur. Constraint in a control hierarchy also creates freedom for the system it regulates from the vagaries inherent in that system's exchanges with the environment and is, in part, an internal development. Constraint as a liberating aspect of control must also exist in an incipient form at the interstices between the shift from an obligate stage to a facultative one in self-simplication . . . or the shift would never occur.

For example, every step in the growth of a crystal via screw dislocation, or the shell of a conch, amplifies the likelihood that the following step or event will occur at an increase in magnitude (number and speed) over the previous step or event. At a certain threshold, the universe of ions needed for the growth to accelerate in a normal crystal, however, becomes increasingly depleted as a reciprocal of the rate that they are being added to it, until the process slows to naught and rigidifies. In the case of the growth of living organisms (like the conch), an event occurs which changes the rate of the events of accretion in such a way that the final outcome of the process is not absolute or rigid. "In other words, what we need for a useful control system is a set of constraints that holds between certain degrees of freedom, but that does not lead to completely rigid bodies" (Pattee 1973:83). Otherwise, evolution could not occur. Two primary conditions must be satisfied for such a control hierarchy to arise. First, as has already been implied, the rate of a certain event must change relative to unconstrained rates which would obtain for the same event. Second, the operation of the event must be repeatable without leading to a rigid outcome (Pattee 1973:83). Since the description of control hierarchies requires an alternative level of symbolic (linguistic, mathematical etc.) description, this in turn implies that not only is the control event repeatable, but that an obligate stage requires that the entire process be repeatable at the alternate level of description.

The kind of control I am discussing in the abstract here, and which has been developed in biophysics, biochemistry, and mathematics, epitomizes the role of ritual in Hutterite colony fission as well. The two control features described above, which must obtain for a "control event" to relate the growth of a collective system to the individual elements which comprise it, matches the way ritual relates the individual to the collective in Hutterite society which I think has evolved as a self-simplifying system. This nascent cultural system has evolved a series of descriptions of itself, which moves from the adoption of Hutter's name through the reproductive metaphor of mother and daughter colonies which reconstitute Christ's body itself, in a regenerative symbolism which declares them to be "a people." That ritual is the control event in this scenario is clear but the way individuals' participate in the ritual cycle needs clarification.

**Synergistic Ritual and the Evolution of the Obligate Commune**

The initial intent of the proponents of adult baptism (the Zürich reformers) was that the ritual should serve all members of society. However, its rationale implied that those persons baptized on the basis of knowledge owed little allegiance to the state. As a result, the first adult baptisms were perceived by state authorities to be antisocial and anarchistic acts, consequently, severe persecution was encountered by its practitioners (the *Täufer*). Adult baptism was, with respect to incorporation within the state, the antithesis of a synergistic act. The same act which "saved" a person from damnation and eternal suffering, condemned him or her to a life of suffering at the hands of the same society the person lived in. Not surprisingly then, sects rapidly formed around *the individually oriented ritual* of adult baptism and eventually they began to see themselves as separate societies. Under conditions of extreme poverty, communal sharing of property was proposed and immediately became an issue around which vigorous debate again erupted – this time within the *Täufer* community itself. An emigration of the dispossessed communalists resulted, and after an initial period of foundering, workable communes were established under the powerful tutelage of Jacob Hutter. As soon as Hutter had established viable communes, they were quickly destroyed in the first Moravian persecution and Hutter was cruelly tortured and finally executed by his captors. The persecution eventually subsided and the remnants of Hutter's followers — *now calling themselves by his name* — began to move back onto lesser estates and then progressively onto increasingly powerful ones after the pattern discussed in Chapter II. After years of migration and persecution the Brethren began to decline until finally, Michael Waldner successfully renewed *Gütergemeinschaft*. Waldner's visionary experiences seem to have been at the crux of an evolutionary shift from facultative to obligate states for the Hutterites. Before he established the new *Gemeinschaft*, Waldner had literally steeped himself in the history of his people, so he was certainly aware of the migration/persecution pattern which I have just described. After much meditation, and worry over the lapsed state of the "community of goods," he had a vision during which he was reported to have died, was taken to see both hell and heaven by an angel and told that the only hope of salvation lay in "the ark of the *Gemeinschaft*." After Waldner had his vision he always called himself "a new man," and shortly thereafter began "the new *Gemeinschaft*." The metaphor of the ark, as the communal version of collective rebirth after the death of the world via a purging by water, is central to Waldner's vision. Salvation was no longer just a possibility for those practicing only adult baptism by water, a prerequisite of communal rebirth and life in *Gütergemeinschaft* had been added. After the rebirth of *Gütergemeinschaft* in Russia, the Brethren again migrated to avoid yet another instance of persecution. It may have been simply by chance that they migrated via a ship auspiciously named *The Harmonia* to the "New World" for which they had always been enjoined to search by Saint Peter ("...look for new heavens and a new earth, wherein dwelleth righteousness"). However, the fortuitous does not long coexist with strong faith and many of today's Hutterites find these things to be the source of great inspiration. It is also very likely that the choice of a ship in advance, by its bellweather name, and the choice of "the New World" over a possibly less risky migrations back into Western Europe, were both related to Waldner's vision. Recall, for example, how the Brethren choose new land and that they call their children by the same names as persons who have been protected by God and have had messages revealed to them by his angels. In retrospect, neither the ship's name, nor the choice of America as a destination, seem likely to have been merely chance happenings. The Brethren often put great stock in visions and dreams, although they rarely reveal this to outsiders. In any case, during the mid-19th century, again under the aegis of a government anxious for frontier settlement, the Hutterites migrated to the United States at the peak of the same period which brought waves of other immigrants from across Europe. Amidst the sea of new and sometimes rather exotic people, the Hutterites, dwelling out on the frontier, barely seem to have been visible until yet another war brought them renewed persecution and eventual migration to Canada.

Upon settling in North America the collective rebirth fathered first by Waldner and then Walter and Wipf, became actualized as the mother-daughter colony fission process described in Chapter V. The contemporary method of "branching," "splitting," or "hiving" as the Brethren now variously call the process of group fission, is the result of what can be interpreted as the evolution of a self-simplifying system.

An alternative level of description was first broached by Hutter's death and then subsequently by Waldner, who was followed in turn by Walter and Wipf. After the martyr's death of Hutter, which represents an emulation of the life of Jesus Christ, his followers took his name for themselves (just as Christ's did). This was the first major step toward symbolizing the brethren's collective self-awareness. At that point, more than one dead person (both Hutter and Christ) was sustained by name, in eternal life, as a function of the survival of a group of living persons, as a viable social unit. After first relinquishing *gütergemeinschaft* and then being revitalized by the Carinthians, the Hutterites again gave up communal life in Russia. *As a result of Waldner's vision, however, individual salvation became conditional upon sustained collective successive rebirths through time.* The initial revivals of *Gütergemeinschaft* represented yet another level of description in which the persons renewed bore the occupational names (*Schmiede, Leherer*) or first name (*Darius*) of the person who brought them into being. Since these names were utilized while the leader was still living, (not martyred as was

Hutter) the names were somewhat less formal. The brethren often say that the three different *leute* were "fathered" by men who still lived. For example, when speaking about the *Dariusleut* a Hutterite will often say "*Waldner ist der vater*" [Waldner is the father] or *Manner vaten die leute* [men fathered the groups]. When speaking about the actual fabrication of a new colony, Hutterites will say *Manner machen der Bruderhof* [Men make the "commune," literally "Brother-farm"]. The masculine noun (*der Bruderhof*) is used to refer to the actual entity in this instance but the feminine form (*die kolonie*) is used to describe the fission process (*schwarmen*) as follows: *Die Tochterkolonie ist geboren von die Mutterkolonie* ["the daughter-colony is born of the mother-colony"]. The male name is then the name of a line — just as in kinship reckoning — and the female is the source of the line's continuity through time. Maleness imparts "spirit" to female flesh and the two combine in life renewal. The Hutterite colonies are now obligate *holons* themselves, from which the parts cannot stray, as they were prone to in the past, without losing the salvation which is essentially and solely Hutterian. The part which strays is no longer a part of a body which also suffers without it. The body of Christ now called after his latter disciple, Jacob Hutter, and further specified as *leute*, is kept alive by a group of individuals who regard themselves as lesser beings who "give up" their individual desires to a greater Trinitarian being which they constitute and even ritually feed at "the Lord's Supper."

The ritual which began the self-simplifying entrainment which I have been describing, began as the antithesis of a synergistic act and gradually a new culture has coalesced around that same ritual. The ritual of adult baptism is now the essence of a synergistic act wherein an individual mutually serves both himself or herself and society. The ritual of adult baptism has always been a precondition of individual salvation and responsibility, but it is now collectively recapitulated as rebirth at another level in a hierarchy, which evolved as the growth of the culture repeatedly slowed.

## Beigiessungstäufe and the Cybernetics of Self and Society

The threshold of the division of a colony during the fission process can be regarded as a point at which the ogive curve, which describes its overall growth, intersects the maximal development of its control group of baptized colony managers (the voting council). The managerial group, which comprises most of the council, acts in a conservative and stabilizing manner oriented towards sustaining the colony as it exists, at the apogee of the ogive curve. However, during the initial stages of development, decisions made by the council are directed toward effecting and promoting changes in the colony's internal structure, and its economic relationship to the "outside" world.

In the initial stages of development, decisions tend to be either straightforward executive initiatives, or recommendations are made by executives, which are quickly converted into consensus votes directed in a positive way towards doing things. New buildings are constructed, farm enterprises are enlarged and so on. In the latter stages of development, decisions tend to be negatively oriented, major projects are avoided and new activity is minimized. As well, almost all proposals are voted on after considerable deliberation and debate in council. The number of completely consensual votes diminishes and executive initiative is turned towards finding and recommending a new locale for a daughter colony.

Within the context of this overall shift from individual initiative and consensus to collective decisions and debate, the demand for (and granting of) baptism can be understood as the core of control. Adult baptism is a repeated event which is the necessary antecedent to both marriage (and for Hutterites this almost exactly coincides with reproduction as well) and promotion to the control group. As such, baptism changes the overall rate of growth of the colony over time. However, this is not a simple kind of on/off homeostat like the *Rumbin* rituals of the *Tsembaga* around which events in the fission process revolve because the rate of occurrence of the control event (baptism) changes as well: it too becomes more frequent and less inclusive.

Since the amount of time it takes for information leaving a

sensing device, or cybernetic control in a system, to return to the point of its origination is an aspect of the system's operation itself, each past operation of the control directly constrains its next. This is a kind of primitive "memory," as Bateson (1971) points out, because the immediate past is a prologue to a future, which while slightly different from the past, gains inertia from it. In the case of a Hutterite colony, since the frequency of baptismal occurrence increases as the age of those baptized also increases, a large gap between the ages of the baptized and the unbaptized is prevented from occurring, and this stabilizes the system by vitiating the development of a demographic hiatus between the council and labor force. I believe that this also serves to keep persons involved in the day to day operation of the colony largely unaware of the changes in the age of baptism which accrue over the duration of fission intervals. When I pointed out the patterns represented in Tables 5.9, 5.10, 5.11 and Figure 8.1 to several Hutterite preachers, each said that he had never noticed the pattern before, but thought that there were "religious reasons" for it. When asked what these might be, each first pointed out that there were only a limited number of tasks which, according to the *Ordnungen*, Hutterites were allowed to perform, and that when each of these "jobs" was taken, new ones couldn't simply be invented. When further asked why two men couldn't share in doing the same things, they said that men could only work well together when one was "the boss" and the other "obeyed." Otherwise it was thought that two men would disagree "over even the littlest things."

These kinds of indigenous explanations of the lag between mean age at baptism for cohorts at different stages of colony development are *non sequiturs* with respect to what might cause delays in individual motivation to seek baptism, but nonetheless they reveal several important facts. First, an attempt to maximize harmony in colony life is thought to be consistent with a rather rigid and individuated hierarchical authority structure. Such a structure is graphically represented in: the proxemics of everyday church ritual; the distribution of bread and wine at *Abendmahl*; seating arrangements at dinner; mourning behavior; and even in access to washing machines. Second, the statements reveal the critical importance of individual tasks as venues where responsibility can be demonstrated: authority and responsibility are therefore ineluctably joined. Converting what was formerly a "one man operation" into the shared responsibility of two men would constitute an usurpation of the responsibility-authority quotient which accretes to an individual as he or she ages. A newly baptized person would also wish to demonstrate his newly acquired responsibility and that would lead to conflict with the authority already invested in the incumbent person. Obviously, such a conflict could badly damage colony solidarity.

The decision to seek baptism is also an important aspect of the increased control of the colony at the peak of its growth. Most of the young people I talked with who could be said to be staving off asking for baptism, were not aware that they were, in fact, doing such a thing. They tended to regard themselves as simply normal with respect to their age and development and said that they were "not ready for it" yet and that the spirit had not as yet "come upon" them. Several persons, who married shortly after their baptism, pointed out that they knew they were ready because they had seriously considered marriage for several years. One insightful and troubled young man said that "since I don't want to get married yet it would be bad to ask for baptism even if the spirit came to me. There is nothing to do here that I need to be baptized to do."

At least for that one young man, a classic "double bind" existed because responsibility could only be demonstrated by *not* asking for baptism yet the demonstration of responsibility should ultimately have led to baptism. Most young Hutterites with whom I have spoken are simply unaware of the increase in the age at baptism over the course of development of a colony. This is because the rate of colony growth parallels their own personal growth and social development owing to a slow slippage in the age of the candidates with the frequency at which they are baptized. This stochastic situation produces slight increments in the age of the general population and leaves no serious gaps between adjacent cohorts of candidates. It is the relative insignificance of the change from one cohort to the next which becomes significant over the "long run" of the colony through the interval of its fission time.

The decision to seek baptism is only measurable in a positive sense as an actual baptism or the (rare) rejection of a petition for it. From the viewpoint of the majority of young Hutterites it appears that rarely is a decision actually made not to seek baptism. Baptism results from the "coming of the spirit" into individuals in most instances. It is also important to remember that baptism must be granted by those already baptized, therefore baptism is not merely a function of the desires of individual candidates but represents the sum of a set of *di*vidual, not *in*dividual, concurrences between the candidate and each baptized council member. The multiple perspectives from which one may regard baptism are crucial to an understanding of how it effectively controls the life of the commune. Perhaps I can best illustrate this simultaneous patterning of perspective with the following quote from John Steinbeck's *The Log from the Sea of Cortez* (1951:35):

> We put on heavier coats and hung about the long bench where the helmsman sat. The little light on the compass card and the port and starboard lights were our outmost boundaries. Then we passed Point Sur and the waves flattened out into a groundswell and increased in speed. Tony the master said, 'Of course, it's always that way. the point draws the waves.' Another might say, 'the waves come greatly to the point,' and in both statements there would be a good primitive exposition of the relation between giver and receiver. This relation would be through waves; wave to wave, each of which is connected by torsion to its inshore fellow and touches it enough, although it has gone before, to be affected by its torsion. And so on and on to the shore, and to the point where the last wave, if you think from the sea, and the first if you think from the shore, touches and breaks. And it is important where you are thinking from.

Steinbeck's illustration of the effect of waves upon waves varying in frequency as they approach a point from two perspectives is analogous to the point I am attempting to make with respect to ritual as a control in Hutterite society. By trying to comprehend baptism from the perspective of the successive cohorts of candidates (the boat) and simultaneously the successive cohorts of councilmembers (the shore), we may better approximate the synergistic nature of the communal behavior which surrounds *Beigiessungstaufe*. The few councilmembers who had ever opposed baptisms said that they did so because it was their "sacred trust" to insure that only a person who "had truly received the spirit" was baptized. This was done for the "good of the person" and for "the preservation of the body of Christ." The baptized must exert their own responsibility by either encouraging or discouraging petitions for baptism as a syneidesis of their own baptisms. Although few persons are actually rejected for baptism, they can be dissuaded from seeking it by those who already are baptized, and particularly by those who recently were baptized. In one colony with which I worked over several years, just prior to division, baptism was described in such serious tones by virtually everyone in the previous cohort that one had the impression that life was extremely difficult and unrewarding after it had happened. However, immediately following division I heard several of these men in the newly formed daughter colony also variously describe baptism as "a relief," "joyful," "peaceful," and "bringing serenity and fulfilment." The amount of criticism leveled at persons for behaving "childishly" also seems to have greatly subsided after division. Teenage children were actually performing jobs or being trained to do things (like driving a large earthmoving machine) which in the mother colony only baptized adults had done.

The ritual of adult baptism is central to a kind of cybernetics of self with society, in which persons on either side of its occurrence, by guiding themselves and their behavior with respect to it, also have their society steered by it. Responsibility for one's acts via a *"giving-up-ness"* [*gelassenheit*] of personal desires, constitutes a control of the individual which is synergistic with the persistence of the life of the obligate collective – the body of Christ reborn. The issue of "consciousness," or "cognized" vs. "uncognized" action, can be seen as deriving from a far too simplistic construction of mental life which can not be reduced to basic either/or states of awareness. There are many kinds of consciousness – and ritual consciousness is but one kind – which by being collective forms of awareness should not be reduced to a state termed "uncognized" which precludes further analysis and excludes any real meaning from the lives of the very persons affected. That rituals may act like "on/off" switches does not mean that the consciousness which informs them is likewise a digital expression of thought and action.

## "Closed" and "Open" Perspectives on Hutterite Culture, 1529-1977: History vs. Evolution

The Hutterites' own interpretation of their past may be found in their two *Geschichtbuchen* which allude to a waxing and waning of the impact of "The Spirit" upon them. According to the Hutterites, "The Spirit" is easily lost and only constant vigilance can preserve both it and *Gütergemeinschaft*. Under the pressure of persecution, when the Brethren were first forced to flee Moravia, it is noted in their literature that many people gave up *Gütergemeinschaft* and returned to their former ways of life. However, the primary waning of "The Spirit" was thought to have occurred from the second Moravian expulsion which began in 1621 and lasted through the 30-Years' War (1618-1648) and the reign of the Catholic Empress, Maria Theresa (1740-1780). Andreas Ehrenpreis was the last strong *Vorsteher* during this period and it was he who saved many of the original documents of the Brethren from destruction. Both Ehrenpreis and the author of the Great Pentecost Sermon of the Hutterites, Hans Friedrich Kuentsche, who preached at Kesselsdorf, Slovakia from 1641 to 1659, explicitly warned the Brethren about the ease with which "The Spirit" could be (and was being) lost (see Anderson, 1972, Vol. 1:212-216). The return of "The Spirit" to the Brethren was manifested at the rebirth of communal life under Michael Waldner in Russia.

Peter (1975) has interpreted Hutterite history as a dialectical process in which periods of dominance by the nuclear family, alternate with periods of dominance by the commune. In Peter's schema the seeds for the successive phases are sewn in each preceding one in a neat, Hegelian series of thesis-antithesis-synthesis transformations. Peter's interpretation is grounded in the Hutterites' own interpretation of the eternal struggle that goes on within the individual and which has been writ large on their history as a group. The dialectical-historical interpretation suffers from both a too casual dismissal of warfare as a mitigating factor in the persistence of *Gütergemeinschaft,* and an inability to pinpoint in contemporary society those factors which supposedly wrought the dialectic in the past.

Peter (1975:104) quite rightly points out that the Brethren had persisted through "more severe" persecutions than occurred during the 30-Years' War (specifically around 1547). However, factors such as famine and disease (particularly the plague) which were accessories of the 30-Years' War, received no attention in his analysis. A brief, severe persecution during an apocalyptic and eschatological phase of the reformation could understandably have been survived by a culture (indeed, I am suggesting it was the primary catalyst for its development) which later foundered through nearly 200 years (1593-1782) of steady exposure to disease, pestilence, starvation and migrations, punctuated by repeated and vicious episodes of persecution. Peter's evaluation of Hutterite history also suffers from an inability to relate this supposed dialectic to local conditions in anything remotely resembling an empirical way, even for the present day Hutterites. His conclusion regarding the Hutterites at present is rather ambiguous because although he is forced to admit that the colonies are now "much more sophisticated and balanced" (Peter 1975:113), the dialectic gives no indication of how such a change could have come about.

Diener (1974:615) has suggested that the Hutterites have survived because they have occupied a particular kind of niche throughout the more widespread evolution of capitalism itself.

> The Hutterite culture, then has not survived because of its unique value system nor due to the efficient adaptation of the population to any local environment. Rather, for over four centuries, the Hutterites have occupied a unique evolutionary niche: the rural frontier region of expanding capitalism. Like a surf rider balanced precariously upon a gigantic wave, the Hutterites have found a point of stability in what appears to be an avalanche of change, and thus have remained static while the world about them was transformed.

In a very general way I agree with Diener, but all of this amounts to a fairly superficial statement. Few would argue that the Hutterites have not occupied such a niche but their adaptations have also been rather different from one locale to the next and their values have certainly played a paramount role in their development. The Brethren have been more than an accidental contingency of capitalist expansion and they have certainly not "remained static." The fact that the Brethren have survived does not permit us to say that they remain unchanged. Their ideology is fundamentally the same now as over 400 years ago but it has evolved as well. Practices like "the ban," and arranged marriage have disappeared altogether, as have many occupations (most notably *Sendbote*) and certain rituals have been developed and/or elaborated (notably funerals and "shivarees"). From the Hutterian viewpoint (that of an optimal society) and from ours (as an utopian venture) the Brethren may give the illusory appearance of being "static." Instead, the Hutterites are "a people," and like any other "people" in diaspora — the Jews or the Gypsies for example — they have actually changed a great deal, yet retain their communal identity, partly as a function of having persisted against such incredibly great odds.

While Peter's (1975) interpretation of Hutterite history fails to deal adequately with the effects of external factors which have impinged upon Hutterite life and he describes a strain which even the Hutterites recognize as perennial, Diener does not deal at all with their specific evolution in its internal dimension. Diener (1974:615) does note, very perceptively I think, that "human culture is distinctive in that the unit undergoing adaptive radiation must be genetically, behaviorally, ecologically, and *symbolically* defined." (my italics)

I have suggested that the relationship between the World and the Hutterites themselves, or what they term "the inside" and "the outside," must be examined from a self-simplifying perspective to make sense of the evolution of Hutterite society (Stephenson, 1978). Diener *et al* (1980) have also recently suggested that self-simplication might prove a fruitful model for the establishment of not only the Hutterites, but of Islam as well. Bennett (1967:161-198) has shown that there is a complex interplay between both external and internal factors which ultimately combine and allow successful fission to take place. These variables which Bennett describes, include the carrying capacity of the land registered in terms of productivity, its regional availability, rates of financial savings, rates of population growth, and what he later summarized (1976:183) as "various religious beliefs and social practices." Exactly what these beliefs were and how they were enacted has until now remained obscure. The assumption that seems to be passing unnoticed here is that these beliefs and practices are somehow completely internal factors when, in fact, they are neither completely internal nor external, partaking of both worlds to make sense of life.

It must be emphasized that the symbolism of Hutterite society, by which it separates itself from "the world" are, like its economics, only understandable within a self-simplifying, *open* systems' approach. This is because the absence of symbols as an antimaterialist representation in and of itself has taken the form of an inversion of the icons of the churches of "the outside world." As such, Hutterian symbolism depends as much on "the outside" for a semantic foil as their crops do upon its markets as a source of profit. Even their word for Christmas is a pun based on this contrast. The structure of Hutterian symbols of rebirth (spirit, water and blood) and the use of silence and absence, are based on a coupling of their past with existential universals: they describe life in general, and their lives in particular.

The classic structuralist analytical device of mutually exclusive binary oppositions, should not merely be regarded as a disposition of the mind to always classify material things in such a manner. Each structure also represents a retrospective of its own ontogeny. I suggest it is also a diachronic look back down the ogive curve of its own development. The sequence [-, -/+, +] should then be understood to represent a transition from the absence of a thing into its presence over time and corresponds to the heap - facultative - obligate evolutionary sequence. Thus, the spirit [-], water [-/+], blood [+] structure of *Täufer* baptismal symbols corresponds to: the Trinity object of worship; their history (Spiritualists, *Täufer*, Persecution); individual lives (birth, life, death as well as, revelation, baptism, martyrdom); Christ's life; and ultimately, to the universal symbols of birth itself (gestation, breaking water, placenta). (See Figure 5.1). I shall return to the existential motifs of Hutterian ritual momentarily, for the present it should suffice to point out that not only does the formal structure of Hutterite symbols recapitulate their development, but semantically they are also concerned with development, so form and content mutually affirm one another through them. Before moving more completely into Hutterian symbolism, a few brief additional historical notes are called for.

From the outset, the boundaries of the Hutterian culture itself have been contingent upon the performance of the ritual of adult baptism. Vayda and Mackay's (1975) offhand suggestion that individual Hutterites could have saved themselves from persecution by giving up their faith seems erroneous to me because of their very dependence on adult baptism and a willingness to suffer persecution for it. Anyone who did not participate in the ritual, or who would not risk persecution would not be a Hutterite anyway. From the Hutterite point of view, they would not even be a true Christian.[3]

The nature of the Hutterians' relationship with "the outside" world stabilized during their "Golden Age" in Moravia. I have described this as a *sendboten*/convert exchange. It is important to stress that a large influx of converts means that the population and its growth in Moravia was largely open and connected to the "outside" world and not very free from it. Hutterian economies at this point were also involved with "the outside" although they were certainly diversified and self-supporting as well. The Brethren were estate managers and the sales of craft items were also very significant (see Chapter II). The celebration of important rituals (Easter, Pentecost, and Christmas) took place during this period but the sermons which fully explicate these events in the Hutterian context were only then being written.

Hutterian social organization has been absorbed by their ideology in such a way that individuals now see themselves as contingencies of the group whereas at the outset the group was seen as a creation of individuals. Today's Hutterite population still depends on the "outside" as a market and as a semantic foil for symbolic meanings, but it no longer needs converts. Today's task is not to create a following through "commitment" via ritual conversion, it is to socialize the children of an existing people.

The old ritual of conversion is now a culmination of childhood socialization and the prelude to adult life as a "child of God." This transition could only be accomplished after the *sendboten*/convert exchange had ended and was itself a precondition of the system of colony fission. Once the Hutterites are recognized as constituting a people unto themselves, the concept of commitment as a useful analytical device should be supplanted by the examination of actual beliefs, and the symbols which bring meaning into being. The Hutterian Brethren may be communal but it makes no more sense at this point to ask why they continue to exist than it does to ask why the Gypsies, Jews, or Navaho exist. Perhaps I should rephrase this to say it makes the same kind of sense to ask *how* all persecuted peoples persist, rather than *why* they exist.

The metaphor of the group as the unit of reproduction is realized in the fission process which began as a result of Waldner's vision. This process is regulated by "sacred" ritual. The metaphor of the group as an actual being, also occurs among other well established communal groups with strongly religious or moral philosophies. For example, the *Yamagist* communalists of Japan (the largest group in that country) have been successful from their inception (1953) and have come to call their society *ittai seikatsu* ["way of living-as-one-body"]. The *Ittoen* ["Garden of Light"] group — Japan's oldest communalists (since 1906) — have even convinced the government to tabulate their membership (about 300 people) as a single household in the Japanese census (Plath 1969:1-17). The goal of one of the late '60s communes which survived into the '70s is also a collective *uber-mensch*: "The organism of many who act as one" (Hollenback 1973:430-431, 1971).

The feeling of "oneness" is a very real psychological component of attempts at communal living which fail as well. In these latter groups, the metaphor of the group as one reproducing unit may have failed to develop, but the emotions which help to bring it into being are certainly well known. Concerning the "Sunrise Hill" community, Gordon Yaswen (1973:456), one of its members, wrote:

. . . there was, in me, not only the pride of each other member as a
brother or sister, but also a pride in the something that bound us all
together; the thing we were building in the air between us and above
us. It was a sense of something *more* than just a COLLECTION of
beautiful people; our groupness was an entity in its own right; an
entity composed of our separate beings combined, and therein was a joy
I had never sampled before. This Community, Sunrise Hill, was an act
of love between us all; it was a group coitus. The Community was a
continuing gesture of communion, and the fruition of our regard for
each other.

When these feelings are given consistent metaphysical
expression and reach their apotheosis in the symbols of sacred
ritual, consider the centripetal effect on a culture which this can
engender. I am discussing the effect of ritual on the integration
of a culture through the effects it has on the self-concept —
indeed, the *non*self-concept — of its members. For example, in
discussing the annual Hutterian celebration of the "Lord's
Supper," as opposed to the weekly "mass" of Catholicism, I had
the following exchange with one of the Brethren; here called
"Thomas":

Peter:        . . . but do you really claim anything different [from Roman
Catholics]? I mean, at mass a person becomes at one with
Christ?

Thomas:     No, there's a difference and this is what it is . . . the
Catholics, they try to make Christ be a part of them so they
chop him up . . . that's true, that's why they say they eat
his body . . . that way they can say he's a part of them. Us
Hutterites, it's different . . . we become part of Jesus . . .
that's why the Catholics' thinking they're eating Jesus is so
wrong.

Peter:        You mean it's just the opposite, that you must sustain Christ,
not that he should sustain you?

Thomas:     Of course! All of these people who say 'Bring Christ into your
life' You know? The ones who sell newspapers in Calgary.

Peter:        Yeah, Jehovah's Witnesses maybe.

Thomas:     Them. They're wrong too . . . you can't make Jesus part of
you . . . that's selfish . . . we are supposed to be in his life,
his suffering.

## Metanoia: New-Life Ritual and Existential Symbolism

As indicated earlier I tend to think of ritual as a kind of maelstrom or vortex of evolutionary change which condenses frequencies of experience into symbols which become increasingly foreshortened via continual repetition. A range of redundancy can then be said to exist for symbols at different stages of evolutionary incorporation within a ritual. The compacted symbols are then to be regarded as being in various stages of imparting the information they represent to the unconscious where it becomes a form of "shared awareness" and as such is an unexamined assumption in the culture-specific epistemology or *eidos*.

Ritual, when it is regarded as performing in this manner, is open to inspection at both a "surface" level and a "deep" level. It is not a matter of ritual acts being either conscious or unconscious at all: they are both and so they are also partly mystifications and partly revelations. In my own analysis, the surface level corresponds to the cybernetic, systemic integration of society via ritual acting as a control. However, the variables which are controlled by ritual are not controlled in such a way that the system is completely homeostatic. Nor are the individuals automatons of some kind: they ask for baptism after long and probing self-examination and are granted it after conscientious deliberation.

It is evident from the graph in Figure 5.6 that the size of the colony represented in it is diminishing over time. This is probably due to increased costs in production and increases in consumption expenditures related to a modernization of plumbing and other "comfort" items. As a result of this, the optimum size of colonies seems to be dropping into the range of an extended family farm population. This drop threatens the communes *qua* communes, not because of defection due to a rise in importance of the family incurred through a loss of "the spirit," but because an extended family farm is not really much of a commune even if its members do live in *Gütergemeinschaft*. To avoid this fate (and the Brethren do worry about it), smaller families and the adoption of intensive production of new crops via hot-housing or even hydroponics might conceivably result. A lack of "we feeling" is risked by a Hutterite colony which is no more than an extended family farm. This also endangers the group by making them susceptible to the ecstatic preaching of pentacostalist sects. Indeed it is to such groups that most Hutterite apostates "defect" (See Peter *et al* 1982).

At a "surface" level of analysis, the ideas expressed in the beliefs which attend ritual must be related to the events which it controls; and at a deep level, to a more universal substratum of existential significance.

The existential motifs of initiation ritual (a denial of death via a new birth of the individual which guarantees eternal life) are readily apparent in the Hutterian baptismal synoptics. There is "a dying of the old man and a putting on of the new" which also projects *de novo* the collective image of the eternal life of Christ of which "the new man" is a component part. The symbolism for this ritual ultimately refers to the symbols of birth itself.

In the analogic milieu of proxemic behavior with which this digital symbolization merges, it is evident that at *Beigiessungstäufe* prior to marriage, single, unmarried persons; and then later at *Zusammengeben* marrying pairs, assume the proxemic (analogic) position of infants. Immediately following each of these rituals there is a ritual meal. In the first instance (*Beigiessungstäufe*), the obligate collective is fed by the ingestion of a staple food (bread) and a mildly mood altering drug (alcohol, wine). In the second instance (*Zusammengeben*), the nuptial pair eat in public, seated together for the only time during their lives. Buried deep within the Hutterian ritual of adult baptism, but rendered evident by the absence of iconic surface symbolization, is a characteristic of initiation rituals which has not previously been discussed. Many authors have noted that initiation is a rather universal prelude to marriage. It has also been widely noted that initiates tend to be kept apart from the general population and in many cultures are often naked as they pass from one status to another. Turner (1969), following Van Genep (1960), called this structural limbo which lies at the interstices between recognized social statuses "liminality." I would suggest that while "liminality" is certainly an aspect of the position which initiates occupy, they are not merely "betwixt and between" different loci in the social hierarchy – they can also be representations of the infants which their future potentially holds and constitute a more general celebration of new life. *Metanoia*, or the celebration of new life, is basic to the species and to culture, both of which must be propagated by individuals. In *Ephesians* 5:21- 33 reference to the parallel relation between man to woman on one hand, and human beings to Christ on the other, is said to be "a great mystery." It is exactly this "mystery" which is also one of the primary emotions of religious expression among humankind. That birth symbolism should suffuse the origin of a new culture is then no surprise, but it reveals a profound connection among us all.

When the most basic human experiences – birth and death – are represented in ritual, the depth to which these may penetrate individual consciousness is considerable. Furthermore, since they are universal, they may be said to be a profoundly shared form of awareness which needs little in the way of verbal discourse to reveal itself as "consciousness." The symbols which bring meaning into being in these rituals are quite nearly universal: blood and water. The "Holy spirit," which is omnipresent and invisible, is represented by the relative absence of things which is also the defining characteristic of Hutterian communalism – the low priority of material things.

One must also ask what brings new rituals into being? The Hutterian funeral of today is more elaborate than in earlier times and the "Shivaree" was not always held. The answer inheres in the same proposition: increasingly regularized behaviors breed new rituals in the same manner that they refine older, established rituals. First, early Hutterite marriages were arranged by the group and since the "Shivaree" is an individual and group celebration where courtship occurs (as are funerals), they are not likely to have existed until individual choice or family selection replaced group selection by lot. Funerals were not practiced by the early *Täufer* probably because death was so often a product of persecution. If secret burial later replaced the absence of burials, this would also be consistent with Hutterite history. Not until permanent *Brüderhofes* could be established were funerals practiced. Just as death follows birth in the life of an individual, so must funerals be the consequence of actual social life in groups. Early funerals are said to have been austere and a matter of the spirit. Only in North America have they been elaborated to include a representation of group hierarchy in terms of grief and its expression; and only in North America has the group become a unit which reproduces itself. The unification of hierarchy celebrated at *Abendmahl* is now corroborated at the burial; death is now collective because rebirth is.

## Toward an Hermeneutics of Hutterian Ritual

The interpretation of archaic biblical materials through layer after layer of changes in language has long presented scholars with an imposing problem: that which results after numerous translations is often just so much gibberish in the end (Miller & Stephenson 1980:244). Gadamer (1976) has posed this hermeneutical problem in a much broader context. While interpreting anything, an analyst usually assumes a locus *in absentia* with respect to the material; he represents himself as outside of it. This presents the next analyst to follow, with a problem compounded by the previous one's failure to explicitly include himself in the historical process. The unfortunate outcome of this is that each writer or analyst represents another layer of sediment which obscures his subject from the next. This problem has special ramifications for anthropologists, given our "participant observation" methodology and our unfortunate habitual absenteeism from the ethnography which results. For the most part, this work is not an exception to the rule, although as indicated at the outset, I wished to utilize a literary device by having the form of the work correspond to its basic content. I have attempted to weave analysis into the material after the developmental sequences which give rise to them in the way that symbols themselves rationalize the past and set the stage for the future. Chapter III, for example, is a structural retrospective of the previous two chapters upon which the next chapters in turn depend. The ethnographer enters the scene at the very end of the chapter, in a European city the Hutterites left at the very beginning of their trek through the following five centuries. Chapter IV serves as a contemporary interlocutive device between the first three chapters and the three which follow it. Here, the ethnographer assumes a contemporary first person account to link the Brethren to the outside world, and so my description of them, while it stems from my experience with them, certainly is not their description. It is my interpretation of their descriptions of themselves; and so while it may connect with them, ultimately it is outside of their formative experience. This format is then a kind of self-simplication series itself which moves from a "heap," through a "facultative," and toward an "obligate" stage, which it can never really reach but still must aim for. At the end of this sojourn the reader is faced with the writer in the Epilogue, who is still confronted with the problem of communicating something of what it might feel like to be a Hutterite and get baptized upon professed belief. I cannot simply let the Hutterites speak for themselves on this matter because, from their perspective, it is one of those sacred mysteries concerning which Wittgenstein (1951:189) once remarked, "whereof one cannot speak, thereof one must be silent." And yet, since I am not a Hutterite, it is not a description I could offer with words either: it lies within the realm of the imaginable but out of the grasp of a conventional description. However, I think there still remains something to convey here concerning the involvement of the individual in ritual as a primary emotive experience.

In his *Poetics of Music*, Igor Stravinsky wrote "The more constraints one imposes, the more one frees one's self of the chains that shackle the spirit."[4] Ritual is a constraint which frees both the self and the group in ways and by means which we now only vaguely understand, partly because critical understanding is anathema to actual participation in it. Perhaps we can at least say that the involvement of the person in ritual is time spent in a context where to falsify is itself difficult, and where acts and thoughts may finally merge as perfect praxis. As such ritual is a release from the contradictions of the quotidian affairs of life; ritual mirrors where a people have been and anticipates whither they will go. There is also a complementarity here between the two dimensions of the sacred and the secular. Possibly, in those cultures which strive toward utopian ideals, the magnified difficulties of everyday existence demand an increase in the recuperative power of ritual practice. One of the clearest expressions of the enjoyment which ritual complementarity can bring to the everyday lives of individuals, as opposed to its unfortunate portrayal as simply dull, boring, and monotonous behavior, can be found in Antoine de Saint-Exupery's *Le Petit Prince*:

> 'What is a rite?' asked the little prince.
> 'Those also are actions too often neglected,' said the fox.
> 'They are what make one day different from other days, one hour from other hours. There is a rite, for example, among my hunters. Every Thursday they dance with the village girls. So Thursday is a wonderful day for me! I can take a walk as far as the vineyards. But if the hunters danced at just anytime, every day would be like every other day, and I should never have any vacation at all.'

There is quite simply a limit to how far an ethnographer can push the illusion that both he, and hopefully the reader, have penetrated the understanding of people in another culture without demanding of the reader the suspended disbelief offered by fiction. And this is not fiction. The people are real. The persecutions, executions, tortures, and migrations all happened. Today, the kneeling baptized farmer in black clothes and the laughing children playing "tag" in the setting sun of another long Canadian prairie summer day, are all very real.

I stand, in my memory, atop a knoll overlooking the colony, listening to the sounds of the children playing, and to the cowbells' hollow muffled peals. In the background can be heard the steady thudding of an ancient tractor engine which drives the irrigation system which sprays the garden.

The engine sputters, stops, and the sound of the spray of water ends on the drawn out treble note that every person knows who has ever watered a lawn.

The last of the cows enter the barn and their bells are stilled.

The children have scattered to buildings farther off down the road.

Silence envelops the colony landscape.

I walk down to attend evening services I can hear the whisper of my boots in dry grass.

A pheasant breaks from some bracken in front of me, its wings beating the fluttering note of escape.

Control and inspiration seem so antithetical and yet they seem also to be the internal strain within the condensed metaphors which lie behind the symbols which reside in ritual. What can I say to conclude here, that leaves to the Hutterians that which is only theirs, untrapped by my own attempt to "control" the subject matter in analysis, yet I hope, inspired by my poor art to the reader – the fox at play and the pheasant along my walk to church.

Out of the silence soon will rise the loud voices of the people singing their prison songs, their paeon to the shreds of the past which makes them whole today.

That is their "conclusion." My own is more fragmentary. It is the silence of the bell which beckons me into the absence of things and the presence of a certain spirit. In *On Authority and Revelation*, Søren Kierkegaard put the matter so:

> To find the conclusion, it is necessary first of all to observe that it is lacking, and then in turn to feel quite vividly the lack of it. It might therefore be imagined that an essential author, just to make evident the misfortune that men are living without a conclusion, might write a fragment (but by calling it that he would avoid all misapprehension). Though in another sense he provided the conclusion by providing the necessary life-view. And after all a worldview, a life-view, is the only true condition of every literary production (1966:4).

## NOTES

1 As quoted in Smith's (1973:114) review of synergy.
2 As quoted in Smith (1973:114).
3 Vayda and Mackay's suggestion utilized a quote from Diener's work (1974) which he then took vehement exception to (Diener, Nonini and Robkin, 1980) because once decontextualized, he was being made to sound as if he supported Vayda and Mackay's contention. Thereafter, a bitter exchange in the back pages of *Man* ensued which shed far more heat than light on the subject. Since none of the principals had done fieldwork with the Brethren – and because Vayda and Mackay appear to have understood little about *Täufer* cultural identity during their history – the debate was a sterile one. All of the authors (Vayda, 1981; Diener, 1981; Vayda, 1982) appear less interested in understanding the Hutterian People than they are in supporting their own perspectives on cultural ecology. Using ethnographic descriptions of people who died for their pacifism, like

chesspieces in some private academic battle over paradigmatic hegemony in the field of Anthropology, strikes me as mildly offensive. But the Hutterians whom I know would merely find it amusing, in fact, outright silly, that academics in remote institutions, who had never met any of them, would argue over the meaning of apostasy. Apostasy means not being a Hutterian any longer – something which those who never were Hutterian could know little of in the first place.

4   As quoted by Pattee (1973:74).

# BIBLIOGRAPHY

Anderson, James R.
   1972   Pentecost Preaching of Acts 2 — An Aspect of
   Hutterite Theology, unpublished Ph.D. dissertation (2 vols.),
   University of Iowa.

Arendt, Hannah
   1958   *The Human Condition*. Chicago: University of Chicago
   Press.

Armour, Rollin S.
   1966   *Anabaptist Baptism: A Representative Study*. Scottdale:
   Herald Press.

*Ausbund*
   1955   Lancaster: Press Incorporated.

Bateson, Gregory
   1958   *Naven*. Stanford: Stanford University Press.

   1966   Problems in Cetacean and Other Mammalian
   Communication. In K.S. Norris (ed.) *Whales, Dolphins and
   Porpoises*. Berkeley: University of California Press.

   1967   Cybernetic Explanation, *American Behavioral Scientist*
   10, No. 6:29-32.

   1968   Redundancy and Coding. In T.A. Sebeok (ed.), *Animal
   Communication: Techniques of Study and Results of Research*.
   Bloomington: Indiana University Press.

   1970   Form, Substance and Difference, *General Semantics
   Bulletin* 37.

   1972   *Steps to an Ecology of Mind*. New York: Ballantine.

Beck, Joseph

1883   *Die Geschicte-Bücher der Wiedertäufer in Oesterreich--Ungarn.* Wein: Carl Gerald's Sohn.

Bee, Robert L.
1974   *Patterns and Processes.* New York: Free Press.

Bender, Harold
1950   *Conrad Grebel.* Goshen: The Mennonite Historical Society.

Bennett, John W.
1967   *Hutterian Brethren: The Agricultural Economy and Social Organization of a Communal People.* Stanford: Stanford University Press.

1969   *Northern Plainsmen: Adaptive Strategy and Agrarian Life.* Chicago: Aldine.

1975a Hutterites   Forever,   *Reviews   in   Anthropology* (November):445-457.

1975b Change and Transition in Hutterite Society. In A.W. Rasporich (ed.), *Western Canada Past and Present.* Calgary: McClelland and Stewart West Limited.

1976a *The Ecological Transition: Cultural Anthropology and Human Adaptation.* New York: Pergamon Press Incorporated.

1976b Frames of Reference for the Study of Hutterian Society,   *International   Review   of   Modern   Sociology* 6 (Spring):23-39.

Berger, John
1985   *The Sense of Sight,* Pantheon: New York.

Berlin, Brent, and Paul Kay
1969   *Basic Color Terms: Their Universality and Evolution.* Berkeley: University of California Press.

Bleibtreu, Hermann K.
1964   Marriage and Residence Patterns in a Genetic Isolate, unpublished Ph.D. dissertation, Harvard University.

Bleibtreu, John N.
1968   *The Parable of the Beast.* Toronto: Collier-Macmillan.

Bloch, Maurice
1977   The Past and Present in the Present, *Man* 12:278-292.

Bloch-Lane, Francois
1965   The Utility of Utopias for Reformers, *Daedalus* (Spring).

Boldt, Edward D.
1980   The Decline of Hutterite Population Growth: Causes and Consequences - Comment, *Canadian Ethnic Studies*, Vol. XII, No. 3:111-117.

Bossert, Gustav Jr.
1951   Michael Sattler's Trial and Martyrdom in 1527, *The Mennonite Quarterly Review* XXV (July):205.

Boulding, K.E.
1934   The Application of the Pure Theory of Population Change to the Theory of Capital, *Quarterly Journal of Economics* XLVIII (August).

1956a Toward a General Theory of Growth, *General Systems* 1:66-75.

1956b General Systems Theory — The Skeleton of Science, *General Systems* 1:11-17.

Braght, Thieleman J. Van
1837   *The Bloody Theatre or Martyr's Mirror of the*

*Defenseless   Christians*   (trans.   by   Daniel   Rupp).   Lancaster:
David   Miller.

Brock,   Peter
1970   *Twentieth   Century   Pacifism*.   New   York:   Van   Nostrand
Reinhold   Company.

Buettner-Janusch,   John
1967   *Origins   of   Man*.   New   York:   Wiley   and   Sons.

Canada   Council   for   the   Arts   and   Humanities
1977   Report   on   Ethics   and   Research.   Ottawa:   Queen's
Printer.

Carden,   Maren   Lockwood
1969   *Oneida,   Utopian   Community   to   Modern   Corporation*.
Baltimore:   John   Hopkins   Press.

Cell,   Charles   P.
1974   Charismatic   Heads   of   State:   The   Social   Context,
*Behavior   Science   Research*   9,   4:255-306.

Cherry,   Colin
1952   The   Communication   of   Information,   *American   Scientist*
40:640-663.

1957   *On   Human   Communication*.   Cambridge:   M.I.T.   Press.

Clark,   Peter   G.
1974a   Political   Mobility   Patterns   within   Canadian   Hutterite
Communities,   Paper   presented   at   Canadian   Sociology   and
Anthropology   Association   Meetings,   Toronto,   Ontario,   August
26.

1974b   Dynasty   Formation   in   the   Communal   Society   of   the
Hutterites,   unpublished   Ph.D.   dissertation,   University   of
British   Columbia.

Clarke, Bertha W.
1924 The Hutterian Communities, *Journal of Political Economy* 32:357-374, 468-486.

Clasen, Claus-Peter
1972 *Anabaptism: A Social History, 1525-1618.* Ithaca: Cornell University Press.

1973 Executions of Anabaptists, 1525-1618: A Research Report, *The Mennonite Quarterly Review* XLVII 2 (April):115-152.

Cohn, Norman
1970 *The Pursuit of the Millenium: Revolutionary Millenarians and Mystical Anarchists of the Middle Ages* (rev. and exp. ed.). London: Temple Smith.

Conkin, Paul K.
1964 *Two Paths to Utopia: The Hutterites and the Llano Colony.* Lincoln: University of Nebraska Press.

Conklin, Harold C.
1974 Color Categorization, *American Anthropologist* 75, 4:931-942.

Cook, Robert C.
1954 The North American Hutterites: A Study in Human Multiplication, *Population Bulletin* 24 (December):97-107.

1968 Pockets of High Fertility in the United States, *Population Bulletin* 24 (November):30-40.

Courtis, S.A.
1947 What is a Growth Cycle? *Growth* I, 3 (May).

Deets, Lee Emerson
1939 *The Hutterites: A Study in Social Cohesion.* Gettysburg: Privately Lithoed, republished with additions in

1975 by Porcupine Press of Philadelphia.

De Jouvenel, Bertrand
1965   Utopia for Practical Purposes, *Daedalus* (Spring).

de Saint-Exupery, Antoine.
1945   *Le Petit Prince*. London: William Heinemann Limited.

Devereaux, George
1961   Two Types of Modal Personality Models. In B. Kaplan (ed.), *Studying Personality Cross-Culturally*. New York: Harper and Row.

Diener, Paul, Donald Nonini, and Eugene E. Robkin
1980   Ecology and Evolution in Anthropology, *Man*, 15:1-32.

Diener, Paul
1974   Ecology or Evolution: The Hutterite Case, *American Ethnologist* 1, 4:601:618.
1981   Interpretations of Hutterite Conversion, *Man*, 16:34.

Dirrim, A.
1959   The Hessian Anabaptists: Background and Development to 1540, unpublished Ph.D. dissertation, Indiana University.

Dunn, Judy
1976   How Far Do Early Differences in Mother-Child Relations Affect Later Development? Pp. 481-496 in P.P.G. Bateson and R.A. Hinde (eds.), *Growing Points in Ethology*. Cambridge: Cambridge University Press.

Durbin, Marshall
1972   Basic Terms – Off Color? *Semiotica* VI, 3:255-278.

Eaton, Joseph W.
1963   Folk Psychiatry, *New Society: The Social Science*

*Weekly* (London) 48 (August) 29:9-11.

1964 The Art of Aging and Dying, *Gerontologist* 4:94-101.

Eaton, Joseph W., and A.J. Mayer
1953 The Social Biology of Very High Fertility among the Hutterites: The Demography of a Unique Population, *Human Biology* 25:206-264.

Eaton, Joseph W., and Robert J. Weil
1953 The Mental Health of the Hutterites, *Scientific American* 189 (December):31-37.
1955 *Culture and Mental Disorders: A Comparative Study of the Hutterites and other Populations.* Glencoe: Free Press.

Eibl-Eibesfeldt, Irenäus
1971 *Love and Hate: The Natural History of Behavior Patterns.* New York: Holt, Rinehart and Winston.

Eliade, Mircea
1958 *Rites and Symbols of Initiation: The Mysteries of Birth and Rebirth.* New York: Harper and Row.

1966 Paradise and Utopia: Mythical Geography and Eschatology. In Frank E. Manuel (ed.), *Utopias and Utopian Thought.* Cambridge: Houghton Mifflin Company.

Estep, William R.
1963 *The Anabaptist Story.* Nashville: Broadman Press.

Evans, Simon M.
1973 The Dispersal of Hutterite Colonies in Alberta, 1918-1971: The Spatial Expression Cultural Identity, unpublished M.A. thesis, The University of Calgary.

Firth, Raymond
1973 *Symbols; Public and Private.* London: Allen and Unwin.

Fischer, Chistoph A.
1607a *Vier und funfftzig Echebliche Ursachen Warumb die Widertaufer nicht sein im Land zu Leyden.* Ingolstadt.

1607b *Der Hutterischen Widertaufer Taubenkobel.* Ingolstadt.

Flint, David
1975   The Hutterites: A Study in Prejudice. Toronto: Oxford University Press.

Freud, Sigmund
1918   *Totem and Taboo.* New York: Random House, Incorporated.

1928   *Beyond the Pleasure Principle.* New York: Bantam Books.

Freud, Sigmund, and J. Breuer
1966   *Studies on Hysteria.* New York: Avon Books.

Friedmann, Robert
1943   Adventures of an Anabaptist in Turkey, 1607-1610, *The Mennonite Quarterly Review* 17 (April):73-86.

1957   The Doctrine of the Two Worlds. In G.G. Hershberger (ed.), *The Recovery of the Anabaptist Vision.* Scottdale: Herald Press.

1958   The Philippite Brethren: A Chapter in Anabaptist History, *The Mennonite Quarterly Review* 32 (July):272-297.

1961   *Hutterite Studies.* Goshen: Mennonite Historical Society.

1964   Jacob Hutter's Epistle Concerning the Schism in Moravia in 1533 (trans. by the Society of Brothers, intro. by Robert Friedmann), *The Mennonite Quarterly Review* 38

(October):329-343.

1966 The Re-establishment of Communal Life among the Hutterites in Russia (1859), *The Mennonite Quarterly Review* 39 (April):147-152.

1970 A Hutterite Census for 1969: Hutterite Growth in One Century, 1874-1969, *The Mennonite Quarterly Review* 44 (January):100-105.

1973 *The Theology of Anabaptism.* Scottdale: Herald Press.

Gadamer, Hans-Georg
1976 *Philosophical Hermeneutics.* Berkeley: University of California Press.

Gaster, T.H.
1956 *The Scriptures of the Dead Sea Sect.* New York: Anchor.

Geertz, Clifford
1973 *The Interpretation of Cultures.* New York: Basic Books.

Gluckman, Max (ed.)
1964 *Closed Systems and Open Minds: The Limits of Naivety in Social Anthropology.* Chicago: Aldine.

1965 *Politics, Law and Ritual in Tribal Society.* Toronto, Mentor.

Godel, Kurt
1931 Ueber formal unentscheidbare Satze der Principia Mathematica und verwandtler Systeme I, *Monatschefte fur Mathematic und Physik* 38:173-198 [English] *On Formally Undecidable Propositions of Principial Mathematica and Related Systems I.* Edinburgh: Oliver and Boyd, 1962.

Goffman, Erving
1956    The Nature of Deference and Demeanor, *American Anthropologist* 58:473-503.

Goodhope, Nanna
1940    Must the Hutterites Flee Again? *Christian Century* 57 (November) 13:1415-1417.

Government of Alberta
1972    *Report on Communal Property, 1972*, Select Committee of the Assembly. Edmonton: Queen's Printer.

Gratz, Delbert L.
1953    *Bernese Anabaptists*. Scottdale: Herald Press.

Griffen, D.
1947    The Hutterites and Civil Liberties, *Canadian Forum* 27 (June):125-129.

Grobstein, Clifford
1964    *Strategy of Life*. San Francisco: Freeman and Company.

1973    Hierarchical Order and Neogenesis. In H.H. Pattee (ed.), *Hierarchy Theory: The Challenge of Complex Systems*. New York: George Braziller.

Gross, Paul S.
1954    *Hutterian Brethren: Life and Religion*. Pincher Creek Hutterite Colony: by the author.

1959    *Who Are the Hutterites?* Pincher Creek Hutterite Colony: by the author.

1965    *The Hutterite Way: The Inside Story of the Life, Customs, Religion, and Traditions of the Hutterites*. Saskatoon: Freeman Publishing Company.

Guttmacher, A.F.
1941   Selective Pregnancy, *Human Fertility* 6 (April):30-39.

Hall, A.N. and R.E. Fagan
1956   Definition of a System, *General Systems Yearbook* 1:18-28.

Hall, E.T.
1959   *The Silent Language*. Greenwich, Conn.: Fawcett.

Harada, M.
1968   Family Values and Child Care during the Reformation Era: A Comparative Study of the Hutterites and Some Other German Protestants, unpublished Ph.D. dissertation, Boston University.

Hartzog, Sandra H.
1971   Population Genetic Studies of Human Isolate, The Hutterites of North America, unpublished Ph.d. dissertation, University of Massachusetts.

Hawthorn, Harry (ed.)
1955   *The Doukhobors of British Columbia*. Vancouver: University of British Columbia and Dent and Sons.

1956   A Test of Simmel on the Secret Society: The Doukhobors of British Columbia, *American Journal of Sociology* (July).

1957   The Doukhobors of British Columbia, *Canadian Encyclopedia* Vol. III.

Hays, D.G., E. Margolis, R. Naroll, and D.R. Perkins
1972   Color Term Salience, *American Anthropologist* 74:1107-1121.

Heiman, Franz
1952   The Hutterite Doctrine of Church and Common Life.

A Study of Peter Riedemann's Confession of Faith of 1540, *Mennonite Quarterly Review* XXXV:22-47, 142-160. Originally a Ph.D. dissertation, University of Vienna (1927), trans. by Robert Friedmann.

Hershberger, G.F.
1957 *The Recovery of the Anabaptist Vision.* Scottdale: Herald Press.

Hinrichs, Carl.
1952 *Luther and Müntzer: Ihre Auseinandersetzung uber Obrigkeit und Widerstandsrecht. Arbeiten zur Kirchengeschicte* (ed.), Kurt Aland, *et al.*, No. 29. Berlin: Walter de Gruyter and Company.

Hockett, Charles F.
1963 The Problem of Universals in Language. In J.H. Greenberg (ed.), *Universals of Language* (sec. ed.). Cambridge: M.I.T. Press.

Hofer, Peter
1955 *The Hutterian Brethren and Their Beliefs.* Starbuck: The Hutterian Brethren of Manitoba.

Hollenbach, Margaret
1971 The Family of Taos, New Mexico, unpublished M.A. thesis, Department of Anthropology, University of Washington, Seattle.

1973 Relationships and Regulation in the Family of Taos, New Mexico. Pp. 430-441 in R. Kanter (ed.), *Communes: Creating and Managing the Collective Life.* New York: Harper and Row.

Horsch, John
1931 *The Hutterian Brethren 1528-1931: A Story of Martyrdom and Loyalty.* Goshen: The Mennonite Historical Society.

Hostetler, John A.
1961 The Communal Property Act of Alberta, *University of Toronto Law Journal* 14:125-128.

1963 *Amish Society.* Baltimore: Johns Hopkins Press.

1965 *Education and Marginality in the Communal Society of the Hutterites.* University Park: Pennsylvania State University Press.

1970 Total Socialization: Modern Hutterite Educational Practices, *The Mennonite Quarterly Review* 44 (January):72-84.

1974 *Hutterite Society.* Baltimore: Johns Hopkins Press.

Hostetler, John A., and Gertrude Enders Huntington
1967 *The Hutterites in North America.* New York: Holt, Rinehart and Winston.

1968 Communal Socialization Patterns in Hutterite Society, *Ethnology* 8 (October):331-255.

Huntington, Gertrude E., and John A. Hostetler
1966 A Note on Nursing Practices in an American Isolate with a High Birth rate, *Population Studies* 19 (March):321-324.

Hutterian Brethren of Montana
1963 *The Hutterian Brethren of Montana.* Augusta: The Brethren.

Janowitz, M.
1963 Anthropology and the Social Sciences, *Current Anthropology* 4:139-154.

Jones, N. Blurton

1972    Comparative Aspects of Mother-Child Contact. Pp. 305-328 in N.B. Jones (ed.,) *Ethological Studies of Child behaviour*. Cambridge: Cambridge Univesity Press.

Kanter, Rosabeth Moss.
1968    Commitment and Social Organization: A Study of Commitment Mechanisms in Utopian Communities, *American Sociological Review* 33:499-513.

1972    *Commitment and Community: Communes and Utopias in Sociological Perspective*. Cambridge: Harvard University Press.

1973    Utopian Communities, *Sociological Inquiry* 43 3 and 4:263-290.

Kaplan, Bert, and Thomas F.A. Plaut
1956    *Personality in a Communal Society*. Lawrence: University of Kansas Press.

Kateb, George
1965    Utopia and the Good Life, *Daedalus* (Spring).

Kessler, Johannes
1902    *Sabbata mit Kleineren Schriften und Briefen*. Emil Egli and Rudolf Schoch (eds.). St. Gallen: Huber.

Klassen, P.
1962    The Economics of Anabaptism, 1525-1560, Ph.D. dissertation, University of Southern California.
1964    *The Economics of Anabaptism, 1525-1560*. The Hague: Mouton

Klassen, William
1965    The Child in Anabaptist Theology, paper presented in Chicago (mimeographed).

Koenigsberger, A.G.

1965    The Reformation and Social Revolution. In Joel Hurstfield (ed.), *The Reformation Crises*. London.

Koestler, Arthur
1967    *The Ghost in the Machine*. London: Pan.

Kohler, W.J.
1908    *Flugschriften aus den ersten Jahren der Reformation*, II, No. 3.

Krahn, H.
1969    An Analysis of the Conflict between the Clergy of the Reformed Church and the Leaders of the Anabaptist Movement in Strasbourg, 1524-1534, unpublished Ph.D. dissertation, University of Washington (2 vols.).

Kirsztinkovich, Bela
1962    *Haban Pottery*. Budapest: Corvina Press.

Kroeber, A.L.
1944    *Configurations of Culture Growth*. Berkeley: University of California Press.

1952    *The Nature of Culture*. Berkeley: University of California Press.

Kuhn, Thomas
1962    *The Structure of Scientific Revolutions*. Chicago: University of Chicago Press.

LaBarre, Weston
1954    *The Human Animal*. Chicago: University of Chicago Press.

Laszlo, Ervin
1963    *Essential Society: An Ontological Reconstruction*. The Hague: Martinus Nijhoff.

Leach, Edmund
1954    *Political Systems of Highland Burma.* Boston: Beacon Press.

1965    Two Essays Concerning the Symbolic Representation of Time. In W.A. Lessa and E.Z. Vogt (eds.), *Reader in a Comparative Religion.* New York: Harper and Row.

1970    *Levi-Strauss.* London: Collins.

1976    *Culture and Communication.* Cambridge: Cambridge University Press.

Lee, S.C., and Audrey Brattrud
1967    Marriage under a Monastic Way of Life: A Preliminary Report on the Hutterite Family in South Dakota. *Journal of Marriage and the Family* 29 (August):512-520.

Levi-Strauss, Claude
1966    *The Savage Mind.* Chicago: University of Chicago Press.

Levins, Richard
1973    The Limits of Complexity. In H.H. Patte (ed.), *Hierarchy Theory: The Challenge of Complex Systems.* New York: George Braziller.

Linton, Ralph
1943    Nativistic Movements, *American Anthropologist* 45:230-240.

Livingston, John A.
1973    *One Cosmic Instant: Man's Fleeting Supremacy.* Boston: Houghton Mifflin.

Looney, Patricia
1986    Hutterite Women and Work, unpublished M.A. thesis,

Dept. of Anthropoplogy, University of Victoria, Victoria, B.C.

Lorenz, Konrad
1943 Die angeborrenen Formen moglicher Erfahrung, *Z. Tierpsychol.* 5:235-409.

Mackie, Marlene
1965 The Defector from the Hutterite Colony, unpublished M.A. thesis, University of Alberta.

Mange, A.P.
1963 The Population Structure of an Human Isolate, unpublished Ph.D. dissertation, University of Wisconsin.

Martens, H.
1969 Hutterite Songs: The Origins and Aural Transmission of Their Melodies from the Sixteenth Century, unpublished Ph.D. dissertation, Columbia University.

Marcuse, Herbert
1964 *One Dimensional Man.* Boston: Beacon Press.

Marx, Karl, and Frederick Engels.
1951 *Selected Works* (2 vols.). Moscow: Foreign Languages Publishing House.

Maslow, Abraham H., and Larry P. Gross
1964 Synergy in Society and in the Indiviudal, *Journal of Individual Psychology* 20 (November).

McCulloch, Warren S., and Walter Pitts
1943 A Logical Calculus of the Ideas Immanent in Nervous Activity, *Bulletin of Mathematical Biophysics* 5:115-133.

Mead, Margaret
1972 Changing the Requirements in Anthropological Education, *Western Canadian Journal of Anthropology* III

3:19-23 and response, 80-85.

Mecenseffy, Grete
1956   *Geschicte des Protestantismus in Osterreich*, Gratz: Köln.

Middleton, Robert G.
1969   *Computers and Artificial Intelligence*. New York: Bobbs-Merril and Howard W. Sams.

Miller, Ann and Peter H. Stephenson
1980   Jacob Hutter: An Interpretation of the Individual Man and His People, *Ethos 8*, 3:229-252.

Moore, John Allen
1955   *Der Starke Jorge*. Kassel: J.G. Oncken Verlag.

Moore, W.E.
1963   *Social Change*. Englewood Cliffs: Prentice-Hall Incorporated.

Moorhead, P.S., and M.M. Kaplan
1967   *Mathematical Challenges to the Neo-Darwinian Interpretation of Evolution*. Philadelphia: Wistar Institute Press.

Murphy, Robert F.
1971   *The Dialectics of Social Life*. New York: Basic Books.

Newman, A.H.
1896   *A History of Anti-Pedobaptism*. Philadelphia: American Baptist Publication Society.

Nicolai, J.
1964   Der Brutparisitismus der Viduinae als ethnologisches Problem. Pragungsphanomene als Factoren der Rassen--und Artbildung, *Z. Tierpsychol.*

Nietzsche, Friedrech
1927 *The Birth of Tragedy* (originally published 1872), in *The Philosphy of Nietzsche*. New York: Modern Library.

Olsen, Carolyn L.
1989 The Demography of Hutterite Colony Fission from 1878-1970 Among the Hutterites of North America, *American Anthropology*. 823-837.

Palmer, Howard
1971 The Hutterite Land Expansion Controversy in Alberta, *Western Canadian Journal of Anthropology* 2 (July):18-46.

Parkinson, T.J.
1981 The Relationship between Parity and Longevity in *Dariusleut* Hutterite Women in Alberta, unpublished M.Sc. Thesis, Dept. of Medical Demography, London School of Hygiene and Tropical Medicine, London, U.K.

Parsons, T.
1970 Some Considerations on the Theory of Social Change. In S.N. Eisenstadt (ed.), *Readings in Social Evolution and Development*. New York: Pergamon Press.

Pattee, Howard H.
1972 The Evolution of Self-Simplifying Systems. In Ervin Laszlo (ed.), *The Relevance of General Systems Theory: Papers Presented to Ludwig von Bertalanffy on His Seventieth Birthday*. New York: George Braziller.

1973 The Physical Basis and Origin of Hierarchical Control. In H.H. Pattee (ed.), *Hierarchy Theory: The Challenge of Complex Systems*. New York: George Baraziller.

Peter, Karl.
1966 Toward a Demographic Theory of Hutterite Population Growth, *Variables* 5 (May):28-37.

1975    The Instability of the Community of Goods in the Social History of the Hutterites. In A.W. Rasporich (ed.)., *Western Canada Past and Present*. Calgary: McClelland Stewart West Limited.

1980    The decline of Hutterite Population Growth, *Canadian Ethnic Studies*, Vol. XII, No. 3:97-111.

1987    The Dynamics of Hutterite Society. Edmonton: University of Alberta Press.

Peter, Karl, E.D. Boldt, I. Whitaker, and L.W. Roberts
1982    The Dynamics of Defection among Hutterites, *Journal for the Scientific Study of Religion* 21 (4): 327- 337.

Peters, Victor
1965    *All Things Common: The Hutterite Way of Life*. Minneapolis: University of Minnesota Press.

Piaget, Jean
1963    *The Origins of Intelligence in Children*. New York: Norton.

1970    *Structuralism*. New York: Harper.

Plath, David W.
1969    Modernization and Its Discontents: Japan's Little Utopias, *Journal of Asian and African Studies* 4:1-17.

Polak, Fredrick L.
1966    Utopia and Cultural Renewal. In Frank E. Manuel (ed.), *Utopias and Utopian Thought*. Cambridge: Houghton Mifflin.

Proust, Marcel
1971    *On Reading*. New York: Macmillan (originally published in 1906 as "Sur La Lecture" by Mercure de

France as Proust's preface to his translation of John Ruskin's *Sesame and Lilies (Sesame et Lys)*, Paris).

Radcliffe-Brown, A.R.
1952  *Structure and Function in Primitive Society*. New York: Free Press.

Ramsayer, Robert L.
1970  The Revitalization Theory Applied to Anabaptists, *The Mennonite Quarterly Review* XLVII, 2 (April):102-114.

Rapoport, Anatol
1953  What is Information? *ETC: A Review of General Semantics* 10:247-260.

1972  The Search for Simplicity. In Ervin Laszlo (ed.), *The Relevance of General Systems Theory: Papers Presented to Ludwig von Bertalanffy on His Seventieth Birthday*. New York: Goerge Braziller.

Rappaport, Roy A.
1967  Ritual Regulation of Environmental Relations among a New Guinea People, *Ethnology* 6:17-30.

1968  *Pigs for the Ancestors: Ritual in the Ecology of a New Guinea People*. New Haven: Yale University Press.

1971a Ritual, Sanctity and Cybernetics, *American Anthropologist* 7 3:59-76.

1971b The Sacred in Human Evolution, *Annual Review of Ecology and Systematics* 2:23-44.

1984  *Pigs for the ancestors: Ritual in the Ecology of a New Guinea People*, New Haven: Yale University Press. (enlarged edition)

Raymaker, A.J.

1929   Hymns and Hymn Writers among the Anabaptists of the Sixteenth Century, *The Mennonite Quarterly Review* III (April).

Richards, M.P.M., and Judith F. Bernal
1972   An Observational Study of Mother-Infant Interaction. Pp. 275-198 in N.B. Jones (ed.), *Ethological Studies of Child Behaviour*. Cambridge: Cambridge University Press.

Riedemann, Peter (or Rideman)
1950   *Account of our Religion, Doctrine and Faith (1540-1541)*. English translation by the Society of Brothers, Second Edition, 1970. Rifton: Plough Publishing House.

Roberts, J.M., M.J. Arth, and R.R. Bush
1959   Games in Culture, *American Anthropologist* 61:597-605.

Roberts, J.M. and B. Sutton-Smith
1962   Child Training and Game Involvement, *Ethnology* 1:166-185.

Roheim, Geza
1950   *Psychoanalysis and Anthropology*. New York: International Universities Press.

Ryan, John
1972   The Agricultural Operations of Manitoba Hutterite Colonies, unpublished Ph.D. dissertation, McGill University.

Salisbury, R.F.
1975   Non-Equilibrium models in New Guinea Ecology: Possibilities of Cultural Extrapolation. *Anthropologica* 17(2): 127-147.

Sanders, Douglas E.
1964   The Hutterites: A Case Study in Minority Rights, *Canadian Bar Review* 42 (May):225-242.

Schenkel, R.
1967 Submission, Its Features and Function in the Wolf and Dog, *American Zoologist* 7:319-329.

Schiller, Friedrich
1954 *On the Aesthetic Education of Man* (trans. by Reginald Snell). London: Routledge and Kegan Paul.

Schluderman, Eduard, and Shirin Schluderman
1969a Social Role Perception of Children in Hutterite Communal Society, *Journal of Psychology* 72:183-188.

1969b Developmental Study of Social Role Perception among Hutterite Adolescents, *Journal of Psychology* 72:243- 246.

1971a Maternal Child Rearing Attitudes in Hutterite Communal Society, *Journal of Psychology* 79:169-177.

1971b Paternal Attitudes in Hutterite Communal Society, *Journal of Psychology* 79:41-48.

1973 Developmental Aspects of Social Role Perception in Hutterite Communal Society. In L. Brockman, J. Whiteley, and J. Zubec (eds.), *Child Development: Selected Readings.* Toronto: McClelland and Stewart.

Schmid, Walter
1952 *Quellen zur Geschichte der Täufer in der Schweiz.* Zurich: S. Hirzel Verlag.

Schuler, Melchior, and J. Schulthess (eds.)
1828 *Huldreich Zwingli's Werke.* Zurich: Fridrich Schulthess.

Schwartz, Hillel
1971 Early Anabaptist Ideas about the Nature of Children, *The Mennonite Quarterly Review* 102-113.

## 258 BIBLIOGRAPHY

Shannon, Claude E., and Warren Weaver
1949 *The Mathematical Theory of Communication.* Urbana: University of Illinois Press.

Serl, Vernon C.
1960 Stability and Change among the Hutterites. In H.C. Taylor (ed.), *Research in Progress.* Bellingham: Western Washington College of Education, Graphic Arts Press.

1968 Stability and Change in Hutterite Society, unpublished Ph.D. dissertation, University of Oregon.

Sherif, M., and C.I. Hovland
1961 *Social Judgment: Assimilation and Contrast Effects in Communication and Attitude Change.* New Haven: Yale Univesity Press.

Simmel, Georg
1968 *The Conflict in Modern Culture and Other Essays.* New York: Teachers College Press.

Simon, H.A.
1962 The Architcture of Complexity, *Proceedings of the American Philosophical Society* 106, 6.

1973 The Organization of Complex Systems. In H.H. Pattee (ed.), *Hierarchy Theory: The Challenge of Complex Systems.* New York: George Braziller.

Smith, Henry C.
1927 *The Coming of the Russian Mennonites.* Berne: Mennonite Book Concern.

1950 *The Story of the Mennonites.* Newton: Mennonite Publication Office.

Smith, Robert A.
1973 Synergistic Organizations. In Julius Stulman and

Ervin Laszlo (eds.), *Emergent Man: His Chances, Problems and Potentials*. London: Gordon and Breach.

Snow, C.P.
1964 *The Two Cultures: And a Second Look* (sec. ed.). Cambridge: Cambridge University Press.

Starbird, Ethel A.
1977 A Way of Life Called Maine, *National Geographic* 151 6 (June):727-756.

Steinbeck, John
1951 *The Log from the Sea of Cortez*. New York: Penguin Books.

Stephenson, Peter H.
1973a Color: Its Apprehension and Symbolic Use in Language and Culture, unpublished M.A. thesis, The University of Calgary.

1973b The Evolution of Color Vision in the Primates, *Journal of Human Evolution* 2:379-386.

1974 On the Significance of Silence for the Origin of Speech, *Current Anthropology* 15, 3:324-326.

1975 Becoming a Hutterite: The Cybernetics of Ritual in a communal Society, ms., research proposal on file, University of Toronto 11 pp.

1976 A Strophe on Structuralism and Neurology: Color Salience and the Tricolor Traffic Signal, paper presented at Canadian Ethnology Society Meetings, February 21, Victoria, B.C.

1978a Like a Violet Unseen – the apotheosis of absence in Hutterite Life, *The Canadian Review of Sociology & Anthropology*, No. 4:433-442.

1978b A Dying of the Old Man and a Putting on of the New: The Cybernetics of Ritual Metanoia in the Life of the Hutterian Commune, unpub. Ph.D. dissertation, Department of Anthropology, University of Toronto, Toronto, Ontario.

1979a Hutterite Belief in Evil-eye: Beyond Paranoia and Towards a General Theory of Invidia, *Culture, Medicine, and Psychiatry* (Sept.), 3-247-265.

1979b Color Salience and the Tri-Color Traffic Signal, *American Anthropologist* (Sept.) 81:643-647.

1979c A note on the Dialectical Evolution of Human Communications Systems, *Journal of Human Evolution*, 8:581-83.

1980a The Significance of Silence: On the Evolution of Human Communications, *Dialectical Anthropology*, 5:47-55.

1980b *Pshrien*: Hutterite Belief in Evil Eye and Concepts of Child Abuse. In J. Ryan (ed.) *Canadian Ethnology Service Paper No. 62*, Ottawa: National Museum of Man, National Museums of Canada (Mercury Series Monographs).

1981a Introduction to Intuition Aesthetics and the Art of Interpretation. In Marie-Francoise Guedon and D.G. Hatt (eds.) *Canadian Ethnology Service Paper No. 78*, Ottawa: National Museum of Man, National Museums of Canada (Mercury Series Monographs).

1981b The View from Rattenburg-on-the-Inn and the Ethnography of Intuition. In Marie-Francoise Guedon and D.G. Hatt (eds.) *Canadian Ethnology Service Paper No. 78*, Ottawa: National Museum of Man, National Museums of Canada (Mercury Series Monographs).

1983 He died too quick. The Process of Dying in a

Hutterian Colony, *OMEGA: Journal of Death & Dying*, Vol. 14, No. 2: 127-134.

1985   Gender, Aging, and Mortality in Hutterite Society: A Critique of the Doctrine of Specific Etiology, *Medical Anthropology* 9, 4:355-365.

1986   On Ethnographic Genre and the Experience of Communal Work with the Hutterian People, *Culture* Vol. VI No. 2, 1986.

Stoesz, W.
1964   At the Foundations of Anabaptism: A Study of Thomas Muntzer, Hans Denck, and Hans Hut, unpublished Ph.D. dissertation, Columbia University.

Tambiah, Stanley
1985   *Culture, Thought, and Social Action*. Cambridge M.A.: Harvard University Press.

The New English Bible
1970   *The Apocrypha*. Cambridge: Oxford University and Cambridge University Presses.

Thom, Rene
1975   *Structural Stability and Morpho Genesis*, trans. by D.H. Fowler. W.A. Benjamin Incorporated.

Thompson, D'Arcy W.
1952   *On Growth and Form* (sec. ed.). Cambridge: Cambridge University Press.

Thompson, Robert T., and James V. McConnell
1955   Classical Conditioning in the Planarian *Dugesia Dorotocephala*, *Journal of Comparative and Physiological Psychology* 48:65-68.

Tillich, Paul

1966   Critique and Justification of Utopia. In Frank E. Manuel (ed.), *Utopias and Utopian Thought.* Cambridge: Houghton Mifflin.

Tinbergen, W.
1951   *The Study of Instinct.* Oxford: Oxford University Press.

Trivers, R.L.
1971   The Evolution of Reciprocal Altruism, *Quarterly Review of Biology* 46:35-57.

Tschetter, Michael
1913   *Trauungs Verhandlung fur Zusammenstellen, u. Zusammengeben, Dariusleut,* document trans. by Else Reist (1965), printed as Appendix VIII in John A. Hostetler (1974), *Hutterite Society.* Baltimore: Johns Hopkins Press.

Turner, Victor W.
1969   *The Ritual Process.* Chicago: Aldine.

Ulam, Adam
1965   Socialism and Utopia, *Daedalus* (Spring).

Unruh, John D.
1969   The Hutterites during World War I, *Mennonite Life* 24 (July):130-137.

van Genep, Arnold
1960   *The Rites of Passage.* Chicago: University of Chicago Press.

Vayda, Andrew P.
1971   Phases of the Process of War and Peace among the Marings of New Guinea, *Oceania* 42:1-24.

1981   Interpretations of Hutterite Conversion, *Man* 16:144.

1982    Interpretation of Hutterite Conversion, *Man* 17:546.

Vayda, Andrew P. and Bonnie McCay
1975 New Directions in Ecology and Ecological Anthropology, *Annual Review of Anthropology*, 4:293-306.

von Bertalanffy, Ludwig
1950a The Theory of Open Systems in Physics and Bilology, *Science* 3:23-29.

1950b An Outline of General System Theory, *British Journal for the Philosphy of Science* 1:134-165.

1962    General System Theory – A Critical Review, *General Systems* 7:1-20.

Waldner, Jakob
1974    Diary of a Conscientious Objector in World War I, *The Mennonite Quarterly Review* 48 (January):73-111.

Wallace, Anthony F.C.
1956    Revitalisation in Movements, *American Anthropologist* 8:264-281.

1966 *Religion: An Anthropological View.* New York: Random House.

Walpot, Peter
1957 A Notable Hutterite Document Concerning True Surrender and Community of Goods, *The Mennonite Quarterly Review* XXXI (January):22-62.

Washburn, S.L., and I. Devore
1961 The Social Life of Baboons, *Scientific American* 204:62-71.

Wenger, J.C.
1947a *Glimpses of Mennonite History and Doctrine.* Scottdale:

Herald Press.
1947b Two Kinds of Obedience, *The Mennonite Quarterly Review* XXI:18-22.

Wiener, Norbert
1950 *The Human Use of Human Beings: Cybernetics and Society*, Boston: Houghton Mifflin Co.

Williams, G.H., and Angel Mergal (eds.)
1957 *Spiritual and Anabaptist Writers.* Philadelphia: Westminster Press.

Williams, Julia
1939 An Analytical Tabulation of the North American Utopian communities by Type, Longevity, and Location, unpublished M.A. thesis, University of South Dakota.

Wilson, E.O.
1975 *Sociobiology: The New Synthesis.* Cambridge: Harvard University Press.

Wynne-Edwards, V.C.
1962 *Animal Dispersion in Relation to Social Behaviour.* Edinburgh and London: Oliver and Boyd.

Yaswen, Gordon
1973 Sunrise Hill Community: Post Mortem. Pp. 456-472 in R. Kanter (ed.), *Communes: Creating and Managing the Collective Life.* New York: Harper and Row.

Zeeman, E.C.
1976 Catastrophe Theory, *Scientific American* 234 4 (April):65-83.

# Index

## 268   *Index*